Shakespeare's Schoolroom

Rhetoric, Discipline, Emotion

Lynn Enterline

PENN

UNIVERSITY OF PENNSYLVANIA PRESS

PHILADELPHIA

Published by
University of Pennsylvania Press
Philadelphia, Pennsylvania 19104-4112
www.upenn.edu/pennpress

Printed in the United States of America on acid-free paper
10 9 8 7 6 5 4 3 2 1

Library of Congress Cataloging-in-Publication Data
Enterline, Lynn, 1956–
    Shakespeare's schoolroom : rhetoric, discipline,
emotion / Lynn Enterline. — 1st ed.
        p. cm.
    Includes bibliographical references and index.
    ISBN 978-0-8122-4378-9 (hardcover : alk. paper)
    1. Shakespeare, William, 1564–1616—Knowledge and
learning.   2. English drama—16th century—Classical
influences.   3. Education, Secondary—England—
Curricula—History—16th century.   I. Title.
PR2903.E58 2012
822.3'3—dc23
                                        2011023528

Contents

Introduction

"Thou art translated"

This book places moments of considerable emotional power in Shakespeare's poetry—narrative and dramatic portraits of what his contemporaries called "the passions"—alongside the discursive and material practices of sixteenth-century English pedagogy. The analysis moves between grammar school archives and literary canon, using linguistic, rhetorical, and literary detail to put pressure on institutional goals and effects. And it brings evidence about the theatricality of everyday life in humanist grammar schools to bear on Shakespeare's representations of character and emotion—particularly expressions of "love" and "woe." Throughout the book, I rely on the axiom that rhetoric has two branches that continually interact: tropological (requiring formal, literary analysis) and transactional (requiring social and historical analysis). Humanist training in rhetorical *copia* was designed to intervene in social reproduction, to sort out which differences between bodies (male and female) and groups (aristocrats, the middling sort, and those below) were necessary to defining and producing proper English "gentlemen." But the method I adopt in this book brings out a rather different story from the one schoolmasters invented to promote their new pedagogical platform and argue for its beneficial effects on the commonwealth. That is, when Shakespeare creates the convincing effects of character and emotion for which he is so often singled out as a precursor of "modern" subjectivity, he signals his debt to the Latin institution that granted him the cultural capital of an early modern gentleman precisely when undercutting the socially normative categories schoolmasters invoked as their educational goal.

Each chapter traces the classical texts, rhetorical techniques, and school disciplinary practices that enabled Shakespeare to invent characters and emotions so often taken to resemble modern ones, demonstrating in the process that *seriatim* genealogy cannot possibly account for the startling literary and social effects of sixteenth-century pedagogy. Rather, a more complex temporal perspective is required to explain the evident modern appeal of Shakespeare's characters—dependent as they were on ancient examples absorbed in an educational institution that, while laying the foundation for what we now call "the humanities," trained and disciplined its students in ways quite alien to our own practices and expectations. This analysis leans forward and backward in two ways. First and most generally, by highlighting the ancient rhetorical models and texts that made Shakespearean emotions possible, I put the retrospective force of "re-naissance" (a rebirth from the classical past) into productive tension with the prolepsis implicit in the now widely accepted label "early modern studies." Second, I pay attention to many of the early Latin lessons that helped shape Shakespeare's portraits of personal character and emotion. But I also read those portraits back into grammar school archives, assessing that institution's disciplinary and discursive practices by way of Shakespeare's frequent engagement with early Latin training. Here I take my cue from Freud, whose evolving ideas about "psychical reality" led him to suggest that a memory, as an event arising within the subject, might produce a "more powerful release" of affective energy "than that produced by the corresponding experience itself."[1] Implicit throughout this book is the idea that Shakespeare's affectively charged returns to early school training in Latin grammar and rhetoric are so emotionally powerful precisely because these personifications reenact, or reengage, earlier institutional events, scenes, and forms of discipline that were not fully understood or integrated when they occurred.

One scene from *A Midsummer Night's Dream*, a play intimately engaged with classical antecedents, will help capture how much school discipline reveals about character and the passions in Shakespeare's texts and vice versa. "Bless thee, Bottom, bless thee! Thou art translated" (3.1.118–19): Peter Quince's frightened outburst still makes audiences laugh—even though "translation" no longer calls up the intense, embodied memories and emotions it must once have done for writers and audiences trained up in Latin grammar and rhetoric at the hands of humanist schoolmasters. Rather than merely act a part in a play based on a Roman poem, as many schoolboys had been required to do before him, Bottom also undergoes a physical, classically derived metamorphosis that his peers understand in terms of translation, a common sixteenth-century lesson in Latin vocabulary and grammar. On a daily basis, schoolboys were set to translate passages from English to Latin and back again; and a master backed up his demand for such linguistic agility by the sting, or the threat, of his birch.

Such early lessons in bilingual translation were the basis for more advanced training in the tropes and, eventually, physical gestures of an orator—the embodied aspect of rhetoric called *actio* thought necessary to the performance of eloquence. As numerous schoolmasters had it, "Eloquence and wisdom are one." Read in light of the discursive and disciplinary school practices that once made Bottom's metamorphosis viscerally funny to contemporaries, "translation" in a play that shuttles between the classical world of Athens and the vernacular world of English fairies is not merely a matter of moving from one language to another, or from one cultural context to another. Translation involves social, emotional, and bodily change too: It offers the Mechanicals the possibility of any interaction whatsoever with Athens's aristocrats; signifies terror when the literary history they have imitated comes alive; and allows Bottom, in his classically altered dream state, to see, act, touch, taste, and take imaginative as well as sensory pleasure in *Midsummer*'s woods of desire.[2]

Much like the sixteenth-century schoolboys trained up in the techniques of verbal, vocal, and bodily performance necessary for eloquence, Bottom tries to memorize a dramatic rendition of a Latin precursor (in this case, Ovid's story of Pyramus and Thisby) only to embark on an emotional experience made flesh. Translated from his early conviction that he is *not* the same thing as the Ovidian part he is playing ("I Pyramus am not Pyramus" [3.1.20]), Bottom soon loses any such certainty: "Methought I was—there is no man can tell what. Methought I was, and methought I had . . ." (4.1.207–8). His metamorphosis changes organs of perception, makes him an "ass," and thereby mediates the vernacular world of English fairies through the eyes and ears of a new head derived from precedent classical texts. When Bottom wakes up and reaches for synaesthesia to capture his translation's ecstasy, not only do sensations cross, but so do word and body: "The eye of man hath not heard, the ear of man hath not seen, man's hand is not able to taste, his tongue to conceive, nor his heart to report, what my dream was" (4.1.211–14). Acts and threats of flogging at school vividly joined early lessons in Latin grammar to a boy's physical experiences of learning that language; more advanced lessons continued to connect ancient words, tropes, and stories intimately to his body, and did so in ways that required him to co-ordinate all its parts to gain social approval and advancement. As we'll see in Chapter 2, grammar school training in rhetorical delivery (*actio*), as well as rehearsing for school theatricals, drilled boys in the techniques of Latin eloquence through exercises in physical as much as verbal imitation. Schoolmasters required young orators to learn how to use and refine the chief tools of their trade: eyes, ears, hands, tongues. As pictured in a mid-century treatise on "manual rhetoric," *actio* was closely associated with synaesthesia like Bottom's: An orator's outstretched palm displays a fountain of water (eloquence) pouring from an open mouth (Figure 1). The collected individual hands depicted at the bottom of the engraving reinforce that larger image, illustrating particular aspects of oratorical success with specific body parts centered in the palm—a tongue, an ear, an eye. If well synchronized, a schoolboy came to know through practice, these organs might combine to achieve rhetoric's chief aspiration: the ability to move minds and hearts.

Expanding our standard view of early training in Latin as a rather silent, solitary drilling in reading and writing, I argue throughout this book that humanism's platform of *imitatio*—the demand that boys imitate the schoolmaster's facial movements, vocal modulation, and bodily gestures as much as his Latin words and texts—was designed to train young orators in physical as well as verbal techniques that would touch the "hearts" of those who heard and saw them. And as we will see, humanist masters understood, and integrated in various ways into their educational program, the ancient premise that true eloquence also relies on the power of emotions. As one sixteenth-century schoolboy wrote in his notebook's section on *actio*, "Cicero saith yt is almost impossible for an Orator to stirre up a passion in his Auditors except he be first affected with the same passion hymselfe."[3] Success in becoming a Latin-speaking gentleman involved not merely the good memory and bodily deportment necessary to theatricals, which Bottom immediately evokes when he wakes up from his dream: "When my cue comes, call me, and I will answer. My next is, 'Most fair Pyramus.'" (4.1.200–1). Social success also required a boy to imitate movements of eye, ear, hand, tongue, and heart in persuasive performances of the passions; a transfer of emotion was the desired end, and bodily and verbal facility the practical means, that schoolmasters offered a boy for obtaining a position of esteem in the school's carefully structured hierarchy. The organs that coalesce in Bottom's list of body parts are those that schoolboys were disciplined to bring together effectively enough to give life to memorized Latin scripts, imbue old words with emotion, and achieve the transfer of feeling necessary to persuasion. Whether such transfers of feeling worked in precisely the way schoolmasters believed they would is a question I raise throughout this book.

Which is the Latin "ass" through which Bottom experiences the world of English fairies? Did his night with Titania rival the sexual exploits of Apuleius's Lucius? The unusual situation certainly solicits such a comparison. Does he hear through the ears of Ovid's Midas? Shakespeare intimates as much in a joke on

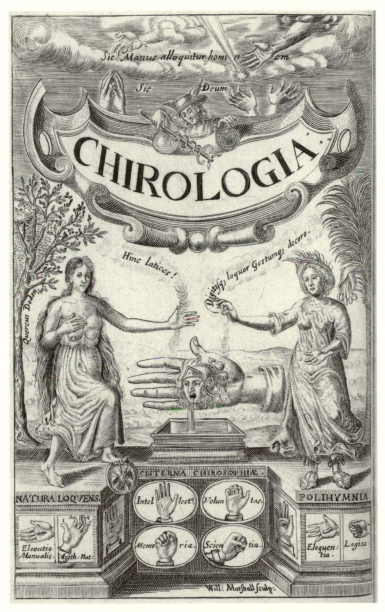

Figure 1. Title page to John Bulwer, *Chirologia: or the Naturall Language of the Hand* (London: Thomas Harper, 1644). Reproduced by permission of the Folger Shakespeare Library.

Bottom, who boasts to Titania, "I have a reasonable good ear in music" (4.1.28). That Bottom has no idea that in the *Metamorphoses* Midas got his ass's ears as punishment for judging Pan's music superior to Apollo's only increases the incongruous conjunction between Shakespeare's weaver and the Latin texts he doesn't know. Or is Bottom speaking in the voice of an *asinus*, the derogatory name given in some grammar schools for those who lapsed into English too many times in one day? Whether mediated through any one of these Latin asses or all of them, the joke at first seems to be on Bottom. Yet it quickly becomes more than funny. Bottom's metamorphosis may frighten his friends; and it may have caused former grammar schoolboys in the theater to laugh at the surprising intersection between a weaver and the Latin texts he wouldn't have been able to read. Perhaps for some it brought back memories of their own first attempts to take part in school plays. But it also allows Bottom alone of the Mechanicals a transforming, erotic "vision" comparable to those shared that night in the woods by the play's aristocratic lovers (4.1.205). As I demonstrate in the chapters that follow, Shakespeare was not alone among contemporaries in the distinctly sexual hue he gives to the language, texts, and rhetorical techniques he learned to imitate during puberty. But this book also shows that the many kinds of "love" intimately connected with Latin pedagogy in Shakespeare's texts are no more predictable, nor socially useful, than the one experienced that night in Athens's woods between an ass and a fairy queen.

If the synaesthesia of "Bottom's Dream" speaks to the complex way the school's verbal and physical training transmitted the texts of the Latin past to the bodies and minds of its students, it is important to remember that Tudor schoolmasters explicitly designed these lessons to "train" their boys "up" the social ladder. Read in light of the school's announced goals, Bottom's translation also speaks to the school's carefully planned intervention in social reproduction. His vision takes flight from both the texts and the techniques of humanist pedagogy, but at the same time it reveals the new dissonances that the humanist curriculum and program introduced into sixteenth-century society. As is well known, schoolmasters distinguished between popular and elite culture by dismissing English vernacular tales ("old wives' fairy rubbish") in favor of ancient Latin stories. Out of such a hierarchical distinction—one that privileged a "father" over a "mother" tongue—schoolmasters claimed that their new pedagogical method of constant imitation would benefit the English commonwealth and grant Latin initiates a certain degree of upward mobility. Bottom's translation, however, recalls the school's valued social distinctions while moving all too easily between the ancient past of Ovid's *Meta-morphoses* and the vernacular, English world of "fairy rubbish." His classical translation, that is, quickly ushers Bottom into the very world of English fairies that schoolmasters asked young boys to abandon for the world of Latin and of men. Like the many passionate characters I take up in this book, Bottom would have been an unlikely candidate for grammar school training: Both the status of the character himself and the stories that make up this "rare vision" force the social and discursive categories of contemporary education to collide. *Shakespeare's Schoolroom* looks at the classically inflected, embodied passions of many other characters like Bottom—characters who would have been excluded from grammar school training but whose words, bodies, and emotions nonetheless have a great deal to tell us about the institution that made them possible.

Each chapter takes up scenes in which Shakespeare draws on schoolroom texts and practices to personify passions at some considerable distance from the socially normative position—never mind bodily and vocal deportment—for which English schoolboys were actually being "trained up." In the case of *A Midsummer Night's Dream*, Shakespeare marshals not only translation, but also the tropes and transactions of school training in oratory, to portray the Mechanicals: In so doing, Wall's author doubly proves himself capable of the verbal "wit" that could get a schoolboy out of trouble. First, "Wall" is "the wittiest partition" that Demetrius "ever . . . heard discourse" (5.1.167–8) precisely because he personifies the idea of "partition," a rhetorical term for a section of an oration (*partitio*).[4] Second, and consonant with school training in *prosopopoeia*, he picks up and expands the apostrophe to the wall in Ovid's *Metamorphoses* ("'*invide*' *dicebant* '*paries*,'" "they said, 'envious wall'" 4.73) into a dramatic personification ("That I am that same Wall; the truth is so" 5.1.162).[5] As I show throughout this book, habits of personification—from advanced lessons in the techniques of *prosopopoeia* to other exercises in grammar and translation—permeated school training in rhetorical skill at every level of instruction. But in contrast to humanist claims that their program in imitation conferred gentlemanly identity and mastery on its initiates, this method of reading the texts of former schoolboys back into the educational institution that made them possible indicates that the cumulative effect of grammar school instruction in socially sanctioned language, expression, and bodily movement was to establish in students a significant detour between event and feeling, orator and the passions he imitated for the sake of persuading and pleasing others. Indeed, school training engrained what I have come to call "habits of alterity" at the heart of schoolboy "identity." Even early lessons in translation, conducted in the silence of written exercise, gave boys a proto-dramatic part to play in dialogues with peers, parents, or masters: Latin textbooks called *vulgaria* offered boys a Latin *ego* in sentences for translation that put that "ego" in quotation marks from the beginning. And more advanced training in the art of declamation, as well as the habit for school theatricals thought useful for training young orators, required students to mimic—indeed, to embody— a host of passions that were not their own. From first to last, the humanist disciplinary regime pulled against the drive to verbal, corporal, and affective self-mastery schoolmasters advocated. Their debt to the theatrical nature of the very rhetorical tradition they taught means that rather than strengthen the stability of masculine identity, the grammar school's daily demand for verbal and bodily mimicry performed in public under the threat of punishment would produce rhetorically capable "gentlemen" only by keeping such identity at a distance.[6] To put this problem in Bottom's memorable summary of his translation, "it shall be called 'Bottom's Dream,' because it hath no bottom in it." My aim throughout *Shakespeare's Schoolroom* is to take the Latin linguistic turn, as well as the social goals, of sixteenth-century pedagogy literally and seriously. By contrast to the current tendency to accept humanist claims about their success in cultivating obedience and respect for authority and hierarchy, I show that when Shakespeare's representations of character and emotion most profit from school training, they also warn us, as does "Bottom's Dream," to be cautious about taking schoolmasters entirely at their word.

Chapter 1

Rhetoric and the Passions
in Shakespeare's Schoolroom

"Do you love me, master? no?"
—Ariel to Prospero

Of Questions and Methods

A brief catalogue of lines will evoke a sense of this book's topic—Shakespeare's career-long fascination with the idea, practices, and effects of contemporary pedagogy: "Schoolmasters will I keep within my house" and "I am no breeching scholar in the schools" (*Taming of the Shrew*); "I read it in the grammar long ago" and "I was their tutor to instruct them" (*Titus Andronicus*); "O learn to love, the lesson is but plain" (*Venus and Adonis*); "Wilt thou be the school where Lust shall learn?" (*The Rape of Lucrece*). And one final retort to one of Shakespeare's most bookish teachers: "You taught me language, and my profit on't / Is, I know how to curse" (*The Tempest*). Sixteenth-century humanist schoolmasters claimed that their methods of teaching Latin grammar and rhetoric would turn boys into gentlemen, that the eloquence and wisdom garnered at school would directly benefit the English commonwealth. In the chapters that follow, I explore what Shakespearean poetry and drama tell us about such claims while asking, at the same time, how the all-male grammar school affected the emotional registers of early modern masculinity. I began my research for this book by asking what the nuances of Shakespearean emotion reveal about the grammar schools' curriculum, methods of instruction, and forms of discipline. But it was not long before another, related question emerged: When read from the vantage of archival evidence about the Latin schoolroom that made them possible, what do the texts of schoolboys and former schoolboys tell us about the experience of being "trained up" as a "gentleman" in the period? We have long accepted the word of humanist teachers and theorists about the effects of their pedagogy. It is time to listen to the testimony of grammar school students.[1]

The chapters that follow bring evidence about the minutiae of daily life in sixteenth-century schoolrooms to bear on Shakespeare's representation of character and emotion and investigate, in turn, what his rhetorical and meta-rhetorical portraits of the passions reveal about the institutional curriculum and pedagogical practices that made them possible. More specifically, these chapters challenge three influential assumptions in English studies: first, that London's new, commercial stage was more indebted to popular morality drama than to the "elite" Latin culture of humanism;[2] second, that the grammar school "fostered in its initiates a properly docile attitude toward authority" and effectively produced, as the masters said they would, subjects who believed unreservedly in upholding England's existing social hierarchies;[3] and third, that the school's training in Latin grammar and rhetoric successfully instituted a rigid distinction between male and female language, behavior, and feeling.[4] By contrast, I found that when Shakespeare creates convincing effects of character and emotion, he signals his debt to the institution that granted him the "cultural capital" of an early modern gentleman precisely when undercutting the socially normative categories schoolmasters invoked as the goal of their new form of pedagogy.[5]

A lengthy tradition of historical, philological, and literary inquiry documents the distinctive shifts in theory, method, and imagined outcome that shaped sixteenth-century teaching practices.[6] Humanist schoolmasters replaced the method they claimed to have inherited from medieval precursors—Latin training by rule or "precept"—with lessons in imitation. And they vigorously pronounced that their new method and curriculum would train young gentlemen for the good of Britain. In the text that by 1534 had become the standard school grammar in most English schools, Dean John Colet gives the most concise version of this new pedagogical platform: "[L]atyn speche was before the rules, not the rules before the latyn speche. Besy imitacyon with tongue and penne, more auayleth shortly to get the true eloquent speche, than all the tradicions, rules, and precepts of maysters."[7] Usually described as the product of a "war between grammarians" and strongly associated with the Magdalen School (whose members "monopolized the production of textbooks for school use" throughout England), as well as with Colet and the St. Paul's School (whose statutes were widely emulated in provincial schools), humanism's emergent program for teaching Latin grammar and rhetoric reformed the discursive and material practices of sixteenth-century education.[8] As we know well, this new approach to Latin pedagogy changed the course of English literary history. But in addition it meant that as drilling in *imitatio* began to alter literary taste and technique, it began to govern pedagogical and interpersonal relationships.[9]

Throughout *Shakespeare's Schoolroom*, I compare school training to literary invention, institutional practice to theatrical performance, in order to explore the kind of impact the classical rhetorical tradition had on character and emotion in the sixteenth century. Famous and lesser-known records from the schools themselves appear alongside an array of Shakespearean characters and emotions that either directly allude to, or more generally draw upon, various forms of grammar school training in Latin eloquence. The argument proceeds dialectically: I read literary texts in light of common school books, procedures, and exercises; and I reinterpret those texts and procedures in light of the poetry and drama its former students went on to compose. Such a method reveals a crucial, yet unpredictable, connection between humanist rhetorical training and early modern experiences of subjectivity, sexuality, gender, and the inner life of personal feeling. When I first began to work this way, asking what we could tell about early Latin training from the poems and exercises boys read and wrote at school, as well as the vernacular poetry and drama written later in life by former students, I realized that the grammar school's impact on sexuality, affect, and gender was far more ambivalent and contradictory than schoolmasters asserted—or than we, in turn, have yet acknowledged. Indeed, I demonstrate that when read alongside a variety of school materials, the poetic and dramatic production of at least one former schoolboy reveals considerable resistance to the school's regime precisely when most profiting from its training. There are times when questions of genre and larger trends in literary production (particularly epyllia in the 1590s) require me to examine Shakespeare's texts in relation to those of other contemporary authors. But Shakespeare's work remains my primary focus for two reasons: It constitutes one of the largest bodies of evidence by a former grammar schoolboy about rhetoric and the passions; and Shakespeare is one of the few among the era's most successful and prolific writers whose formal education did not extend beyond grammar school. There is not room enough in one study to examine university practices as well, a job I leave to others.

A famous passage from Roger Ascham's *The Scholemaster* will help ground the following discussion. Bristling with associations between school training, hierarchy, and classical *imitatio*, the passage sketches Ascham's ideal version of how a master should teach grammar and translation. With respect to grammar, Ascham writes that a master must "construe" Latin "into Englishe," for his student so often that "the childe may easilie carie awaie the vnderstanding of it." He must then "parse" the Latin "ouer perfitlie." More important, the "childe" is to follow his teacher's footsteps exactly: first construe, then parse ("[L]et the childe, by and by, both construe and parse it ouer againe"). Even the act of rote memory at the basis of a grammar lesson requires a relationship of imitation, both textual and personal. The next step—often quoted with respect to "double translation" and the purported humanist preference for gentleness over corporal punishment—also turns on imitation. But now a third party is involved in the transaction. The "childe" is to translate into English from Latin; an hour later, he translates back into Latin; after that, his master points out how far his words deviate from what "Tullie" would have said:

> the master shall haue good occasion to saie vnto him: N. Tullie would
> have vsed such a worde, not this: Tullie would have placed this word
> here, not there: would haue vsed this case, this number, this person,
> this degree, this gender: he would have vsed this moode, this tense, this
> simple, rather than this compound . . .

The scene connects master and student via the student's likeness to Tullie and his particular habits of speech. The preeminent personification of a rhetorical master in many texts written in, for, and about the school, Cicero triangulates the pedagogical encounter through Rome as Ascham's final authority for a boy's edification. His recommended technique for good language teaching moves literally and imaginatively between text and persons—or rather, to anticipate the theatrical aspect of this argument, *personae*. It gives the student a precise role in a complex social relation of performance, judgment, and address founded on acknowledging hierarchy and honoring the authority of historical precedent. In a popular dictionary, *An English Expositor* (1616), we get a concise indication of how easily imitation's formal and social senses might collide:

> *Imitate*. To follow.
> *Imitation*. A following.
> *Imitator*. A follower of another.[10]

In Ascham's ideal humanist lesson, a student follows first his schoolmaster and then a personified classical authority. In the process, the "childe" imbibes the art of mimicry in a way that turns on both a real and an imaginary social hierarchy.[11] He earns his master's approval by perpetuating the confusion between text and human, past and present, the linguistic and the personal—a hierarchy and a confusion that become the royal road to learning proper Latin grammar and, eventually, rhetorical eloquence. We will see this confusion again—in more advanced lessons in oratory but also in Shakespeare's narrative and dramatic poetry.

The influential humanist scholar Juan Luis Vives claimed that Latin training would turn a "beast" into a "man." And in the view of virtually every humanist educational theorist who commented on the matter, instruction in classical grammar and rhetoric would substantively benefit the English commonwealth.[12] In the 1940s and 1950s, critics like T. W. Baldwin, Donald Clark, and R. R. Bolgar demonstrated this educational program's profound impact on England's literary Renaissance.[13] In the 1970s, Joel Altman and Emrys Jones expanded this work by drawing attention to important habits of mind—particularly the school's fondness for arguments "on either side of the question" (*in utramque partem*)—that shaped Tudor writing in general and Shakespearean drama in particular.[14] In the last twenty years, however, historians and literary critics have turned their attention to the school's active participation in the ongoing process of social reproduction.[15] This book is deeply indebted to both critical approaches. But I expand the first by taking archival evidence about the school's material practices into account when analyzing subsequent literary history; by pressing further the theoretical as well as the practical alliance between rhetoric and drama in the eyes of schoolmasters; and by specifying a few pervasive, classically derived tropes that, much like *imitatio*, produced long-standing literary as well as social and personal effects. And I expand the second critical approach—humanism's intervention in social reproduction—by bringing psychoanalytic questions about subjectivity, language, gender, and sexuality to bear on the texts its schoolboy subjects produced. In other words, by taking the schoolmasters' emphasis on Latin grammar and rhetoric literally and seriously, I explore the significant overlap between literary history and the widespread institutional effort to teach Latin as a means to uphold—indeed, inculcate—the categories most important to the period's explicit formulations about a properly functioning social order. These readings therefore put considerable interrogative pressure on the normative distinctions between genders, erotic practices, and social classes that authors in the period presume when representing to themselves, and to each other, what counts as a functioning, healthy "body politic."

These chapters move beyond humanist theoretical treatises to consider schoolroom dynamics as revealed in texts used in schools or written by students, placing what we can gather about daily pedagogical routines alongside Shakespeare's numerous experiments with—or better yet, meta-critical meditations upon—the ancient art of *imitatio*. My aim is to rethink the school's literary and social effects, some of them intended and some of them probably not, while developing two related arguments: First, the way Shakespeare represents character and emotion (in drama and in verse) reveals as much about his resistance as his indebtedness to the theatricality of the Latin institution in which he learned the art of rhetorical facility. Second, close attention to matters usually deemed strictly literary—specific rhetorical tropes, choices of genre and precedent topic, techniques of imitation and translation, habits of allusion, revisions of and choices between classical exemplars—affords a properly historical understanding of this institution's impact on early modern English masculinity. A theoretical foray into a huge archive, this book aims to be suggestive rather than comprehensive. I move between a variety of important tropes, characters, and emotions in these texts in order to open up new ways of understanding the myriad connections among humanism's institutional practices, the classical past, and what we have come to call Shakespeare's characteristic "subjectivity effects."[16]

I advance both these arguments—the pertinence of rhetoric to a historical account of masculinity and the crucial difference that the Latin grammar school's daily practices made to Shakespeare's representations of character and emotion—to extend Kent Cartwright's observation that our critical consensus about the commercial theater's indebtedness to popular morality drama has prevented us from fully appreciating humanism's impact on that theater's productions. Cartwright's project is to reassess humanist *drama* beyond the Aristotelian strictures through which it has long been understood and beyond the either/or choice of "popular" versus "elite," since this crude distinction fails to do justice to the capacity of early modern drama to "absorb and refashion a range of influences"[17]—or, I might add, to the range of literary and social gradations lying between the ends of this stark opposition. I hope to move his renewed attention to early modern classicism further into the domain of humanism's social transactions, asking how its pedagogical program, as theorized and practiced by England's emerging class of professional scholars, influenced the students who became poets as well as playwrights for the commercial stage. When I read Shakespeare's convincing effects of character and emotion in light of school training, it is to offer a psychologically and rhetorically nuanced account of the social and personal consequences that attended the humanists' attempt to *produce* their distinctive version of what counted in sixteenth-century Britain as the difference between "popular" and "elite."

Before the next chapters take up schoolroom practices and some of their unintended consequences, a general outline of current approaches to the grammar school's forms of social reproduction is necessary. As the result of an emerging class of (often lowborn) professional scholars searching for financial and social advancement—and a fortuitous battle between Henry VIII and canon lawyers—command of Latin became a significant form of cultural capital in early modern England.[18] In the words of Lisa Jardine and Antony Grafton, humanist schooling "stamped the more prominent members of the new elite with an indelible cultural seal of superiority."[19] Funding for new and reestablished grammar schools in England came largely from merchant capital; and the majority of students were drawn from landed or merchant classes. And yet even the largest, most prestigious schools ensured support for at least a handful of "poor students" every year.[20] The grammar school's curriculum and training, as well as the new, public mix of boys from different stations therefore did more than "signif[y] an already existing class system." Rather, as Richard Halpern points out, schools "intervened in the system itself, transforming both the ruling groups and the very nature of class distinction."[21] The humanist desideratum of rhetorical *copia* became a distinctive way of marking significant social differences, differences that their training was designed both to produce and to police.[22]

As an all-male institution that separated young boys from their families to bring them up as Latin-speaking gentlemen, moreover, the Tudor grammar school institutionalized a historically distinctive, hierarchical division between "mother" and "father" tongues. Establishing a socially significant opposition between English and Latin, maternal and paternal spheres of language and influence, schools self-consciously sought to intervene, materially and discursively, in the reproduction of normative gender categories.[23] And indeed, a crude misogyny does inform many school textbooks, which often distinguish a boy's coddling mother from the bracing discipline of his Latin schoolmaster. But whether *all* boys who read and translated such passages from and into Latin felt the way the authors presumed they would about leaving their mother's care for the schoolmaster's discipline is far from obvious (here we might remember one Shakespearean schoolboy, "creeping like snail / Unwillingly to school").[24] Of course, it does not take exhaustive research to show how profoundly the linguistic and rhetorical basis of the school's curriculum influenced commonplace, dismissive views about female inferiority. For example, a former schoolboy published the following comment in 1577 about his own attempt at versification and wives:

> Take in good parte these triflyng toyes,
> good Reader which I write:
> When I was a boye with boyes,
> these toyes I did indite.
> Tushe, tushe, thei foolishe are thou saiest:
> I graunt, thei are in deede:
> But where are thy wifes wondrous workes,
> now where are thei to reede?[25]

For this former grammar school student, "boyes" are the gender privileged to "indite" poetic "workes," women the gender to bear the burden of mute anonymity. Boys, moreover, learn their craft among a community of "boyes" presumed to persist beyond school—to constitute the future "readers" to whom a man will address himself as the writer does here. Such attitudes will not surprise readers familiar with early modern England's gender norms. And yet I have found that a careful look at the grammar school's texts and material, discursive practices undermines the simple gender dichotomy on which such standard sentiments rest. In the chapters that follow, I hope to make a well-known literary history a little less familiar. That is, if we read Shakespeare's texts from the perspective of school language training, the socially sanctioned community and prima facie meaning of "a boye with boyes" sometimes took turns the boys' teachers did not seem to expect.

Halpern observes that measuring the school's relationship to social reproduction means stepping outside a literary perspective on the "Renaissance" long enough to question the social illogic of an educational institution devoted so narrowly to linguistic arts—first to grammar, then to techniques of rhetoric and style.[26] Departing from an earlier, untroubled appreciation among twentieth-century literary historians for the rise and dominance of an educational institution dedicated to inculcating skills amenable to playwrights and poets, recent critics draw attention to the social function of the humanist school and its legacy. And some have begun to point to a few significant contradictions between the school's announced mission and its actual practice. Grammar schools trained boys in the arts best suited for states-manship, the clergy, the law, and international trade; but masters rarely, if ever, seemed concerned about the fact that many of their students would never pursue such careers. As an important survey of provincial grammar schools attests, fathers from a far greater array of professions than those for which rhetorical training was truly practical enrolled their sons in these new schools: At Hull, for example, the fathers' professions ranged from clergy, counselors-at-law, merchants, and traders to a mix of "tailors, cordwainers, butchers, clerks, surgeons, innkeepers, master mariners, tobacco cutters, milli-ners, grocers, customs officers."[27] And so for Halpern, it is "no longer obvious why Tudor society would allocate a substantial part of its resources" to an insti-tution whose investment in rhetoric made it a "miracle of impracticality" when viewed in light of the kind of training many of these vocations actually re-quired. Though humanist teachers often objected in print to severe corporal punishment, publicly advocating gentler forms of training and persuasion, a host of evidence suggests that corporal punishment hardly vanished from the schools—and that flogging (or the threat of it) was used right alongside the gentler art of inculcating respect for authority by training a boy to imitate or "follow" an exemplary model. Pursuing such evidence in his sociologically oriented study of contemporary objections from families to harsh corporal dis-cipline at school, Alan Stewart observes that "the value of the educational ex-perience of a young man as a rite of passage" in early modern England was "threatened by that experience itself."[28]

To this recent critique of the distance between humanist theory and practice, I would add that a relatively untroubled twentieth-century consensus that the school succeeded in consolidating normative gender categories stems largely from Walter Ong's influential observation that Latin training was a kind of "male puberty rite."[29] Yet it is only in recent years that feminist and queer theorists have questioned the way assessments like Ong's rely on the terms *male* and *female* without fully interrogating their historically and cul-turally variable significance. As will become clear from my analysis in the next chapter, the same might be said of *puberty*. While feminist and queer critique have changed the kinds of questions we bring to bear on Shakespeare's plays, they have only begun to alter our account of early modern pedagogy. Far less widely remembered, moreover, is Harold Newcomb Hillebrand's 1929 account of school theatricals in *The Child Actors*. From his extensive documentation we learn that training in acceptable gentlemanly behavior at school included the indirections, displacements, and emotional excesses of the theater—for which some students were being paid by members of the public as early as 1518 and for which a number of schools became well known—and that whatever *male* signifies in this institutional/ritual context, its meaning must be flexible enough to include the widespread practice of cross-dressing. With great frequency over the course of the sixteenth century, schoolboys preserved—indeed, extended—the long-standing medieval custom of playing female parts on holidays. And they did so as part of their induction into the successful performance of genteel masculinity. In the grammar school attached to Magdalen College, Oxford, boys in the choir acted in plays as early as 1509; in 1518, the master of the choir was paid after his boys' play for providing a costume for Christ and "*pro crinibus mulieribus*" ("for women's hair"). On November 10, 1527, boys from the St. Paul's School, under the direction of their master, John Rightwise, presented a Latin morality play at Greenwich before Henry VIII and several French ambassadors; the dramatis personae include a mix of historical figures (Luther, Luther's wife, St. Peter, Paul, Wolsey) and several female personifications: Lady Peace, Lady Quietness, Dame Tranquility, Ecclesia, Veritas, and Heresy. As I examine in greater detail in Chapters 3 and 4, evidence of cross-dressed playing in the schools increases rapidly after 1525, beginning at Eton.[30] In one arresting case that does not entirely comport with Ong's observation (or received opinions derived from it), the "very loose behaviour" of the schoolmaster's daughter at the King's School in Ely drew considerable parental ire in the town. Evidently, this daughter "would not stick to put on boys apparel" in her father's absence and "lett boyes putt on hers"; she then liked to dance, so dressed, "amongeste the boyes."[31] Whether advanced in the form of a theoretical critique of cross-dressing's impact on the boys subject to such training in Latin rhetorical facility or a historical investigation into the particular details of school events and customs, current accounts of this institution cannot pass too quickly over the term *male puberty rite*. It is time to think in further historical and theoretical detail about what, precisely, we might mean by invoking *male*, *puberty*, or *rite* to describe the social and literary impact of a humanist education.

Impractical though it may appear to some now, and provoking as it appeared to some then, the grammar school's program of inculcating Latin grammar and rhetoric through practices of imitation virtually guaranteed that something we recognize as a literary "Renaissance" occurred as an unintended side effect of its program for the "training up of children" to become "gentlemen" whose "wits" would "aunswereth best the monarchie" and "help" Britain become "the best of common weales."[32] In the following pages, I explore the contradictions between the grammar school's declared purpose, practices, and effects further still, asking what texts written for and in the schools themselves have to say about this institution's social and personal effects, as well as what they reveal about the oblique—yet historically significant—associations that schoolmasters forged on a daily, disciplinary basis among language, subjectivity, gender, body, and emotion. With respect to the world of feeling, I discuss the historical and theoretical differences between the terms *passion*, *emotion*, and *affect* in some detail at the end of this chapter in order to explain my reasons for using one term over another at a given moment in my analysis. But perhaps it does not go without saying that I try not to collapse these words or use them simply as synonyms. Rather, I put them in productive tension because they enter the English language at different moments bearing distinctly different meanings and histories. For now, let me observe simply that taking stock of the grammar school's social, literary, and personal effects requires attention to the intersection between classical rhetoric's chief aim—to "move" audiences in ways that are not purely cognitive—and sixteenth-century understandings of the body and the passions.

To conduct this investigation, I have developed and maintained a theoretical framework flexible enough to address these (ostensibly) disparate areas of early modern experience: classical rhetorical practice and instruction; masculinity; and the embodied life of the passions. To push our account of the school's role in social reproduction further, I rely on the axiom that rhetoric has two branches that continually interact: tropological (requiring formal, literary analysis) and transactional (requiring social and historical analysis).[33] Ascham's personification of Cicero as imagined interlocutor in a scene of grammatical instruction has already suggested as much. Imitation, in Ascham's hands, is a literary and pedagogical practice deploying the animating fantasy of *prosopopoeia* (understood in its Roman sense as a speech "impersonating" that of another) in a grammar lesson that has narrow designs on a student's grammatical abilities and broader aspirations for the formation of his character.[34] Guiding his own speech according to "what Tullie would have said" allows a boy to succeed and win his master's approval. Assessing the grammar school's impact on its gentlemen in the making therefore means taking formal and tropological analysis very seriously—at least as seriously as humanist schoolmasters did—while expanding historical critiques of gender and sexuality in relation to nuances of literary and rhetorical technique, form, and style. This book assesses the claims schoolmasters made about their new program in relation to several kinds of textual evidence: the various texts the boys read and used in their lessons (i.e., dictionaries, *vulgaria,* grammars, commonplace books, rhetorical manuals); extant exercises and poems students wrote while attending a school; the kinds of physical and verbal training the records suggest they received in acting and declamation; and, finally, the literary texts such students went on to compose later in life. Grammar schools declared themselves to be in the business of responding to historical social norms with classical literary and rhetorical examples that would mold those norms in light of the past. For example, in a 1592 London edition of the widely disseminated rhetorical manual that introduced boys to a host of ancient figures and formal rhetorical techniques, Aphthonius's *Progymnasmata*, a student's dutiful inscription reminds us of the extent to which classical rhetorical facility was directly linked to social and personal ends: "disburst to me by my tutor last term for the mending of my youth."[35] The technical path to such "mending" in the *Progymnasmata* consisted of a series of general and then practical instruction in how to imitate such techniques as *fabula* (drawn from Aesop and Hesiod), *narratio* (stories about "persons, deeds, times, places, causes") *chreia* ("anecdote"), *sententia* ("aphorism"), *restructio* ("refutation"), *confirmatio* ("proof"), *locus communis* ("commonplace"), *laus* ("praise"), *vituperatio* (in Shakespeare's translation, "dispraise"), *comparatio* ("comparison" of "persons, things, times, places, animals, plants"), *ethopoeia* ("character making"), *descriptio/ekphrasis* ("where persons, things, times, places, animals and plants are brought before the eyes") and *thesis* ("deliberation of general or abstract questions," i.e., "whether to marry?").[36] The way schoolboys and former schoolboys deployed the ancient forms they were trained to imitate therefore has a great deal to tell us about their experience of being turned into Latin-speaking gentlemen.

The grammar school's belief in language's productive force clearly invites comparison with Jacques Lacan's theory of the Symbolic's determining effect on sexual difference, but I am not the first to notice the resemblance.[37] Schoolmasters and Lacan agree on at least one thing: Language precedes and shapes character rather than the other way around. Since Lacan's return to Freud, moreover, much contemporary psychoanalytic theory has moved between the tropological and the transactional, between semiotic analysis and transpersonal effects. Such movement attests to its complex indebtedness to the history of rhetoric, and it is primarily in light of psychoanalysis's leavening proximity to rhetoric that I invoke it here.[38] More generally, however, Lacan's claim that the subject is an effect of signification, as well as his corollary critique of mastery, is particularly apt for an institution devoted to cultivating a boy's character by means of his submission to—indeed, as we shall see in Chapters 3 and 4, especially, "loving"—his master.

In my view, comparing the grammar school's belief in rhetoric's formative power to Lacan's notion of the Symbolic's shaping force is promising for a study of early modern masculinity, but it is only a beginning. As numerous psychoanalytic, feminist, and queer theorists writing in light of Lacan have suggested in a variety of ways, he left much unanswered about the body's complex embedding in language—particularly with regard to the way specific institutions and the habits they inculcate through repetitive practice grant individuals their social existence and induct them into a given culture's norms about which bodies, actions, thoughts, and emotions "matter"; which do not; and in what ways.[39] It will also become clear that I draw, as have others, on Pierre Bourdieu's definition of *habitus* as an "acquired system of generative schemes," a "product of history" that "produces individual and collective practices."[40] Each chapter detects, and asks how one might interpret in the Shakespearean text in question, the "active presence of past experiences . . . deposited" in schoolboys "in the form of schemes of perception, thought, and action."[41] But *habitus*, like "the Symbolic," works at a level of abstraction that begs historical specificity. In particular, the exclusively rhetorical heart of the Latin schoolroom requires a precise *formal* account of a schoolboy's formative "schemes of perception, thought, and action." I therefore focus in each chapter on the particular tropological and generic questions each text raises with regard to the "active presence" of early school experience in the future writer's habits of invention and impersonations of feeling.

In the readings that follow, a number of important discursive techniques and figures allow me to bring the schoolroom into texts and literary texts back into the schoolroom. In addition to the ubiquitous technique of *in utramque partem* argument so effectively brought to bear already on Renaissance drama, I follow two particular figures in Shakespeare's poetry that are tropologically as well as transactionally revealing about grammar school training, gender, and the passions: *prosopopoeia* (and its early modern umbrella term, *ethopoeia*) and *ekphrasis* ("description"). As the following chapters detail, the art of impersonation and description—judged by ἐνάργεια, or "liveliness," in which a speaker "does not narrate so much as depict, the reader does not *read* so much as *see*"—were standard lessons in advanced oratorical exercise.[42] The confusions of ear and eye, the ability to impersonate characters on demand, were crucial components of school exercises in oratory. It hardly takes a professional Shakespearean to see how important such training in impersonation and "liveliness" might be—for both the dramatist and the narrative poet. I maintain this tropological and transactional focus not simply because rhetoric is one of the period's distinctive and pervasive institutional practices, a peculiar form of early experience to which many texts indebted to school training attest. I do so because Latin rhetorical training—as an elaborately defined set of discursive, corporal, and affective exercises—allows us to reconsider early modern classicism in its literary and social aspect, and therefore to understand the material role ancient texts played in the history of subjectivity, gender, and sexuality in late sixteenth-century England.

An exploration of rhetorical form allows us, in short, to ask what the particular details of literary and school texts, taken together, reveal about the way early modern schoolboys internalized (indeed, embodied) grammar school training. As the next chapter clarifies, the disciplinary program within which boys were educated, from early grammar lessons to advanced training in oratory, makes it impossible to separate language lessons from embodiment; matter rendered significant through time and practice from thought and perception; or affect from the "generative" social "schemes" to which schoolboys were subject during their years under the eye, and birch, of a humanist rhetorical master. The following chapters are designed to show that accounting for symbolic determination, both historically and psychoanalytically, means acknowledging the school's extraordinary cultural reach while at the same time keeping an eye out for its immanent contradictions. As I hope to show, the literary and school texts adduced here reveal a deep, unstable conflict at the heart of the very regime of identity and difference (between girls and boys, mother and father tongues, vulgar and learned) that its avatars worked so hard to install.

Pedagogy, Erotics, Alterity

My opening question—how did grammar school training influence what counted as genteel masculinity in the period?—raises another: How did early modern pedagogy affect experiences of sexuality and desire? Such a question bears directly on a variety of school texts, as we shall see. But it becomes more urgent still in Shakespeare's many dramatic renditions of schoolroom dynamics, as well as in less explicit reflections on rhetorical practice that draw, nonetheless, on early Latin training. Indeed, the more I explored the school's forms of instruction—ranging from lessons in translation to guidance in acceptable gesture, intonation, and affect for convincing oratorical performance—the more frequently I found myself asking, why is Shakespeare so fond of turning contemporary pedagogy and its classical curriculum into a matter of sex? Why is *love* the word he links most frequently to *master* or *mastery*? The affective resonance in the following (by no means exhaustive) list of scenes ranges widely, but each dramatizes the school, its Latin curriculum, and its devotion to language training in a distinctly sexual context.[43] In *Titus Andronicus*, teaching based on Roman poetry leads only to rape and dismemberment: "Indeed I was their tutor to instruct them," boasts Aaron about his lesson in Ovidian imitation that leads Chiron and Demetrius to turn Lavinia into another Philomel (5.1.98). In *The Tempest*, pedagogy leads to near rape: Prospero, erstwhile master and language tutor to Caliban, rebukes his former student for trying "to violate/The honor of my child" (1.2.347–8). Lucrece reacts to Tarquin's threat of rape by asking if he would make himself a "school" for "Lust" (617). In *The Taming of the Shrew*, translating Latin allows Lucentio, disguised as a schoolmaster, to woo Bianca over a line from the *Heroides* and to style himself as a "master" in the "art of love." In *Henry V*, Shakespeare expands *The Taming of the Shrew*'s connection between pedagogy, translation, and seduction beyond Latin to French. When Katherine becomes a beginning language student, her first lesson, like any English schoolboy using a bilingual Latin-English vocabulary, is to learn the names for parts of the body. In at least one school, masters were required by statute to conduct the nightly exercise of having the boys rehearse the Latin names for all parts of the body: "the schoolmaster shall every night teach their scholars their Latin words with the English signification . . . begin[ning] with words that concern the head reciting orderly as nigh as they can every part and number of the body and every particular of the same."[44] Here one sees that the penchant for anatomizing in the period may have more than a literary (Petrarchan) heritage. And the sexual edge surrounding persuasion and deferral in the scene where the king proposes marriage derives largely from jokes about their respective "tongues" and, more generally, problems in bilingual translation. In *Venus and Adonis*, a "lesson" based on "old treatises" from Rome—in this case, Ovid's *Metamorphoses* and *Ars amatoria*—takes a turn toward sexual harassment when Venus plays the role of an Ovidian *magister amoris* to a pupil who "hates" her lesson and describes himself as an "orator too green" to imitate the ancient examples she offers. And in the "Induction" to *The Taming of the Shrew* and *A Midsummer Night's Dream*, impromptu exercises based on Roman poetry gesture toward provocatively undefined and therefore potentially expansive pleasures. Sly learns a lesson in lordly behavior when he hears about pictures of *amor* drawn from the first and tenth books of the *Metamorphoses*. Perhaps it is Mistress Quickly who best cuts to the chase: Hearing young William decline "the genitive case," "*horum,*

harum, horum," Quickly mishears, transforming Latin lessons into a decidedly disreputable erotic encounter. "Vengeance of Jenny's case! Fie on her!
Never name her, child, if she be a whore" (4.1.52–57).

Two acute readers of *Titus Andronicus* point out that Shakespeare can be
savagely critical of humanist claims for the civic and moral benefits of the
school's classical curriculum. In that play, imitating Ovid leads only to cultural, familial, and sexual mayhem.[45] Chiron and Demetrius may show
themselves to be poor Latin scholars, but their stupidity hardly excuses their
teachers or their texts. Caliban's "profit" from his teacher's lessons suggests a
similarly bitter assessment of language training's effect on its students. But two
of Shakespeare's more diffuse (though under-examined) habits confront us
with less overtly political, but nonetheless intractable, questions about the after-
effects of school training. Why does he so often turn pedagogical scenes and
the Latin curriculum behind them into erotic (sometimes violently erotic)
encounters? In addition, when literary and rhetorical concerns about classical
imitation arise, why does he so often engage at the same time in dense, meta-
rhetorical reflections on character, voice, and emotion? Perhaps the most
concise way to evoke both the breadth and the obliquity of Shakespeare's engagement with contemporary pedagogy and its cherished Latin texts is to recall
that he has a pronounced tendency to interrogate the grammar school's language, curriculum, and disciplinary methods for achieving eloquence by giving
a voice to the emotions of precisely those whom its rhetorical training was designed to exclude: women (Venus, Lucrece, Katherine, Bianca, Kate, Lavinia);
"barbarians" (Aaron, Tamora, Othello, Caliban, Ariel, Cleopatra); and characters who could never aspire to gentility (Sly, Bottom, Mistress Quickly).[46]
If this book does the work I hope it will do, other readers will find more
characters to add to such lists.

Perhaps it does not go without saying that these three categories ema-
nate from the school and are not the imposition of modern concerns. The
grammar school was the exclusive domain of men and boys, but Shakespeare
frequently dramatizes aspects of contemporary pedagogy through the voices of
passionate—and often troublesome—women. And these female characters are
not exclusively relegated to the role of docile student or comical *ignorans*.[47]
Chapter 3 examines the scandalous erotics of *Venus and Adonis* in light of two
observations: Venus represents herself as trying to teach Adonis a "lesson" in
love reminiscent of the very first lesson in Lily's ubiquitous *A Short Introduction
of Grammar*: *"amo magistrum"* ("I love the master"). "Barbarism" was a school
commonplace for translating your Latin badly: As Lily's *Grammar* declares,

for instance, "All barbary, all corruption, all Latin adulteration which ignorant, blind fools brought into the world . . . and poisoned the old Latin speech of the early Roman tongue will not be allowed entrance to the school."[48] But Shakespeare is quite capable of inventing "barbarians" like Aaron or Othello who know their classical tradition very well indeed. Where Aaron plays Ovidian "tutor" in *Titus*, Othello's far from "rude" speech wins Desdemona's "love" and "pity": Othello thus imitates Aeneas, whose tale of travel and peril so beguiled Dido in *Aeneid* 2, and whose story stood above almost any other in humanist writing as essential to a boy's education.[49] Caliban's protest about the benefits of Prospero's "language" training, moreover, has long struck readers and audiences as one of *The Tempest*'s most memorable lines. Finally, the school's classical curriculum was shaped by humanist disdain for popular and folk culture. But as I have already suggested, Shakespeare gives an exquisite pleasure in Latin textuality to the likes of Sly and Bottom—and at times seems to cling, like Mamillius, to precisely the "old wives' fairy rubbish" their classical curriculum was designed to supplant.

I discuss some of these characters; I might have chosen others. Their ubiquity suggests how frequently Shakespeare is inclined to provide a classical frame for characters and passions at some considerable distance from the socially normative position—never mind bodily and vocal deportment—for which schoolboys were actually being trained. It is therefore crucial to think beyond the school's explicit categories and social distinctions. The next chapters demonstrate that school training in Latin rhetoric inculcated something one could call a habit of alterity, even though its teachers probably did not anticipate some of the directions in which a talent for impersonating other voices would lead. Characters like those enumerated above indicate how much Shakespeare benefited from this habit. But I believe that his penchant for using school techniques against the institution's explicit representations of a properly functioning social body is a distinctive touch.

By habit of alterity, I mean not only that school training encouraged a general disposition toward impersonation, and hence a propensity for drama. I also mean that if read back into the schoolroom that made them possible, Shakespeare's representations of the passions indicate that early school training encouraged in pupils a highly mediated relation to emotion, a tendency to experience what passes for deep personal feeling precisely by taking a detour through the passions of others (particularly those classical figures offered as examples for imitation). To do justice to this habit of alterity, I analyze the discursive and material practices of sixteenth-century pedagogy according to historically specific representations of social "others" while also keeping in mind psychoanalytic speculation about the effects of the "other" in speaking subjects. Unexpected characters like Venus, Adonis, Bianca, Kate, Aaron, Othello, Caliban, Sly, Bottom, and Mistress Quickly—caught up in the language and dynamics of the schoolroom while acting within sexual fantasies that range from the appallingly violent to the obscene, the bawdy, and the evanescently erotic—tell us that Shakespeare's engagement with the humanist grammar school goes well beyond explicit political and moral critique.[50] In the pages the follow, I show that it is especially in Shakespeare's depictions of character, feeling, and desire that we detect traces of his ambivalent indebtedness to the institution that gave him the classically inflected rhetorical facility of an early modern gentleman.

Emotion and Character

I have been arguing that early modern classicism testifies to a deeply fraught social and transpersonal struggle for verbal, social, and erotic power. Shakespeare and others often call this a struggle for "mastery." What might appear to us to be merely formal decisions in the texts of the period were, rather, embedded in a complex institutional history with immense influence on gender, sexuality, and the passions. Recent cultural and literary critics working on the history of emotion call attention to language's "constitutive role in any culture's emotional universe," an idea captured in Katherine Rowe's apt phrase, "emotion scripts."[51] Among other things, this insight means that before assuming we know what a particular feeling means or how it signifies in a given text, we first require a careful philological account of the changing significance of words used to designate and assign values to emotions across cultures and time periods. The pages that follow understand grammar school training to have provided a fountain of influential emotion scripts. Before turning to the relationship between school practices and Shakespeare's representation of "the passions," however, I must briefly distinguish between it and two other more modern words for the inner life of feeling: *emotion* and *affect*. The medical strain of early modern discourses about the passions derives emotional life from bodily disposition: In humoral theory, one's corporal existence has a determining effect on states of feeling. As much recent scholarly work suggests, Shakespeare's representations of the passions are indebted to the Galenic medical tradition. But we have not yet investigated fully enough why his reflections on the passions involve meta-theatrical or meta-rhetorical reflections on classical figures, texts, and traditions: Hecuba, Niobe, Philomela, Lucrece, Venus, Adonis, Actaeon, Apollo, Daphne, Narcissus, Dido, Aeneas, Sinon, and Medea (among others) provide the Latin mythographic template from which his scenes of overpowering feeling derive their force.[52] In Chapter 3, for instance, I ask two related questions of *Venus and Adonis*: Why is the narrator's exercise in *prosopopoeia* (understood as giving a voice to mythological characters) deliberately framed as a lesson in "love"? And what does the rhetorical contest between the two main characters have to tell us about the affective and erotic contours of the poem? Chapter 4 analyzes an example of *ekphrastic* description—"wanton pictures" of Venus, Apollo, and Io offered to Sly—in light of Shakespeare's critique of "mastery" and the schoolroom in *The Taming of the Shrew*. And in Chapter 5 I examine the crucial role that Hecuba plays in school rhetorical training and thus in Shakespeare's reflections on *imitatio* and "woe" in *The Rape of Lucrece, Hamlet*, and *The Winter's Tale*. In Shakespeare's hands, the passions have a distinctly classical cast; part of the project of this book is to demonstrate why.

With respect to the difference between the modern terms *emotion* and *affect*, I try to use our own modern and familiar term, *emotion*, to designate a commonsense understanding of personal feeling, one that often presumes emotions to be (relatively) transparent indicators for interior states. Deriving from the Latin *emotus*, a "moving out" or "perturbation" (and used in several Latin school texts in ways close to our own modern sense), *emotion* still did not emerge as an English word in its own right until the late seventeenth century. Eventually bifurcating from *passion*, whose significance slowly narrowed from its early modern provenance to signify only intense, overpowering, and amorous feelings, *emotion* supplanted the earlier term and served to distinguish certain feelings "from cognitive or volitional states of consciousness."[53] After the late seventeenth century, *passion* was no longer used, as it was from the fourteenth century until roughly 1680, to designate corporal sensations as much as states of mind: For example, the OED cites "a bely ache or passion" (1547). The early range and subsequent narrowing of *passion* is a telling index of how important it is to remember that school discipline was a corporal as well as verbal affair.

When I use *affect*, by contrast, I aim at a range of related meanings that derive from both early modern and psychoanalytic discourse. The earliest English meanings for *affect*, relatively faithful to the Latin *afficio* from which it derives (especially with the ablative, "to cause a person to be affected by an emotion . . . to stir, to be strongly moved"), were "a mental state brought about by influence; the action or result of affecting the mind in some way; an emotion, feeling."[54] Perhaps transmitting the Latin sense of an individual being acted upon in some forceful way, Richard Hooker links "affection" to appetite rather than reason, describing such strong feeling as a mystery "not altogether in our power," at times a desire for something even if it "be . . . never so impossible."[55] In the rest of this book, I therefore use *affect* in one of two ways. First, I draw on its early modern sense of an intense, sometimes mysterious state of feeling (for example, Leontes's famously enigmatic declaration that "affection" is a force that "stabs the center" and "communicates" with dreams). Indeed, a number of the classically inflected passions analyzed here, however powerful, seem "not altogether in the power" of those who experience them and run counter to commonsense or intuitive assessments of inner life.

Second, I am also drawing on a modern psychoanalytic understanding of *affect* (also with a Latinate origin) to signify moments of opacity in emotions. Psychoanalytic theory detects a distance between putative cause and (emotional) effect that stems from our blindness, as speaking subjects, to the most significant events of our own history.[56] Several of Freud's important theories turn on affect's enigmatic quality: He generally uses "affect" to distinguish an event, idea, or sign from the quantity of psychological energy "bound" to it. Indeed, his insight into the "separation" of affect from idea, or idea from affect, was that "they were sure to follow different paths."[57] For example, Freud's quantitative analysis of the dream work theorizes a transfer of affective energy from one (forbidden) sign to another (permissible) one; his analysis of the death drive studies repetition's deeply compelling yet impenetrable significance for the subjects of trauma. His early encounter with hysterics led him to distinguish between traumatic event and the "proportionate discharge of affect" that is nonetheless disassociated from it. Perhaps most important for my question about what pressure a schoolboy's past might exert on his literary production as an adult—an issue that exceeds the scope of *habitus*—is that Freud's investigations into hysteria led him to posit a notion of "psychical reality" in which a *memory* might produce a "more powerful release" of affective energy "than that produced by the corresponding experience itself."[58] Such an insight is suggestive about the retrospective force that literary representations of the passions might have had on audiences and authors "trained up" by the humanist grammar school. In each of his analyses of "affect," Freud found nuances to emotional life that evade conscious understanding, require significant semiotic analysis, and defy the linear narratives of developmental models. Based on such an understanding of emotion's mobility, obliquity, and resistance to *seriatim* explanation, I use the word *affect* to indicate that the "passion" I am considering—especially when indebted to the Latin schoolroom—may well be less transparent than it seems.[59]

Throughout this book, then, I use *affect* rather than *emotion* to point toward a coincidence between the school's theatrical training and psychoanalytic theory: Repeatedly imitating others' words and emotions in public, under the scrutiny of many monitoring eyes and the threat of possible punishment, would be an efficient way to blur the seemingly obvious line between the intensity of an actor/orator's expressions from the actual speaker's feelings. I will suggest that the inventive fantasies of writers who were engaging their past school training (whether consciously or not) could take surprising turns—detours that are nonetheless affectively moving and intense. To put the matter another way, acts of poetic ventriloquism, in this period, could be at once profoundly moving and deeply enigmatic; and they therefore testify to the heuristic pallor of the term *persona*. The cumulative effect of school training in proper language, behavior, and affect was to institutionalize numerous kinds of detours and transfers between event and feeling, speaker and audience, orator and the passions he imitated. It is these detours and transfers—the domain of the theater, the school, the poetry of former schoolboys, but also the unconscious—that prompt me to distinguish between emotion and affect when reading early modern representations of character and the "passions." One of the stranger aspects of grammar school practice is that the humanist effort to discipline language and affect produced rhetorically skilled subjects whose technical proficiency in evoking assigned passions, from themselves and from an audience, meant that a boy's connection to his own feelings might become tenuous at best. And prone, moreover, to preposterous reversals of cause and effect. From the perspective of the school, scholars achieved their place in their social world by being drilled in the art of feeling and conveying passions that came from somewhere else and someone else. From a psychoanalytic perspective, early modern schoolboys were trained in techniques that distanced them from their own experience in both language and time; the substitution of a new, "father" tongue for an earlier, "mother" tongue only exacerbated the retrospective work of puberty's displacements. To preserve my double focus on school practice and psychoanalytic theory, I maintain this mutually informing pair of terms—*emotion* and *affect*—to convey both the intensity and the opacity of early modern "passions."

Earlier, I invoked Bourdieu's notion of *habitus*, or "structuring dispositions," to suggest that the school's theatrical forms of corporal and verbal
discipline might incline its students toward emotionally charged practices of
imitation, personification, and multiple identifications in adult life. As I'll
explore in the next chapter, the school's structuring dispositions might further incline a former schoolboy to experience poetic or rhetorical invention as
an adult as if he were still performing for an audience or judge. Bourdieu's
theory gives "disproportionate weight to early experiences," arguing for "the
active presence" of a past that "tends to perpetuate itself into the future by reactivation in similarly structured practices."[60] At least three pasts are important
in this book: the classical past activated in schoolroom exercises in imitation;
the student's individual, familial past as it intersects with the disciplinary and
discursive methods of the school; and the transpersonal, collective past "reactivated" in the literary inventions of an adult schoolboy. The result, as Bourdieu
observes, is not a "mechanical determinism" but rather a historical, identifiable
set of constraints that put limits on the field of possible inventions, emotions, and subject positions available to the boys who earned their place as
"gentleman" by means of facility in Latin.

Though I find Bourdieu's ideas about the continuing after-effects of institutional practices extremely helpful for thinking about the texts of former
schoolboys, there are times when *habitus* is not capacious, or perhaps nuanced, enough for my topic. The passions represented in the literary texts of
former schoolboys—classically inflected representations of grief, love, rage,
disgust, wonder, and fear in which normative categories of gender and desire
vanish—suggest the kinds of affective excess, opacity, and displacement traced
in psychoanalytic theory. As the next chapters illustrate, moreover, normative
boundaries between genders and erotic practices often turn to shifting sand in
these texts. And at the same time, the ostensibly clear distinction between
pain and pleasure tends to disappear when Shakespeare's eroticized versions
of *imitatio* take a turn toward violence. These ambivalent associations require
a theoretical position that not only accounts for the structuring habits of past
practice, but also attends carefully to future retrospection—to the links between the conditions of cultural intelligibility, the odd temporality of puberty,
the vicissitudes of memory, and the enigmatic effects of punishment and cultural taboo.

Finally, thinking through Shakespeare's school for the passions leads to
what I have found to be one of the more complex after-effects of rhetorical
training, by which I mean "character," whether personal or literary. Shaping

a boy's character along socially useful lines lay at the heart of humanist pedagogy; virtually every schoolmaster who commented on the social utility of a
classical curriculum insisted, after Cicero, that eloquence and wisdom were the
same thing and therefore useful to the commonwealth. I use the word *character*
advisedly throughout—not entirely in the sense of twentieth-century "character criticism" (reading literary texts according to a sense of "individuality impressed by nature and habit; mental or moral constitution"). Nor do I use it
entirely in its dominant sixteenth-century association with external signs: a
"distinctive mark impressed or engraved; a brand, stamp, graphic sign, or style
of writing."[61] Instead, I use it in the sense fostered in school texts and practice
because it is in the schools that future poets and dramatists first became ac-
quainted with the rhetorical notion of *ethos* (a term originating with Aristotle
and with a long life in rhetorical theory). As a technical term widely circulated
in the schools by way of a chapter in Aphthonius's *Progymnasmata* on "character making" ("*etho-poeia*"), ἔθος was not merely a matter of intellectual history
but also became a category important to schoolboy practice.[62] In Aphthonius's
scheme, which was partially preserved in the schoolmaster Richard Sherry's
Treatise of Schemes and Tropes (1550), *ethopoeia* (impersonating historical and
mythological characters) is closely allied to two other kinds of speech making:
prosopopoeia (impersonating abstractions or "things unknown") and *idolopoeia*
(impersonating dead people).[63]

As we will see in Chapter 5, Aphthonius's lesson in character-making is
very likely the route by which Hecuba and Niobe became such a compelling figures of grief for Shakespeare. Furthermore, in its "emotional" form,
ethopoeia designates a speech that follows "the motion of the mind in every
respect" ("*quae prorsus animi significant motum*")—for example, "words such
as Hecuba would say at the fall of Troy."[64] As deployed in early modern education as a lesson in imitation, *character* therefore designates a revealing historical switch point where Latin rhetorical training contributes to the word's
bifurcation in two directions. First, it moves inward, swerving away from the
external signs of writing to the sense of interiority that has dominated since
the mid-eighteenth century: "personality; the moral or mental qualities" of
an individual. Second, it moves classical *ethos* into English fiction, signifying
"the personality or 'part' assumed by an actor on the stage" and, eventually,
literary character *tout court*.[65] Many of the poetic and dramatic moments this
book surveys participate in that historical shift, revealing how tightly rhetorical training in the Latin schoolroom tied rhetorical *effects* of "character" to
the life of "the passions," and at the same time, how profound the confusion

between texts and persons became. But before I can comment further about this switch point in its social, personal, and literary aspects, I must first take a closer look at daily life in the Tudor grammar school—particularly the disciplinary practices surrounding early lessons in imitation and imperson-ation. At this point in my analysis, however, I hope it is clear that following "the motion of the mind in every respect" was one lesson in imitation that Shakespeare learned well. Perhaps instead of seeing a single-handed "inven-tion of the human,"[66] we might see in Shakespeare's convincing subjectivity-effects an eloquent, "gentlemanly" index of the Latin schoolroom's material, discursive, and disciplinary interventions in early modern culture.

Chapter 2

Imitate and Punish

The Theatricality of Everyday Life
in Elizabethan Schoolrooms

All that was to me a pleasure when I was a childe while I was undre my
father and mothers kepyng, be tornyde now to tormentes and payn. For
than I was wont to lye stylle abedde. . . . What sport it was to take my
lusty pleasur betwixte the shetes, to behold the rofe, the beamys. . . . But
nowe the worlde rennyth upon another whele. For nowe at fyve of the
clocke by the monelyght I most go to my booke and lete sleepe and slouthe
alon. And yff oure maister hape to awake us, he bryngeth a rode stede
of a candle. Here is nought els preferryde but monyshynge and strypys . . .
> —Grammar school lesson for translation into Latin,
> Ms. Arundel 249

Imitate and Punish

"Imitation is a principle that animates not only humanist stylistics but also humanist pedagogy."[1] Richard Halpern's formulation succinctly captures two important strands of early modern thinking about the grammar school. First, as we began to see in the passage from Ascham's *Scholemaster*, imitation structured the humanist approach to teaching both grammar and rhetoric. Perhaps contemporary satire best captures the ongoing tension, as well as the uneven development, that characterized "the grammarians' war" over the benefits of teaching Latin through imitation as opposed to memorizing rules and precepts. As late a play as *Cupid's Whirligig* (1616), performed "sundrie times" by the Children of the Revels, depicts pedagogy as rote learning when four boys recite grammatical rules and examples from memory.[2] But the earlier *Parnassus* trilogy (1598–1601) satirizes contemporary pedagogy in its distinctly humanist guise: A teacher is one who "interprets" a common schooltext, *Pueriles confabulationes*, "to a companie of seven-yeare-olde apes."[3] Along these lines, Skelton is more succinct: "Speak, Parrot!" Second, grammar school ordinances consistently demand that the headmaster himself model exemplary behavior for his students: The humanist idea of authoritative model and imitation, in other words, also structured the school's hierarchy of personal relations. As Thomas Elyot puts it, a teacher should be "such a one as the child by imitation following may grow excellent."[4] School ordinances usually put their expectation for a master's exemplarity in a rather more pragmatic, cautionary light: "The masters shall not be common gamesters, nor common haunters of tavernes or alehouses or other susspect houses or places of evell rule or of other knowne vice at the tyme they be elected."[5] At Oundle, these ordinances extend to boarding houses, where those running them should "give example to the scholars not to follow gaming or other vain pastimes not meet for students."[6] The Renaissance discourse of exemplarity pervades school ordinances about personnel. But it is important to remember that because its "new" pedagogy turned on imitation, the Latin grammar school gave exemplarity— and its related habits of mind and conduct—considerable institutional and material support.[7]

Imitation could intervene in the school's daily routine in yet another, more theatrical and disciplinary way. Public exercises in grammar, translation, and speechmaking revolved around a master who was the final judge of a boy's worth. A scholar from the seventh form at the Westminster School wrote a detailed "Consuetudinarium" (ca. 1610)—an account of daily life—one of the few extant accounts of its kind written by a student rather than a school authority. It gives a pupil's perspective on how imitation operated in the school's daily economy of reward and punishment. The young scholar's pronouns vacillate between "them" and "us," revealing someone poised between ranks— being a student and a master in the making:

> . . . *they* were all of them (or such as were picked out, of whom the
> Mr made choice *by the feare or confidence in their lookes*) to repeat and
> pronounce distinctlie without booke some piece of an author that had
> been learnt the day before. Betwixt 9 and 11 those exercises were reade

which had been enjoyned *us* overnight (one day in prose, the next day in verse); which were selected by the Mr; *some to be examined and punished, others to be commended and proposed to imitation.*[8] (Emphasis mine.)

In such a setting, a boy's choice is stark: imitate "some piece of an author" well or be beaten. Verbal skill is the medium through which one proves oneself worthy of esteem ("commended") or unworthy, which means facing the threat of being "punished." A student could, in fact, look forward to the exact hour of potential punishment on a daily basis. The "Consuetudinarium" is as precise as a book of hours: "Betwixt 9 and 11. . . . Betwixt one to 3. . . . Betwixt 3 and 4 they had a little respite." The Bailiff's ordinances at Shrewsbury establish a similarly predictable schedule. The tolling of "the schollers' bell" signaled that the master would arrive within the hour to punish students "for negligence accordinge to his discression and their deserts."[9]

In another, better known, report of what it felt like to go to school at St. Paul's and Eton, Thomas Tusser makes Latin and flogging equivalent:

From Powles I went, to Aeton sent,
To learn straightwayes the Latin phraise,
Where fifty three stripes given to mee
     At once I had.
For fault but small, or none at all,
     It came to passe thus beat I was,
See, Udall, See, the mercy of thee
     To mee, poor lad.[10]

That Tusser's complaint moves from "Latin phraise" to "fifty three stripes" in epideictic verse (*epideixis* being the rhetorical term for words spoken in blame as well as praise) reveals how thoroughly the school equated punishment with rhetorical performance.[11] Sanctioned forms of verbal facility, even in the guise of an English rather than a Latin complaint against one of its masters, suggests that the author was, in fact, a "poor lad" who tried hard enough to deserve better.

The "Consuetudinarium" also reveals how imitation shaped Westminster's elaborate, hierarchical organization for supervising and controlling what counted as acceptable speech (e.g., three slips into English would provoke punishment). Older boys were appointed as surrogates for the master to "monitor" and reprimand the younger boys' linguistic performance in his absence. In addition to imitating the master in front of their peers, these boys appear to have been required to give a weekly, public account of their classmates' linguistic lapses:

> These Monitors kept them strictly to speaking of Latine in theyr several commands; and withall they presented their *complaints or accusations* (as we called them) everie Friday morn: when the punishments were often redeemed by exercises or favours shewed to Boyes of extraordinarie merite, who had the honor (by the *Monitor monitorum*) manie times to begge and prevaile for such remissions. And so (at other times) other faultes were often punished by scholastic tasks, as repeating whole orations out of Tullie, Isoc.; Demosth.; or speaches out of Virgil, Thucyd., Xenoph: Eurip &c.[12] (Emphasis mine.)

Corporal punishment and imitation (in the narrow linguistic sense) are equivalent: "Punishment" is "redeemed by exercises"; "remission" for whipping is a "scholastic taske," as in "repeating whole orations out of Tullie." The chance to perform rhetorically—by "begging and prevailing" for exemption from flogging—is said to be an "honor" for boys of "extraordinarie merit." And once set in motion, imitation (in the broader sense of one person copying another's example) proliferated: *magister, monitor, Monitor monitorum.* All of this hierarchy of discipline was devoted to the hourly and weekly regulation of verbal competence: Latin speaking, translation exercises, cases brought against, pleas advanced ("complaints or accusations" valuing the form, forensic skill, over the actual content of such utterances), and the "repeating of whole orations."[13]

The phrase the Westminster student uses to describe the scheduled, weekly event of a master's surveillance—"By the feare or confidence in their lookes"—does more than reveal the close link, in practice, between imitation and the threat of either public shame or corporal punishment.[14] It suggests the young *monitor*'s identification with his master. "Their lookes" rather than "our" looks: The phrase divides the writer from his (now former) classmates by means of a hierarchy of imitation that moves him up the ranks from the supervised to the supervisor. Psychoanalytically speaking, the phrase reveals the student's identification with, or desire for, the place from which he is seen—which is also the place from which he is judged and loved—as well as the accompanying internalized divisions that characterize Freud's topographic description of a composite, fractured psyche.[15]

Both the unnamed Westminster scholar's and Tusser's accounts of a day at school suggest we would do well to reexamine the interweaving of affective and institutional histories implicit in Renaissance rhetorical pyrotechnics—a personal and transpersonal history in which performance, formal technique, socially specific criteria for judgment, and fantasies of mastery and address are intertwined. If nothing else, it might produce intriguing reflection on the period's fondness for such literary forms as the complaint, the lament, and the satiric "scourge."[16] More particular still for several texts in the next three chapters, literary representations of the "passions" frequently emerge in ekphrastic descriptions or, more generally, passages engaged in what classicists call "programmatic" reflection on the text's own representational and rhetorical strategies. While there are powerful literary reasons for the "enduring" nature of ekphrastic *paragone*[17] and meta-poetic reflections, the distinct preference for such formal self-display in the epyllia of former schoolboys, as well as Shakespeare's plays, is suggestive about the school's hierarchical, disciplinary, and theatrical structures. What better way did a student have to fulfill the charge successfully to imitate classical exemplars before an audience of peers and masters than to point to his own verbal skill (the tendency to programmatic reflection)? What more effective way to persuade an audience to pause for thought, rather than rush to judgment, than to suggest that one's words can rival other arts? Or to lay claim to the verbal and visual demands of good oratory, the training for which I describe below, than to stage an ekphrastic comparison between the arts of speaking and seeing?

Here we encounter an early modern institutional practice resembling the triangular structure that W. J. T. Mitchell detects in the "social structure of *ekphrasis*" more generally: "if *ekphrasis* typically expresses a desire for a visual object (whether to possess or to praise), it is also typically an offering of this expression as a gift to the reader."[18] Or, in this setting, it is a gift to one's master or peers. Verbal paintings invite an audience to shuttle between aesthetic admiration and interpretive labor, a state of suspended attention a schoolboy could surely turn to his social advantage. And if Mitchell is right to discover in ekphrastic turns *qua ekphrasis* an unpredictable vacillation between an impossible, utopian desire (for the image to be present to the reader or audience) and a "counter-desire or resistance (the fear of paralysis and muteness in the face of a powerful image),"[19] then the affective intensity allied to verbal and visual interplay implicit in ekphrastic display might have been of considerable social value for young orators. For as I describe in the next section, a boy's success depended on his ability to stir up passions in his audience by means of his acquired set of verbal and visual skills. Ekphrastic turns can and do convey many subtle messages—and often prompt modern audiences to become precisely the careful readers that their authors hoped to create out of contemporary ones.[20] Read in light of the institution that taught boys to imitate similar passages in their classical forebears, however, early modern ekphrases preserve something of the external and internal rivalries implicit in the school's social scene, with its decidedly punitive methods for teaching Latin; its master who sat in judgment; and the divided, self-monitoring schoolboy subjects who strove to find a place in their world by living up to the master's daily demands and exercises.

Actio, Actio, Actio

The Westminster *monitor*'s phrase, "by fear or confidence in their lookes," attests to the school's still more diffuse, yet for that no less daunting, disciplining of socially acceptable affect. Records from a variety of schools similarly indicate that humanist discipline included lessons in proper intonation as well as physical deportment; masters gave a boy's voice and gestures strict attention and training. Beyond Westminster's requirement that boys perform memorized passages publicly "without booke," one of John Brinsley's rules for ideal teaching was that the master should pronounce clearly so that his boys might imitate after him: A teacher must "utter before them what they cannot." A commonplace book from the 1630s suggests the extent to which humanist training made the vocal techniques of rhetorical training routine: As the student dutifully records, "Rhetorick consists in adorning speech with tropes and figures *and pronouncing it* according as the differing nature of those tropes and figures require" (my emphasis).[21] Verbal skill, in the eyes of humanist masters, had as much to do with the bodily mechanics of *pronuntiatio* and *actio* as with memory.[22] Indeed, training in how to move one's body often coincided with training in the physical motions of tongue and throat. Among Richard Mulcaster's recommended daily exercises in running and wrestling and dancing is the practice of "loud speaking"—an exercise in vocal modulation ("first begin lowe, and moderately, then went on to further strayning, of their speeche: sometimes drawing it out . . . sometimes bringing it backe, to the sharpest and shrillest . . .") derived from the ancient oratorical practice called "vociferation." In Lily's *Grammar*, which outlines and gives specific names to common, "ugly" faults of pronunciation, the boys found in a section called "Orthoepia" a specific exercise for refining the motions of their "chattering" tongues (*balbutiens . . . ora*): Errors of pronunciation "may bee amended by quickly pattering over som ribble rabble made hard to pronounce on purpose, as, *arx, tridens, rostris, sphinx, praester, torrida, seps, strix*."[23] I quote from Charles Hoole's English rendering here, because he thought highly enough of what was originally Lily's exercise in tongue-tripping to recommend it to other schoolmasters (*Grammatica Latina in usum scholarum adornata* [London, 1651]).

School records, moreover, indicate that humanist masters often moved beyond trying to discipline a boy's memory, voice, and tongue to giving more general instruction in the art of socially acceptable gesture and physical demeanor. Indeed, the Westminster student's comments about his fellows' "looks" suggest that discipline extended even to the performance of certain kinds of facial expression. In classical rhetorical theory, the nuances of physical deportment are called *actio* and thought crucial to persuasive oratory. And so in John Stanbridge's *Vulgaria* (a text designed to teach students Latin by means of double translation), boys were to translate from one language to another and also to imbibe a lesson in bodily demeanor: "Also see yt the gesture be comely with semely and sobre movyng : sometyme of the heed / sometyme of the hande / and fote: and as the cause requyreth with all the body."[24] Richard Sherry, the headmaster of the Magdalen School from 1534 to 1540, compares rhetorical skill to bodily demeanor by means of one word: "Scheme," Sherry writes, is a "Greke worde" that signifies first "the maner of gesture that daunsers use to make" and second "the fourme, fashion, and shape of anye thynge expressed in wrytynge or payntinge . . . a word, sayynge, or sentence, otherwyse wrytten or spoken then after the vulgar and comen usage."[25] Dancing, in his view, becomes a communicative activity in which the body's "gestures" signify just as much as spoken words or written sentences; it is therefore one of many physical activities recommended for the training of effective orators. In a commonplace book from the 1590s, begun while the writer was still at school, a collection of phrases gathered under the heading "*actio*" begins with Demosthenes's often quoted maxim: "the principall part of an oration was *actio*, the second the same, the third noe other." The writer then records that persuasion stems from the emotions conveyed by a speaker's facial and bodily movements: "the passion wherewith the Orator is affected passeth by the eyes, *for in his face we discover it & in other gestures*" (emphasis mine). More evocatively still for the school's impact on drama, he translates *actio* as "action" and calls it "eloquence of the bodye, or *a shadowe of affect*" (emphasis mine). Rhetorical technique, in such a translation, exercises a precedent and determining force on human passions and actions. Finally, this young writer records that rhetorical excellence arises from "three springes which flowe from one fountayne": "*vox, vultus, vita*. Voyce, countenance, life."[26] Faces, as much as voices, required proper training.

The Westminster student's account of daily life indicates how far the school's highly articulated hierarchy governed the repeated exercises that were to establish, within each boy, a set of approved gestures, tones, and facial expressions. And it was based on a stark distinction: One is either the *monitor* or the monitored—watching and judging or speaking and performing. Acquiring socially sanctioned habits of speech, movement, and affect in such a disciplinary setting means that a scholar learned to adopt the verbal and corporal behavior of others and also learned to monitor his own performance while imitating those examples. Or indeed, as in the case of the young writer from Westminster, he learned to supervise the social and rhetorical performance of others while in the middle of monitoring his own. Such daily practices, it seems to me, might instill within schoolboy subjects a self-reflexive division reminiscent of what Harry Berger identifies in many of Shakespeare's plays as a character's "internal auditor."[27] "*Monitor monitorum*" ("the monitor of monitors"): The school's regulatory version of self-reflection in the daily performance of Latin eloquence suggests that Berger's meta-theatrical definition of Shakespearean subjectivity—the constant activity of an internal auditor whose imagined overhearing turns dramatic monologues into attempts at self-persuasion—may derive from an earlier institutional scene of affective discipline. "Past experiences" of judgment, emulation, and admonition at school remain internally active in adult life, continuing to define what it means to be a social subject from within. From *monitor monitorum* to internal audition—such a trajectory from one institutional scene of performance and judgment (the schoolroom) to another (the commercial theater) resembles the divisions central to psychoanalytic theory's model of the self-censoring subject. I am proposing that such a division—an intrapsychic scene folded inward as a persistent interpsychic system—was an important consequence of the grammar school's methods for training in Latin eloquence. And that it was realized not only in depictions of characters on the commercial stage, but also in the everyday lives of Renaissance schoolboys.[28]

What I call the theatricality of everyday life in the sixteenth-century grammar schools does not derive solely from the Westminster student's account. Other kinds of training in rhetoric are similarly suggestive. For example, the ordinances at Shrewsbury required frequent public performances from the boys. On the occasion of a master's election, the ordinances join rhetorical skill directly to the public performance of submission: In the presence of school bailiffs, "the master elected and admitted shall . . . make a Latin oration; one of the best scholars shall welcome him with a congratulatory Latin oration, *promising obedience* on behalf of the school" (emphasis mine).[29] The frontispiece to Alexander Nowell's *Catechismus paruus* (London, 1573) shows a scholar gesturing and declaiming some memorized text before the schoolmaster and an audience of his classmates (Figure 2). A birch sits prominently at the master's side while fellow students are seated around the orator, reading along as he performs his speech without aid of his book.[30] The woodcut captures the school's strict disciplinary hierarchy, as well: The boys are arranged in ascending sizes up through the speaker, and all of them gather before the largest figure of all—the master, who sits at the head of the room, resembling nothing so much as a judge in court.[31] Much like the "Consuetudinarium," this woodcut attests to how far humanism's disciplinary training in imitation relied on the memorial, verbal, bodily, and affective techniques of public performance.

The theater's ubiquitous presence in schoolroom practice may have gone relatively unexamined in part because of a long-standing, anachronistic distinction between rhetoric and drama. Critics have not attended as thoroughly as they might to the school's intimate, habitual association between rhetoric and play acting.[32] Schoolmasters thought both acting *and* declamation were good training in eloquence and the art of gentlemanly behavior. In several ordinances, "declame" and "play" are virtual synonyms. The Shrewsbury ordinances declare that "Everie thursdaie" scholars "shall for exercise *declame and plaie* one acte of a comedie," while St. Saviour's Grammar School in Southward required, in 1614, that "on play days the highest Form shall *declaim* and some of the inferior Forms *act* a scene of Terence or some dialogue" (emphasis mine).[33] A student at Merchant Taylors' described the stage as a "means" to teach "good behaviour and audacitye," while John Bale praised the headmaster of the grammar school in Hitchin for building a large, permanent stage because it allowed him "to train the young and babbling mouths of his students" and "to teach" these future orators "to speak clearly and elegantly."[34] Eton's headmaster from 1560–63, William Malim, admits that theatricals may be a "frivolous art" only to argue that they are essential to the development of *actio*: Nothing is "more conducive to fluency of expression and graceful deportment" than the theater (*ad actionem tamen*

CATECHISMVS

paruus pueris primùm Latinè
qui ediscatur, proponendus
in Scholis.

LONDINI
Apud Iohannem Dayum Typo-
graphum. An. 1573.

Cum Priuilegio Regiæ Maieſtatis.

Figure 2. Title page to *Catechismus paruus pueris primum Latine . . . propo-*
nendus in scholis (London: John Day, 1573). Reproduced by permission of the
Folger Shakespeare Library.

oratorum, et gestum motumve corporis decentem). Christopher Johnson, head-master of Winchester in the 1560s, is more expansive still. As recorded in one of his students' notebooks, he reminded his boys what they should learn "from those stage plays which we have lately exhibited to the view":

> I think you have derived this benefit besides others, that what must be pronounced with what expression, with what gestures not only you yourselves learned, but are able also to teach others (if need were). For there should be in the voice a certain amount of elevation, depression, and modulation, in the body decorous movement without prancing around, sometimes more quiet, at others more vehement, with the supplosion of the feel accommodated to the subject.[35]

Some twenty-five years later, Charles Hoole is similarly enthusiastic. Acting prepares boys "to pronounce orations" and thereby to "expel that subrustic bashfulness and unresistible timorousness which some children are naturally possessed withal, and which is apt in riper years to drown many good parts in men of singular endowments."[36] Given the proximity between Latin oratory and dramatic performance in such accounts, the number of schoolboys "impressed" (i.e., kidnapped) into service at Blackfriars theater cannot surprise. Who better to take to the stage than "seven-yeare-olde apes"? The most minutely recorded case is a complaint brought by Thomas Clifton's father against those from the Chapel Royal theater who "carried off" his son on his way to school and, like their humanist predecessors, required him to learn their "sayd playes or enterludes . . . by harte."[37]

Since T. W. Baldwin's study, however, secondary accounts often describe school training in Latin as a solitary, scholarly activity: "read, read, read; and write, write, write."[38] Mary Crane pursued the written side of school training in careful detail, tracing the "notebook method" of schoolwork that required students to pursue "the twin discursive practices" of "gathering" important "textual fragments and 'framing' or forming, arranging, and assimilating them." In such a practice—a "central mode of transaction with classical antiquity"—Crane detects "an influential model for authorial practice and for authoritative self-fashioning."[39] So, too, does Peter Mack focus primarily on the activities of reading and writing in his account of school rhetorical training.[40] My aim here is to build on this work, to add to the solitary and scribal model (the textual habits associated with *inventio* and *copia*) the corporal and vocal aspects of Latin performance that were necessary for *actio*. I add this dimension to my discussion of school *habitus*, however, while keeping in mind Mitchell's point that when considered as modes of signification, "there is no essential difference" between visual and verbal texts, that speech acts "are not medium-specific."[41] And it is in rhetoric's intertwined verbal and visual practice—the embodied, performative aspect of training in Latin grammar and rhetoric (crucial to the development of London's commercial theaters and resistant to our own text- and performance-based dichotomy)—that I find most reason to question how successful schoolmasters might have been in their announced goal of teaching students to occupy seamless, "authoritative" subject positions by means of rhetorical facility.

Understood alongside the way schoolmasters habitually compared acting to declaiming as an important means for disciplining the young bodies and "babbling mouths" of students, the Westminster "Consuetudinarium" indicates how deeply the theater informed school training in Latin grammar and rhetoric. In other words, the many ways boys were required to demonstrate several skills in speaking "withoute booke" tell us that the presence of an actual stage was hardly necessary. The Westminster student's account of carefully supervised speech—of begging, prevailing, and speaking whole orations out of "Tullie and Demosthenes" as punishment—indicates that a theatrical *habitus* shaped the school's disciplinary practices; its real and phantasmatic hierarchies; and its drilling in socially acceptable forms of eloquence, movement, and affect (e.g., "good behavior and audacitie" rather than "subrustic bashfulness," "fear," or "prancing around"). While ensuing chapters explore specific questions of genre, trope, linguistic form, and imitation in relation to this *habitus*, my point here is not simply that humanist schools made language training an increasingly public activity. Rather, the form this increasingly public education took became, thanks to its indebtedness to ancient rhetorical theory, a process of moving from stage to page and back again—a process that turned England's schoolrooms into a kind of daily theater for Latin learning. And it turned early modern schoolboys into self-monitoring, rhetorically facile subjects who modulated their performances of acceptable speech, bodily deportment, facial movement, vocal modulation, and affective expression by taking the institutional scene of judgment inside, as their own. Another way to put this observation: One might describe a student's sense of inwardness as a phantasmatic, retrospective engagement with the school's theatrical social relations. His emotional life became part of an ongoing "internal audition" derived from early experiences in an institution where one's voice, body, gestures, and emotions came to make sense—became socially legible to oneself and to others—in relation to a hierarchical distinction between audience and actor, judge and speaker, master and student.

In an exceptional study that explores the deep links between "acting, rhetorical gesture, and ancient physiological theory," Joseph Roach traces the influence of Quintilian's conception of the "bodily incarnation of the inward mind" onto the seventeenth-century stage as well as in John Bulwer's *Chirologia* and *Chironomia*. He aims to put to rest "the tiresome debate over the relative formalism or naturalism in seventeenth-century acting style," a debate that "can be traced to the disinclination on both sides to understand the historic links between acting, rhetoric, and ancient physiological doctrines."[42] One of the chief instruments for preserving those links as embodied experience rather than as intellectual history, I would argue, is the grammar school—understood as the place where specific exercises inculcated on a daily basis brought ancient ideas about rhetoric and the passions into practice. Roach draws out the impact of Bulwer's medical background since Galen's view of expressive gesture founds his treatises, but it is important to notice, too, that *Chironomia* ("the art of manuall rhetoric") prominently evidences its institutional origins and aspirations. Like any good former schoolboy, Bulwer derives his invention from classical authority. He says he has added something that was missing from Aristotle's *Rhetoric*, while also stressing, like most schoolmasters, how important eloquence is to the good of the commonwealth: "the Gestures of the Body, which are no lesse comprehensible by Art, and of great use and advantage, as being no small part of civill prudence." He observes that the institutions forming the basis of such prudence are many, but his list begins with "the school":

> Prevalent Gestures accomodated to perswade, have ever been in the Hand; both the Ancient Worthies, as also Use and daily Experience make good, it being a thing of greater moment than the vulgar thinke, or are able to judge of: which is not onely confined to *Schooles, Theaters, and the Mansions of the Muses; but doe appertaine to Churches, courts of Commonpleas, and the Councell-Table.* (Emphasis mine.)

Perhaps it is worth remembering in conjunction with Bulwer's fascination with hand gestures that early school vocabularies frequently begin with bilingual lists of body parts as an easy way for boys to learn Latin nouns. At least one, John Holt's *Lac puerorum* (1507), included a picture of the hand as a kind of chart by which to organize the parts of speech.[43] *Chironomia*'s opening illustration presents four figures associated with "Grandiloquentia" (see Figure 3). Three watch, while one of them, the orator Demosthenes, rehearses. With his back to us in the foreground, Demosthenes observes his own gestures in a mirror held up before him by Andronicus (the Byzantine emperor associated as much with rhetoric as with terror). On the other side of the mirror stand Roscio, the Roman actor against whose theatrical performances Cicero's speeches were famously judged, and Cicero.[44] On the mirror's frame appears the inscription, "*Actio—Actio—Actio.*" Given my account of the theatricality of everyday life at school, Bulwer's immediate association between "schooles," "rhetorick," and "theaters" suggests that his metaphor for the human hands as "two Amphitheaters" for "the voluntary motions of the mind" is less an early modern fantasy about the ancient past than a figure attesting to the theatrical practices of the humanist grammar school, the institution in which boys learned eloquence of tongue and body by constantly monitoring their own performances while staging the passions of others before multiple audiences.[45] In addition, Bulwer's first triad of institutions includes "the mansions of the muses," which suggests that we begin to think of the link between *actio* and the embodied life of the passions not only in relation to staged plays, but also in relation to the literary habits of imitation future poets imbibed as schoolboys.

In the Latin schoolroom, not just in school plays or the commercial theater, we see a social, rhetorical, and visual staging of affective, embodied subjects. By "staging," I mean to invoke the internal divisions of the divided, "speaking subject" as well as the constant process of self-dislocation—or better yet, constitutive blindness—outlined in the psychoanalytic theory that the subject is subject for and to an Other. Far from consolidating schoolboy subjects as it claimed to do, early modern pedagogy would tend rather to produce divided, rhetorically capable, yet emotionally labile speakers for whom language learning and self-representation entailed the incessant dislocations of the theater. By "dislocations," I mean the constant activity of bilingual translation (an early lesson in language's incessant slippages, about which Shakespeare's Mechanicals are perhaps most eloquent, running in terror from Bottom's "translation"), as well as the daily requirement that boys shuttle back and forth from the silent practices of memory and invention to the gestural and vocal techniques required for effective oratory. At the same time, though, I also mean a process quite familiar to Shakespeareans: the constant internal movement in his characters between seeming and being, *persona* and person, address and self-representation; between assuming, whether successively or

Figure 3. Title page to John Bulwer, *Chironomia: or, the Art of Manuall Rhetoricke . . . the chiefest instrument of eloquence* (London: Thomas Harper, 1644). Reproduced by permission of the Folger Shakespeare Library.

simultaneously, the positions of writer, actor, and audience. Iago's "I am not what I am"—to cite the most famous of many meta-dramatic moments long understood to be an expression of Shakespeare's experience on the commercial stage—may also stem from the daily theater of his early training in Latin.

Rather than "strengthen the stability of subject positions," the grammar school's theatrical demand for mimicry performed in public under threat of punishment would produce rhetorically capable subjects insofar as they found themselves "through displacement."[46] Here we might remember Roach's apt description of the early modern actor, who was admired for producing "the signs" of certain passions "on demand"—in other words, "manifestations of an emotion that he fully embodies, *but at the same time is not really his own*" (emphasis mine).[47] The same might be said of an English schoolboy, imitating the passions of a cohort of ancient characters in order to please his audience of master and peers in multiple kinds of Latin performances. Humanist schoolmasters announced themselves to be in the business of "civil prudence" by consolidating rhetorical mastery and thereby producing proper English gentlemen. But it seems to me that their practice pulled against the drive to verbal, gestural, visual, and affective self-mastery because of their profound indebtedness to the theatricality of the very rhetorical tradition they taught.

A Gentleman Is Being Beaten

The affect performed in the Westminster "Consuetudinarium" is "fear or confidence," but other texts point to other, more ambivalent kinds of affect associated with the punishments meted out for a boy's linguistic error. For instance, in John Redford's *Wit and Science*—a play most likely written for and performed at St. Paul's somewhere between 1535 and 1547—the stock figure of a flogging schoolmaster turns into an immoral woman, Idleness, who seduces her pupil away from Knowledge and leaves him "shamefully blotted" with what appears to be syphilis; Idleness puns (like Shakespeare's Petruchio) on "tail" and "tale" in her battle with Wit and also threatens to "beat" a schoolboy's "arse" because that boy—Ignorance—cannot pronounce his name.[48] In two other stories about flogging, one from John Stanbridge's *Vulgaria* (1520) and another an anecdote about Richard Mulcaster passed down in the St. Paul's School, we find that however much fear the master's birch may have provoked, that rod also could function within what Alan Stewart aptly calls an "erotic economy." His is a promising suggestion, but precisely what kind of erotic economy such scenes convey is rather hard to determine and requires, I think, a closer look in relation to humanist claims about the grammar school's social efficacy.

In Stanbridge's *Vulgaria*, the euphemistic phrase about the master's punishment—"he hath taught me a lesson / that I shall remember whyle I lyue" ("*documentem me edocuit: cuius recordabor dum uiuam*")—refers to a beating: "my buttockes deth swete a blody sweat" ("*adeo ut sanguinem sudorem desudent nates*"). And "marrying the master's daughter" ("*praeceptoris filia mihi inuitissimo nupsit*") refers to the moment of stinging connection between a rod and the buttocks in a flogging.[49] The entire scene is part of an exercise printed in a school text for boys to use—students were asked to translate this sentence (along with numerous others about flogging) from English into Latin and back into English. It is a story that had considerable institutional currency. In the St. Paul's anecdote, Mulcaster was reported to have paused before striking a boy's naked backside due to a "merry conceyt taking him." Instead of whipping the boy, Mulcaster intoned, "I aske the banes of matrymony between this boy his buttockes, of such a parish, on the one side, and Lady Burch, of this parish on the other side." But the boy got off without a stripe when a second scholar, part of the audience for this staged punishment, objected: "all partyes are not agreed." The master therefore "spared the one's fault and th' other's presumption" because he liked the "witty answer."[50] As is also the case in the Westminster "Consuetudinarium," this anecdote tells us that punishment was theatrical: the "marriage banes" are not merely a parody of a marriage ritual; they also become a ritual of their own, enacted before spectators who become actors in the scene they are required to witness. As suggested in Redford's title, "wit" is a boy's only effective tool for evading punishment.

The knot of punishment, theatricality, persuasion, and eroticism in these stories underscores the extent to which, in grammar school training, the performance of verbal dexterity is everything. Lily's *A Short Introduction of Grammar*, which Henry VIII made the standard grammar for "all schools in this realm" for over 150 years, conveys just such an equivalence between flogging and verbal skill: Latin is a language that should "be well and thoroughly beaten in" to a student. The "scholar" in Stanbridge's *Vulgaria* says of his beating, "*canticum hodie canere me edocuit*" ("he hath taught me to synge a newe song to daye"). Not only does the (fictional) scholar in question "sing" as the result of a beating, but he also shows off his learning and wit by parodying Psalms' "I will sing unto the Lord a new song."[51] His song and wit, moreover, are featured in a text composed by a group of humanists for other young boys to use, under further threat of punishment, as translation exercises from English into Latin and back again. ("Singing," of course, is also what both schoolboys and Roman poets do—which means that in this version of flogging, punishment, performance, and classical poetry coincide.) Similarly, the anecdote about Mulcaster, which is just as revealing whether institutional fantasy or actual report, brings together verbal aptitude and harsh disciplinary action. The joke joins a boy's naked buttocks to persuasion as much as a whipping: It is only because the master of rhetoric is moved, because he "likes" the boy's "witty answer," that he turns approving and relents.

The erotic wit associated with school flogging made it at least once into print. *The Loves of Hero and Leander*, a baldly pornographic epyllion published in 1653, concludes with a satiric poem, "On Doctor Gill, Master of Paul's School," and Doctor Gill's answer to it. A raucous satire on the flogging master—"a noble Forker"—the poem portrays a series of different language speakers (from France, Wales, and Scotland) whose verbal gaffs provoke Doctor Gill's punitive rage. The poem's refrain repeats Gill's sadistic glee at each flogging:

> Still doth he cry,
> Take him up, take him up Sir,
> Untruss with expedition.
> Or the Burchin tool
> Which he winds i'th'School,
> Frights worse than an Inquisition.

A poem purported to be a response from Doctor Gill himself follows this satire: In "Gill upon Gill—Or, Gills Ass uncas'd, unstript, unbound," the former St. Paul's schoolmaster upbraids the previous poem's author for mistakes in "orthography," nonsensical "theames," and "barbarous Greek." He aims to punish all these linguistic errors with the same exuberance, beginning with a "saucing" that in such a context draws on the connection between flogging (in *Every Man in His Humor*, a saucing is a beating); appetite (saucing is a way to add a piquant taste to meat); and verbal aggression (in *As You Like it*, Orlando "sauces" Rosalind with "bitter words" [3.5.69]):

> Yes Sir, I'le sauce you openly,
> Before Sound and the company;

And that none at thee may take heart,
Though thou art Batchelour of Art:
> Though thou has paid thy Face
> For thy Degrees:
Yet I will make thy Arse to sneer;
> And now I doe begin
> To thresh it on thy skin,
For now my hand is in, is in.

This volume's schoolboy impertinence turns from an obscene parody of classical *imitatio*—we read that the "loves" of Hero and Leander derive from no lesser an authority than the legendary Greek poet, Musaeus—to an eroticized satire of the language master who made such a parody, and the audience for it, possible.[52]

The sexual charge surrounding flogging, spectacle, and rhetorical facility in all these stories was hardly momentary or fleeting. A poem written by a scholar at the Merchant Taylors' School in 1696 suggests that over the course of the next century, the erotic aspects of school discipline became, if anything, quotidian and institutionalized. Written to be delivered to the members of the school—it is part of a collection of poems by the school's "first boys" to be "spoken upon certain public days of Examination or Election"—this poem was one of several declaimed at a year-end celebration. Entitled "The Birch," it was spoken in the voice of the master's rod, and it staged the connection between rhetoric, punishment, and sex openly before the author's master and peers:

'Tis true I us'd like tortur'd Martyrs
And lay'd about your hinder quarters,
When finding an unlucky Urchin,
(Whose Bum's in cue for putting birch in
Down went his Breeches, up his jerking,
And strait the Whipster fell to forking)
Who ne'er would goe to Schoole, but play
The truant every other day;
. . . .
Be sworn I'le soundly make you smart it,
And suffer too, as many have done.
The laying of a whipping on,

Whipping that's Virtues Governess
Tutress of Arts and Sciences;
That mends the gross mistakes of Nature
And putts new life into dull matter;
That lays foundation for Renown
And all the honors of the Gown:
But one wou'd think there's nothing sillyer
Than with back-side to be familiar,
Tho' I confess my conversation
Has been with the best men in ye Nation;
Their orthodox and primitive doctrine
By me orig'nally was knocked in[53]
My wonders working virtue spread
Itself up strait from Tail to Head,
Thus the ablest disputant and wit
Has by my Influence been bit,
So by my power their learned store
Goes in behind and out before.

. . . .

My dispensations are effectual
I grant to help the Intellectual,
Duly apply'd sance too much vigour
When whipping's us'd in mood & figure.
Thus spiritual mortification
As well as flesh is in fashion,
Further'd by my all powerfull charm
Both to inform and reform
And in this practise there is sense
Confirmed by long experience;
For commonly by whom I cant mend
The Sea, the Camp, or Gallows end.[54]
(Emphasis mine.)

Recorded alongside other less startling poems spoken by other species of "trees" in the annual school records, "The Birch" tells us, like *The Loves of Hero and Leander* and *Wit and Science*, that the connection between sex and flogging was, at best, an open secret. Only the slightest of euphemisms is required to evoke a connection between whipping, student nakedness, and a masterful "forking." The homoerotic undercurrent, in which a boy is allowed to play with the master's rod before the entire school, appears to have been admissible to the extent that he displays the considerable wit he derived from it.

Another couplet, however, introduces a story of "informing" that complicates a univocal reading of the genders associated with the link in "The Birch" between rhetoric, pain, pleasure, and power. Whipping, we are told, "mends the gross mistakes of Nature / And putts new life into dull matter." Such a phrase feminizes a boy's buttocks (and, eventually, mouth and head) along conventional Aristotelian lines: A master's whip becomes the "informing" (or inseminating) principle of a student's newborn "wit," so that, indeed, a "learned store / Goes in behind and out before." The playful pair "to *in*form and *re*form" tells its audience that in contemporary pedagogy, impregnation and punishment are both necessary and the same thing, lest those who pay no heed shall in "The Sea, the Camp, or Gallows end." In this poem written for public declamation, Latin rhetorical training is at once sexual, punitive, and socially efficacious.

All of these texts—school exercise, anecdote, declamation—return historical weight and complexity to our own nearly evacuated cliché, "I'll teach you a lesson." They remind us of the phrase's institutional, yet at the same time deeply ambiguous, erotic and disciplinary origins. The "marriage" scene between the master's "daughter" ("Lady Burch") and a boy's buttocks and the phallic intrusion of the birch's "working virtue" as the violent, staged impregnation of a boy's "dull matter"—each of these fantasies deploy and exceed the reductive taxonomy of binary distinction (male/female, sadistic/masochistic, homo-/hetero-erotic).[55] In addition to what these school texts reveal about the unexpected erotic and gendered slippage that could arise from humanist discipline, a literary one from the 1570s represents a flogged schoolboy and his "master" in a way that shows scant regard for normative distinctions among genders and erotic practices. Published in 1576 and attached to his satire "The Steele Glas," George Gascoigne's "The Complaint of Philomene" anticipates the many kinds of identification between male poetic speaker and female victim that characterize the Ovidian poetry and drama written by former schoolboys in the 1590s (including Shakespeare's two epyllia).[56] While this elegy anticipates discussions of lamentation and cross-voicing in Chapters 3 and 5, I consider Gascoigne's "Complaint" here because it makes flogging's erotic economy—the demand for rhetorical facility, the pains and pleasures of eroticized violence, and the indeterminate fluctuations of gender—yet more explicit and ambiguous than the preceding texts.

Gascoigne's narrator opens his "satyre," "The Steele Glas" with the candid declaration that he is "in dede a dame,/ Or at the least, a right Hermaphrodite." Her/his sister is "Poesie" and s/he bears the name of "Satyra." And in the preface to "The Complaint of Philomene" that follows "The Steel Glas," Gascoigne sustains and complicates his/hermaphroditic voice by comparing Philomela to his narrative persona *and* to the biographical poet who explains why he wrote these verses at a particular time and place. That is, Gascoigne contextualizes the link between "The Stele Glas" and "The Complaint of Philomene" associatively and autobiographically, in a kind of reverie between past and present moments of composition. First, he reminds his patron that he compared himself to Philomela allegorically at the opening of "The Stele Glass"; this learned literary mode then reminds him, in turn, of the elegy he never completed:

> Right noble, when I had determined with myself to write the *Satire* before recited (called the *Steele Glas*) and in myne *Exordium* (by allegorie) compared my case to that of fayre *Phylomene,* abused by the bloudy king hir brother by lawe: I called to minde that twelue or thirtene yeares past, I had begonne an *Elegye* or sorrowefull song, called the Complainte of *Phylomene,* the which I began too deuise riding by the high way betwene Chelmisford and London, and being ouertaken with a sodaine dash of Raine, I changed my copy, and stroke ouer into the *Deprofundis* which is placed amongst my other *Poesies,* leuing the complaint of *Phylomene* vnfinished: and so it hath continued euer Since vntil this present moneth of April.

The preface passes from the specific dates and places of writing, as well as the learning necessary to allegory, to introduce a more technical, rhetorical association developed in the elegy itself around three of Philomela's "notes":

> And bycause I haue in mine *Exordium* to the *Steele Glasse, begonne with the Nightingales notes*: therfore I haue not thought amisse now to finish and pece vp the saide *Complaint* of *Philomene,* obseruing neuerthelesse the same determinate inuention which I had propounded and begonne (as is saide) twelue yeares nowe past. (Emphasis mine.)

By "technical" rhetorical association, I mean the skills required to master the art of *pronuntiatio*: The poet echoes the preface by building his/her "complaint" around what she/he posits were Philomela's first, second, and third syllables.

In the elegy itself, Philomela's song rehearses several exercises in pronunciation as she struggles to tell the story of her rape and her feelings about it. No sooner does he mention the bird rehearsing these syllables than the narrator veers aside. Philomela's feelings about Tereus recall that of a schoolboy, waking up either from or to a nightmare of his master's rod:

> And for hir foremost note,
> *Tereu Tereu*, doth sing,
> Complaining stil vppon the name
> Of that false *Thracian* king.
> Much like the child at schole
> VVith byrchen rodds fore beaten,
> If when he go to bed at night
> His maister chaunce to threaten,
>
> In euery dreame he starts,
> And (ô good maister) cries,
> Euen so this byrde vppon that name,
> Hir foremost note replies.

Flogging turns into the institutional equivalent of rape when Philomela's "notes" conjure up a "child at schole" calling out his master's name for fear; the syllables under comparison, "maister" and "Tereu," tell us how closely technical training in rhetorical practice—in this case, *pronuntiatio*—was tied to flogging. So it seems to me no accident that the boy's outcry—"ô good master"—echoes the very first example of the vocative that sixteenth-century students encountered in lesson one of Lily's *Grammar*: "The vocative case is known by calling up, speaking to: as, *O Magister*, O Master."

The texts I examined earlier flirted with the possible pleasures that could be associated with the master's rod. But in this poem, the next note is "fye"—an expostulation of "disdain" and "disgust" that provides the rhyming note that anticipates the narrator's "I."

> Hir second note is *fye*,
> In Greeke and latine *phy*,

In english *fy*, and euery tong
That euer yet read I.

VVhich word declares disdaine,
Or lothsome leying by
Of any thing we tast, heare, touche,
Smel, or beholde with eye.

Several important points emerge from this constellation of texts concerning schoolmasters and the language skills "well beaten in" to a student. First, a consistent association between rhetorical, punitive, and sexual energy emerges in many texts written at school, as well as those written later recalling that institution. I suggested in Chapter 1 that Shakespeare has a pronounced habit of turning pedagogical encounters into sexual ones; Gascoigne's complaint poem and the preceding school texts suggest he was hardly alone in this reflex. Second, the erotic charge attached to the disciplinary aspect of Latin training varies considerably from text to text, prompting a wide range of affective expression: the pleasures of wit, satire, and pornographic excess; a violent "saucing" or a "sneer" aimed at provoking a reader's laughter; the pathos of the raped and tongueless Philomela; and a "lothsome leying by." So, too, do Shakespeare's sexualized scenes of instruction, as we have seen, span an enormous spectrum of erotic affect. A third and related point is that the constant mix of pleasure in pain and pain in pleasure, a mix that defies sorting, is engrained in the performance of eloquence—from the basic skills required for pronunciation to an ability to use complex rhetorical tropes and strategies.[57] And finally, tropes like "my Lady Burch," Gascoigne's "right Hermaphrodite," and the "learned store" that "comes out before" from the "informed" student depicted in "The Birch" tell us that the distinction between genders central to humanist claims for their curriculum's social efficacy did not always survive a boy's experience of that institution's material practices. The following chapters find similar challenges to normative gender distinctions in Shakespeare's many meta-rhetorical reflections on pedagogy.

All these representations of flogging provoke rather than solve questions. Nor do I mean that these questions are posed simply for us. Schoolboys were between seven and twelve years old.[58] Staged public flogging may well evoke an "erotic economy"—but erotic for whom? When? In what register? With what object? What aim? And with what impact on gender distinctions evoked and evaded in tropes like that of "marrying the master's daughter," "informing," giving birth to the "learned" baby of eloquence, or the "Hermaphrodite" who compares his/her case to Philomela? To answer such questions—or rather, since answering these questions involves the ever disappointing act of naming a fantasy, to take stock of the effect that humanist disciplinary practices had on contemporary discourses of "masculinity"—means thinking about yet another kind of displacement involved in the production of rhetorically capable, early modern "gentlemen." Whether we call it latency or trauma, I use "displacement" to designate the unpredictable intersection between a culture's structuring narratives and the accidents of personal history, an intersection that distances speaking subjects from access to their own experience in both language and time. In the work of Freud, Lacan, and Laplanche, *latency* refers to the unequal relation between the time required to reach physiological sexual maturity and the time required not simply to acquire a language, but to grasp (if indeed one can ever be said fully to grasp) a culture's full range of sexual meanings. For Laplanche in particular, *latency* signifies an unpredictable, historically variable, yet constitutively traumatic misfire between the temporality of human biology and a speaking subject's belated understanding of the codes that give bodies and actions, as well as the genders and sexualities attached to bodies and actions, their culturally specific meaning.[59]

Lacan and Laplanche both contend that for Freud, sexuality is inherently traumatic for speaking beings: With respect to bodily maturity and linguistic skills, we are born too early and understand too late.[60] In other words, if scenes like that of school flogging "can be described as sexual, it is only from the point of view of the external agent, the adult. But the child has neither the somatic requisites of excitation nor the representations to enable him [sic] to integrate the event: although sexual in terms of objectivity, it has no sexual connotation for the subject, it is 'presexually sexual' (Freud, 1950, letter 30)."[61] For such a way of thinking about childhood and puberty, the temporal gap between biological maturity and access to language means that the process through which events acquire sexual significance is not merely uneven; it also continues to resist linear, causal narratives of development. The retrospective process by which bodies and practices become culturally legible, moreover, is subject to the contingencies of particular local histories (familial, personal) that exceed the larger structures (groups and institutions organized around father power) that give individuals the terms within which to lead an intelligible social existence. For this reason, I find it crucial to read the associations I have traced in texts about school discipline carefully and slowly, on a case-by-case basis, and to keep an eye out for the differences between and within writing subjects (whether schoolboys or former schoolboys). Psychoanalytically speaking, the consequences of such enigmatic signifiers are far from predictable, subject to the minute differences of personal, familial, and institutional particularity.

Laplanche's double focus on the temporal and semiotic disarticulations of puberty's translations is pertinent to humanist rhetorical discipline, I believe, because such a theory reminds us of how profoundly "all parties" in these early modern flogging scenes are "not agreed." Despite the considerable erotic charge in all these representations of school beating, this charge is not necessarily (or not yet) erotic for the boys themselves. The exact significance of flogging fantasies, which might well remain indecipherable even to adult minds, is not equally available, or legible, to all. Moreover, schoolboys were subject not simply to one language, *but to two.* The enigmatic world of adult sexuality and fantasy at school was mediated by puberty's temporal displacements, as well as by two languages, symbols, and cultures whose codes for behavior were not always commensurate.[62] Shakespeare's version of this difficulty—sexuality's inscrutable, illegible aspect—is what Eric Partridge called his "bawdy." But a schoolmaster might call it his wit: the penchant for conveying sexual significance by means of double entendre.[63] As the remark of the St. Paul's student ought to remind us, Shakespeare's texts frequently stage their erotic and violent action around words whose several meanings are not equally available to all parties taking part in the conversation.[64]

The extreme (to us) yet clearly familiar (to them) trope of a flogging as a marriage ceremony, or the forcible impregnation of rhetoric and "wit" in the "Intellectual," offers a vivid early modern example of a further difficulty in sexuality that Laplanche is trying to confront directly. In his account of Freud's *Three Essays on a Theory of Sexuality*, sexuality emerges in a series of missed encounters with the unanticipated "intrusions" of adult fantasy— a fantasy that, because undecipherable at the moment of its occurrence, remains an "alien internal entity."[65] If one's accession to a culture's hierarchical ordering of gender and sexuality is traumatic, such trauma exceeds the inside/outside distinctions that lie at the heart of empirical explanations of gender and desire. That is, a child's induction into sexual significance defies empiricism because it arrives, as Laplanche puts it, "both from within and from without":

> On the one hand, in the first stage, sexuality literally breaks in from outside, intruding forcibly into the world of childhood. . . . On the other hand, in the second stage, the pressure of puberty having stimulated the physiological awakening of sexuality, there is a sense of unpleasure, and the origin of this unpleasure is traced to the recollection of the first event, *an external event which has become an inner event*, an inner "foreign body" which now breaks out *from within the subject*.[66] (Emphasis mine.)

On such an understanding of puberty's belated work and breached boundaries, we can interpret the enforced (indeed, institutionalized) adult fantasies about flogging boys' bottoms in early modern grammar schools as indications that for the boys themselves, such scenes are at once familiar *and* foreign, that they are not fully intelligible in their adult sexual sense on first occurrence. Nonetheless, enigmatic signifiers that proleptically anticipate the retrospections of puberty would remain suspended in schoolboy subjects—registered but not entirely available to consciousness, either.[67] Such enigmatic signifiers linger, become alien internal entities ready to signify only when they resurface later and, more unexpectedly still, from inside the subject as memories. A widespread institutional and theatrical ritual through which many boys were required to pass, school flogging reminds us that there is a significant difference, for sexuality, between being taught a lesson and learning it. That difference marks the disruptive temporality of trauma; but as these texts also suggest, it opens a space for erotic fantasy. The various witty turns in these anecdotes and poems tell us that in school flogging fantasies, pleasure goes hand in hand with pain—though it is never predictable when, to whom, or in what way such pleasures and pains will become available. In the retrospective afterlife of these signifiers, flogging's erotic economy means that adult subjects may take their enjoyment, when they can, "precisely there where they suffer."[68]

I have suggested that humanist rhetorical training deployed the displacements of the theater, that the schoolroom's disciplinary stage produced Latin-speaking "gentlemen" out of a constant intersection between address, gaze, and judgment that turned the interpersonal relations of the theater inward as intrapsychic relay. But to this meta-theatrical understanding of the effects of daily school discipline it is important to add the psychoanalytic theory of temporal displacement, or "retrospective action," attending a child's subjection to language and culture. Both perspectives indicate how unstable the culturally normative coordinates for gender and sexuality might become in grammar school training—despite (or because of) the overt effort by school authorities to direct them. In other words, as a staged form of punishment, flogging gives telling evidence that when the labile fluctuations of active/passive, subject/object, looking/being seen, male/female, hetero-/homo- that Freud elaborates so carefully in "A Child is Being Beaten" were institutionalized, they rendered the precise significance of the early modern term *gentleman* increasingly fugitive.[69]

For the early modern schoolboys represented in these texts, writing them, or using them, "whipping's us'd in mood & figure" ("The Birch," line 33). The moods of the verb and the figures of rhetoric are forever intertwined with the sting, the threat, or the performance of flogging. This student's apt pun on "mood" captures the focus of this study, linking, as it does, states of personal feeling with technical exercises in grammar and, eventually at university, logic.[70] "The Birch" links the (proto-) eroticized threat of punishment directly and systematically to verbal skill—be it an exercise in imitation or a "merry conceyt." As Nashe's William Summer famously puts it, "This learning was such a filthy thing . . . When I should have been a school construing *Batte, mi fili, mi fili, mi Batte*, I was close under a hedge . . . I profess myself an open enemy to ink and paper. Nownes and Pronounes, I pronounce you as traitors to boyes buttocks; Syntaxis and Prosodia you are tormentors of wit, & good for nothing, but to get a schoolemaster twopence a weeke."[71] As the unnamed Westminster scholar puts it, a boy's choice is to imitate his precursors well or be beaten. The Merchant Taylors' scholar tells us that the institutionally useful practice of "wit" allows a student the social latitude to satirize, but also the pleasure of performing well under a disciplinary regime in which "a learned store goes in behind and out before." All these texts testify to the considerable emotional and libidinal complexity of grammar school training. And they link discipline, affect, and eroticism directly to rhetoric's formal concerns. More important still, they attest to the punitive history of "masculinity" in the sixteenth-century schoolroom while at the same time revealing undercurrents of gender and erotic *in*difference that pull against the univocal significance of that term. Shakespeare is not alone in giving a sexual charge to the pedagogical scene of Latin instruction. As much of the rest of this book illustrates, his representations of emotion revisit the classical past he encountered at school in a way that deploys normative early modern categories of gender and sexuality only to render them as fluid and unpredictable as the texts I have examined so far. Lily's *Grammar* reminds us that schoolmasters were, after all, teaching boys a language with some room for maneuver on this question: "The Epicene Gender is declined with one article, and under that on article both kinds are figured: as, *Hic paster*, a Sparrow, *Haec aquila*, an eagle, both he and she."

Chapter 3

The Art of Loving Mastery

Venus, Adonis, and the Erotics of Early Modern Pedagogy

> *Amavi, I have loved*
> *Docui, I have taught*
> *Legi, I have read*
> *Audiui, I have heard*
> > —Lesson in "Preterperfect tense singular," Lily,
> > *A Short Introduction of Grammar*

> *It is declined with one article: as* Hic Magister, *a Maister, orels with*
> *two at the moste: as* Hic & haec Parens, *a Father or Mother.*
> > —"An Introduction of the Eight Parts," Lily,
> > *A Short Introduction of Grammar*

One of Shakespeare's most controversial representations of desire, *Venus and Adonis*, bases its sweeping prophecy about the nature of "love"—"Perverse it shall be" (1157)—on the death of a beautiful boy not quite out of puberty.[1] Immensely popular in its own time, the poem has proved troubling to modern readers, in part, because of the marked disparity in age between the two protagonists. As Adonis remarks while trying to evade Venus's sexual aggression,

> Measure my strangeness by my unripe years;
> Before I know myself, seek not to know me,

No fisher but the ungrown fry forbears;
> The mellow plum doth fall, the green sticks fast,
> Or being early pluck'd, is sour to taste.
(lines 524–8)

According to Adonis, the "unripe years" of "sour" youth mean he does not know himself and cannot, therefore, be "known" by another. His blindness to himself with respect to sexuality renders him "strange" to himself or to anyone else.[2]

It is not merely Adonis's "green" inexperience that prompts associations between *Venus and Adonis* and the young boys who learned and imitated Ovid's stories in school. Indeed, at several crucial moments, Shakespeare's Ovidian epyllion portrays Venus's attempt to seduce this "ungrowne fry" as an effort to *teach* him. While assuming the part of a Petrarchan suitor praising his beloved and failing to win his pity, Venus also adopts another, ancient literary role: Ovid's *praeceptor amoris* ("love's teacher") from the *Ars amatoria*.[3] In her pedagogical aspect, of course, Venus embodies the connection between teaching and seducing in the Lucentio-Bianca subplot of *Taming of the Shrew*, which I'll examine in the next chapter. For now, it is enough to notice that in neither the narrative poem nor the play is the would-be *magister* particularly quick witted. Venus especially resembles Ovid's obtuse "teacher" in that she refuses to acknowledge the reality of her situation while eagerly dispensing erotic advice. Borrowing an idea from Ovid's *Ars*—that animals are useful exemplars when teaching humans about sexual practice— Venus tries to develop an *ex tempore* erotic lesson for Adonis. She offers the spectacle of Adonis's lusty "courser" as an apt model: the amatory "proceedings" of a "strong necked steed" equipped with "eares up prickt," "hot courage," and "high desire" preface Venus's didactic plea that her recalcitrant pupil learn from precedent (lines 263, 406, and 276):

> . . . "Thy palfrey, *as he should*,
> Welcomes the warm approach of sweet desire. . . .
> Let me excuse thy courser, gentle boy,
> And learn of him, I heartily beseech thee,
> To take advantage on presented joy;
> Though I were dumb, *yet his proceedings teach thee.*
> > *O learn to love, the lesson is but plain,*
> > And once made perfect, never lost again."
> (385–408; emphasis mine.)

Not only does Venus draw on classical precedent for this "lesson," but her plea is specifically humanist: She asks him *to learn by imitating* the horse's "proceedings." Adonis, however, flatly refuses to copy his steed's example or learn from his *praeceptor amoris*, a rejection that eventually leads to his castration and death.

That Venus models herself on Ovid's erotic instructor is less surprising than it may first appear: The poem may well be following the grammar school's lead. One of the very first lessons any schoolboy encountered in Lily's *Grammar*—a text Shakespeare quotes often and Henry VIII authorized for "all teachers of grammar within this realm"—introduces the cases of a Latin noun as follows:

> The Nominatiue case commeth before the verbe, and answereth to this question, who or what: as *Magister docet*, The maister teaches.
>
> The Genative case is known by this token Of, and answereth to this question, whose or whereof: as, *Doctrina magistri*, The learning of the maister.
>
> The Datiue case is knowen by this token To, and answereth to this question, To whom, or To what: as *Do librum magistro*, I giue a boke to the maister.
>
> *Th'Accusative case followeth the verb, and answereth to this question whom, or What: as Amo Magistrum, I love the master.*[4] (Emphasis mine.)

"I love the master": Lily's inaugural lesson in the accusative case is one Venus would happily teach.

In the pages that follow, I read Venus's failed lesson in classical desire against the background of grammar school training in Latin on which the poem so thoroughly depends. In *Venus and Adonis*, Shakespeare revisits a wide range of school texts, lessons, and methods to create a deliberately provocative portrait of both main characters and their emotions, as well as the origin and nature of "love." My reasons for laying out the poem's decidedly institutional engagements are as follows: Read alongside other Ovidian epyllia written in the 1590s, *Venus and Adonis* attests to considerable contradictions between the stated aims of the Latin grammar school and the actual effects such teaching may have had on its gentlemen in the making. In addition, close study of the way the poem engages with the techniques of contemporary Latin pedagogy reveals several important, and as yet insufficiently recognized, connections between Ovidian erotic narrative and theater history. That is, if we consider the poem's most prominent figural strategies in light of the school texts, exercises, and discipline that made them possible, we begin to see that epyllia in the 1590s are far from the minor genre they are often taken to be—and far more revealing about sixteenth-century theater history than we have yet to acknowledge.

To indicate the kind of critical purchase Ovidian minor epics like *Venus and Adonis* have on two important institutions in Tudor England—namely, the commercial theater and the grammar school—I take my opening cue from humanist schoolmasters, focusing on details of linguistic and rhetorical form. I continue to stress how important rhetoric's tropes and transactions are for a historical account of early modern masculinity, reading the sudden popularity of epyllia in the 1590s against school exercises in Latin grammar and declamation as well as the claims schoolmasters made about heroic po-etry's social efficacy. As I see it, the most important forms at issue for the poem's negotiations with the institution that made it possible are genre (epic) and trope (predominantly *prosopopoeia*, but also *ekphrasis*—the Greek term that often doubled at school for its Latin equivalent, *descriptio*). Overall, I hope to show that the classical lesson gone terribly awry in *Venus and Adonis* has everything to do with the way early modern pedagogy fractured the unity of the masculine identities it was explicitly designed to produce. And if the poem suggests that school training did not always function the way humanist masters thought it would in the realm of social reproduc-tion, however, *Venus and Adonis* also gives telling evidence of the kind of erotic, violent, and transgendered fantasies that might accompany adult returns to rhetorical techniques imbibed at school—particularly the tech-niques of impersonation that would find fuller expression on the commercial stage.

Mothers, Fathers, Masters

Shakespeare's early exercise in Ovidian cross-voiced impersonation begins as a broad satire of Venus's frustrations, excesses, and absurdities. Critics gen-erally note that the poem's joke on Venus stems from the fact that she is trapped by Petrarchan rhetoric ill suited to the occasion. But they have not as yet adequately addressed something else important about her predicament: Not only does she speak from a traditionally male position—a "bold-fac'd suitor" wooing a reluctant object who refuses her pity—but her Petrarchan exuberance turns her desire for a young boy into a desire for a boy precisely to the extent that he is not one, to the extent that he resembles a woman:

> "Thrice fairer than myself," thus she began,
> "The field's chiefest flower, sweet above compare,
> Stain to all nymphs, more lovely than a man,
> More white and red than doves or roses are . . ."
> (7–10)

With these metaphors she is off—busily turning Adonis into Laura, indulging in what Shakespeare's sonnets characterize as the cliché Petrarchan conventions of "beyond compare." When I say that Venus's Petrarchan conceits are ill suited to the occasion, I mean that a literary mode founded on unrequitedness presumes the speaker's disappointment. Contrary to Ovid's version of the story, Shakespeare's poem leaves no doubt that Venus will remain unsatisfied. Given her opening foray into *epideixis*, contemporary readers would not have been surprised to read that her beloved's refusal prompts her to compare Adonis to Pygmalion's statue—"Fie, liveless picture, cold, and senseless stone" (211)—since the figure of stone for the beloved's refusal permeates the *Rime sparse*. Certainly Marston recognized its literary provenance when he wrote *The Metamorphosis of Pigmalions Image* (1598), a poem sometimes taken to be a rather broad satire of Shakespeare's epyllion. Nor would many have failed to notice that when Adonis abandons Venus to hunt the boar, the narrator compares her to Echo, one of Petrarch's favorite figures for conveying the extremity of his predicament and his emotion. Indeed, the narrator turns Venus into the very image of "Poor Petrarch's long deceased woes" when her moans return as echoes:[5]

> And now she beats her heart, whereat it groans,
> That all the neighbor caves, as seeming troubled,
> Make verbal repetition of her moans;
> Passion on passion deeply is redoubled:
>   "Ay me!" she cries, and twenty times, "Woe, woe!"
>   And twenty echoes twenty times cry so.
> (829–34)

"Ill suited to the occasion" has limitations, however, if it suggests a heteronormative frame of analysis for a poem that works to exploit and explode precisely such assumptions. When Petrarchism's binary conventions of address meet Ovid's polymorphous eroticism, the two produce a poem whose plot, tension, and humor depend on the difference between "male" and "female" bodies, identities, and desires while undermining those distinctions at every turn. This both/and dynamic pertains, of course, to both the poem's titular characters. Shakespeare may give Ovid's *praeceptor amoris* a distinctly feminine resonance by turning him into the goddess of love, but Venus's position as unrequited Petrarchan suitor is at the same time conventionally masculine and remains so throughout their encounter. By the same token, Adonis is at once a hunter and fairer than a "nymph," a young boy engaged in hypermasculine pursuits while being, at the same time, "more lovely" than Venus herself.[6] The way the narrator plays with conventional language of gender for both characters means that the poem continually stretches "normal" boundaries, making assumed differences and the desires presumed to be attached to such differences, as well as normative conventions about erotic expectation and practice, hopelessly unequal to the task of capturing either the nature of their erotic quandary or the poem's definition of *love*.

In a move that also takes *Venus and Adonis* beyond its evident Petrarchan engagements, Shakespeare (rather notoriously to modern readers) gives Ovid's Venus a maternal cast. The narrator broadly hints that the relationship between Venus and her beloved Adonis resembles that of mother and son; and these hints derive, in large part, from the stories about incest that precede Adonis's birth in the tenth book of the *Metamorphoses*. As is well known, Ovid tells us that Adonis descended from two such incestuous unions: the one between Pygmalion and his child/statue; and the second between Myrrha, Pygmalion's granddaughter, and her father, Cinyras. Read in terms of literary history, the poem's "juxtaposition of sexuality and parenting" means, as Jonathan Bate puts it, that "Adonis is forced to re-enact, with generational roles reversed," the "incestuous affair between his mother and father in the *Metamorphoses*."[7]

Psychoanalytic critiques have explored this terrain thoroughly, noting among the poem's figures the many "pre-Oedipal" fantasies about Venus's overwhelming maternal power.[8] One of the most prominent of these occurs when Venus's caress evokes an infantile state of symbiotic fusion: "Her arms do lend his neck a sweet embrace; / Incorporate then they seem, face grows to face" (539–40). Later, Venus mourns Adonis's absence "Like a milch doe, whose swelling dugs do ache, / Hasting to feed her fawn hid in some brake" (875–76). At yet another moment, Venus invites her "fawn" to feed and represents this nursing relationship as an erotic one: "I'll be a park, and thou shalt be my

deer: / Feed where thou wilt" (231–32). Of course, such close proximity between mother and child is not without peril. The narrator soon indicates that
Adonis risks being eaten, devoured by a voracious mouth that "glutton-like . . .
never filleth" (548):

> Even as an empty eagle, sharp by fast,
> Tires with her beak on feathers, flesh, and bone,
> Shaking her wings, devouring all in haste,
> Till either gorge be stuff'd or prey be gone,
>> Even so she kiss'd his brow, his cheek, his chin,
>> And where she ends she doth anew begin.
> (55–60)

Here Venus embodies the principle Janet Adelman calls Shakespeare's "suffocating mother," turning into a maternal nightmare who at best engulfs,
and at worst annihilates, her child.[9]

But problems remain for interpretations that define Venus exclusively, or
univocally, as a bad, devouring mother. The poem's decidedly mixed figures
for Venus's gender and her desire erode easy assurance about precisely what
kind of sexual fantasy the narrator is portraying. She may be a "milch-doe"
with "swelling dugs" at one moment, but at another the narrator compares
her to a voracious eagle penetrating Adonis's body with her loving beak. At
yet another, the goddess envies the boar, wishing she could have been the one
to "nousle . . . his flank" and "sheathe" her "tusk in his soft groin" (1115–116).
Such startling transformations give the lie to simple taxonomies that separate
pre- from post-oedipal narratives or hetero- from homo-erotic desires. As
I argued in the last chapter, Laplanche's work on Freud's *Three Essays on the
Theory of Sexuality* is pertinent to the sexual and semiotic complexities of puberty in school training—and here it may further loosen the seemingly inevitable (or universal) association between death and "the mother" that informs
most psychoanalytic interpretations of this incestuous, if unrequited, passion.
That is, Adonis's "unripe years" mean that he neither "knows" love nor can be
"known" unless rudely "pluck'd" before his time. Understood as a temporal
and semiotic conundrum, the phallic invasion of Venus's gender-bending
"beak," the "tusk" that penetrates Adonis's soft "flesh," depicts an encounter
reminiscent of what Laplanche calls the "intrusions of adult fantasy" involved
in even the simplest gestures of childhood care. For a child not yet prepared
to decipher the significance of adult sexual meanings, such intrusions are

illegible. Therefore they remain, but only as "alien internal entities" ready to wound the subject later and from within. Such recursions help us account for the affectively intense, yet exceedingly labile, erotic figures of a poem that engages with the techniques of Latin rhetorical training while giving voices to (and thus fantasizing what it might mean to be or to want) both Venus *and* Adonis. A continuing strand of non-sense in the poem's depiction of both bodies speaks to the enigmatic quality of sexuality for "unripe" boys who read, learned, and imitated stories like this one at school.

On Laplanche's understanding of the retrospective and evasive return of the "pre-Oedipal" mother as "something else" after puberty, moreover, what is at stake in the intersection between a child's inexperience and the cultural meanings awaiting her is precisely *not* the body of any particular empirical mother. In his account, and certainly in the history of early modern education, adults other than mothers become involved in the "presexually sexual" incursions of adult fantasies. Since the fantasies at stake vary from one cultural or historical moment to the next, Laplanche's theory means that knowing precisely which adults do the intruding, in what way, and to what effect requires semiotic analysis undertaken with careful regard for (the not always compatible) details of social, familial, and institutional history. Venus—a looming, ambiguously gendered figure of power—fails either to seduce or to teach this "young fry." An understanding of her desire and her failure requires further attention to the institutional, familial, and tropological coordinates in and around the text of Shakespeare's poem.

And so I want to expand the usual gendered, familial focus on mother-son incest in *Venus and Adonis*—or the dominance of assumptions about familial surrogacy in the period as a strictly female affair—by thinking more generally about the systematic intrusions of adult fantasy that young boys encountered during early years of school discipline. Much historical work on the question of how to historicize psychoanalysis has thus far focused on the important place of wet-nurses in early child care. But on the overwhelming testimony of both parents and schoolmasters, we must add grammar school masters to the list of parental surrogates. The classically inflected fantasies of a school *magister* may have been just as important as parental ones for the famously perplexing depiction of sexuality in *Venus and Adonis*. Shakespeare's sexually provocative departures from Ovid's story (which itself contains no hints of incest, unrequitedness, or difference in age) do more than tell us about the author's agonistic relation to literary history. They also have something important to tell us about the institution in which he encountered, and learned to imitate, Ovid's poetry. As another early lesson in Lily's *Grammar* attests, schoolmasters regularly represented themselves *in loco parentis*. And while they generally prefer to designate themselves as fathers, they could also portray themselves as nurses and mothers if an occasion required: "It is declined with one article: as *Hic Magister*, a Maister, orels with two at the moste: as *Hic & haec Parens*, a Father or Mother." As I mentioned in Chapter 2, a common, set theme for learning to argue on either side of the case came from Erasmus; students were to invent a theme addressing whether a boy owes more duty to his master or his parents. Nothing in the poem's many figures for Venus's parental associations, nor in the institution in which the author first read this story, requires us to fix Venus as any more a "mother" than a "father" to the pubescent Adonis. Indeed, the "parental" role she adopts most explicitly is that of Adonis's *magister*: She styles herself a teacher who can dispense a lesson in "love."

Given the violence implied by Laplanche's term, "the intrusions of adult phantasy," as well as the specter of violence hovering over early modern schoolrooms, it is important to remember that in many of the figures the narrator uses for Venus's attempted seduction, loving Adonis keeps turning into a way to wound him. The association between loving and hurting Adonis becomes so close over the course of the narrative, in fact, that Shakespeare turns Ovid's less than detailed death scene during the hunt into a story about Adonis's death by kiss. As Venus understands it, she and the boar want the same thing:

> 'Tis true, 'tis true, thus was Adonis slaine:
> He ran upon the boar with his sharp spear,
> Who would not whet his teeth at him again,
> *But by a kiss thought to persuade him there;*
> > And nousling in his flank the loving swine,
> > Sheath'd unaware the tusk in his soft groin.
>
> Had I been tooth'd like him I must confess,
> With kissing him I should have kill'd him first.
> (1111–118; emphasis mine)

Most important for the poem's connection to the Latin schoolroom that allowed Shakespeare access to Ovid's story, it seems to me, is the fact that in Venus's lament over Adonis's dead body, she sees herself as just like the "loving swine" because they both were trying to *persuade* Adonis. Overzealous orators both, Venus and the boar turn rhetoric's central preoccupation—persuasion—into erotic action. And they do so in such a way that represents the desired end of "moving" one's audience as a kind of bodily invasion: Kissing is persuading, "loving" is "nousling," and nousling leads to a "tusk in his soft groin." Here the poem's erotically labile imagery blends Venus and the boar while taking a turn toward violence that far exceeds the Latin original that Shakespeare is "imitating." Given the brutality, or threats of brutality, that the last chapter traced in direct relation to imitation at school, I suggest that the link between persuasion and sexual violence in this scene carries in it distinctly institutional memories.

A non-normative psychoanalytic account would argue that the phallic similes in which Venus becomes a ravenous eagle or nousling boar operate not according to a logic of either/or—either male or female, maternal or paternal—but rather according to a logic of both/and: that the poem attests to numerous undifferentiated fantasies about *parental* power. If we read these images of Venus as a voracious *and* penetrating parent alongside the poem's ongoing reversals of sex/gender roles, *Venus and Adonis* becomes particularly suggestive for an anti-foundational theory of sexuality's incessant challenge to normative gender ideologies. For psychoanalysis, and especially in Laplanche's reading of *Three Essays on the Theory of Sexuality*, there is a moment in all our lives when bodies have yet to acquire their culturally assigned meaning, when sexual difference (indeed, what counts as sexual at all) makes no sense. Intimations of this indifference persist despite a culture's—and, in this case, a school's—best efforts to eradicate it. Such a theory helps account for a poem about the nature and origin of "love" in which the imagery is at once rigidly differential and at the same time insistently mutable.[10] With regard to the poem's institutional affiliations, I have suggested that part of Venus's threatening power derives from the opening imperative in Lily's *Grammar*, "amo magistrum"—which association means, in turn, that Venus's role as love's teacher retrospectively makes the master's gender, as much as a boy's, unexpectedly opaque. As I just observed, masters overwhelmingly prefer to speak of themselves as fathers. But they could, on occasion, use maternal metaphors for their pedagogy: One early vocabulary was entitled *Lac puerorum or Mylke for Children* (1427). And there are a few other references in *vulgaria* to teachers as "nurses." The founder of the Magdalen School called instruction in grammar crucial because it is the "mother and foundation of all sciences."[11]

To take a more extended example, John Clarke, headmaster of the Lincoln School from 1622 to 1624 and born the year *Venus and Adonis* was written, published his own lessons for writing and performing orations and declamations in school. In them, he gives some idea how elaborate the fantasies about a master's enigmatic acts of parenting might become in early seventeenth-century schoolrooms. On several occasions, it seems that the town's parents objected to Clarke's pedagogical methods. His examples for theme writing therefore take up the well-worn school topic—whether a boy owes more to his parents or his teacher—in order to resolve the question: According to Clarke, a boy owes most to his teacher. He then records an oration that he imagines appropriate to deliver to parents visiting the school; it proposes an elaborate mythological scene in defense of his teaching methods. Clarke compares outsiders to the slanderous and carnivorous lips of ravenous fathers who, like Saturn, threaten the offspring of a pregnant "Madame School":

> There dwells within this building one who is related to Minerva, and serves her as a lady-in-waiting. Her name is Madame SCHOOL. She has for a long time been married to Priscian, who is the standard-bearer to Apollo; and being also in a state of pregnancy and feeling that her confinement was close at hand, she sent for all her aunts to come from Mount Helicon—the 9 muses, the 3 graces, and the kind Lucina of your presence anew, whom she begs with most humble prayers she can to lend a helping hand and act the propitious midwife. For Madame, when already expectant, was as anxious as any mother-to-be, in case her strength should fail in labor and extrinsic injury befall the unborn offspring. You however will discharge the duty of midwife to perfection if . . . you lend her encouragement and deliver this tender offspring which she is about to give birth to—from her brain. In this latter respect . . . she is not so very unlike her own grandmother Minerva, who as mythology tells us was born from the brain of Jupiter. We hope you will take the newborn into your protecting bosom, and thus save it from the nasty gaping mouth of slanderous detractors, persons who threaten to mangle Madame's literary brood with their foul lips, just like Saturn, famous as the oldest ravener in the world, *who used as we are told to gobble up his own sons.* Grace the interior of Madame's house, in which we hope to exhibit to you . . . something worthy of both your eyes and ears.[12] (Emphasis mine)

Here Clarke turns the space inside school walls into a deeply maternal, domestic one; those who succor Madame School become a series of respectable classical aunties. Those outside its walls are violent fathers, "raveners" ready like Saturn to "gobble up" their sons—an image that should give us pause before we assume that stories of being devoured are necessarily or always linked to mothers for the boys raised on such stories.

Clarke's exercises conclude with a final oration written to welcome parents into the school. Here he again upsets the conventional gender categories on which the social mission of the school was founded by comparing the feelings of headmaster and boys for the boys' parents to those that "love-smitten" Dido once harbored for Aeneas:

> We are like the famous love-smitten lady from Phoenicia, dying of passion from her own Aeneas, from conversation with whom she could hardly ever be torn away; who was told by her sister, "Make hospitality the order of the day, and fashion a chain of reasons for his tarrying." . . . So we have taken care that you should be detained in this school-theater [*in hoc theatro scholastico*], like Phoebus in the sky or Aeneas at Carthage, by what art we could muster . . .

First Clarke represents the school and his methods of instruction as a pregnant mother under threat. Next, he imagines that the boys and their master together resemble Dido, whose passion for Aeneas enables them to ascend to the "art" of persuading a beloved to stay. Clarke's performance is singular among the masters' texts I have found. Nonetheless, these lessons reveal that Shakespeare was not the only one capable of estranging the straightforward gender assumptions one might make about such terms as *master, boy, mother,* and *father*. With regard to the associations between Venus and Adonis and the disciplinary regime they invoke, it is important to note that both Shakespeare's epyllion and Clarke's oration represent a master's acts of parenting and rhetorical performance in terms that are both sexual and violent.

Before I turn to the material school practices that inflected choices of genre and trope in the literary texts of former schoolboys, remember that when Venus offers Adonis an equestrian "lesson" in "love," she too defines that affect in terms of "mastery" and resistance to it. But as she does so, her "plain lesson" from the animal world predicts mastery's inevitable downfall. Developing the narrator's earlier hint about the stallion's resistance to coercion—"The iron bit he crusheth 'tween his teeth, / Controlling what he was controlled with" (269–70)—Venus suddenly remembers a Platonic *topos* ubiquitous in early modern faculty psychology: the battle between the horse of passion and appetite and the reins of reason. In the midst of her lesson in love based on Adonis's exemplary stallion, which is based in turn on examples from Ovid's *Ars amatoria*, Venus becomes just as obtuse as her classical precursor. Trying to press yet another (Platonic) classical precedent into service, she predicts instead the futility of "mastering" anyone's desire. First she advises Adonis, "let" your palfrey's "proceedings teach thee." Then she remarks,

> How like a jade he stood 'tied to the tree,
> *Servilely mastered* with a leathern rein,
> But when he saw his love, his youth's faire fee,
> He held such petty bondage in disdain:
> > Throwing the base thong from his bending crest,
> > Enfranchising his mouth, his back, his breast.
> (391–96; emphasis mine)

Adonis does imitate his palfrey's example to this extent: He treats his would-be master, and her desire to put him into "pretty bondage," with "disdain." In the remaining pages, I follow the lead of Adonis and his stallion, arguing that the poem's unexpected conjunctions—among parenting, rhetorical training, "love," violence, and Ovid's highly ironic portrait of erotic "mastery" in the *Ars amatoria*—are Shakespeare's way of deploying the texts and formal techniques he learned at school against the institution in which he first learned them. Drawing inspiration from early Latin training, he nonetheless manages to satirize the methods, principles, and assumed social effects on which contemporary pedagogy was founded.

Epic, Epyllia, Prosopopoeia

Humanist claims for the political and moral efficacy of a classical education ranged from the broadly civic to the specifically national. Where Mulcaster aims at the good of the commonwealth in general, John Brinsley brought a specifically national concern to bear: He hopes that his translation of Ovid, "dedicated to the good of the schooles," will help in "all the ruder places of the land," "chiefly for the poore ignorant countries of Ireland and Wales." Because in those countries, teaching Ovid's "singular wit and eloquence" will allow schools to "reduce" the "barbarous . . . unto civility" and change "their sauage and wilde conditions . . . into more humanity."[13] The most thoroughgoing, classicizing equation of rhetorical power with good governance is William Kempe's *The Education of Children in Learning* (1588): "great Magistrates" in ancient "commonwealths" captured "the examples and rules of eloquence." Kempe derives rhetoric's civic benefits directly from epic: Homer is "the prince of all poets," because his "precepts and examples" made "Lycurgus and Solon good Lawmakers." He praises "Vergil, Ovid, and Horace, and also Quintilian" as "the only Latin schoolmaisters to all good students euen at this day" and reports that Vergil "did read some part of his booke in the assemblie, [and] the people did no lesse reuerence unto him, then if it had been to the Emperour himselfe." He concludes that Ovid's poetry, "like Orpheus musicke . . . perswaded euen the Getes, a wilde and barbarous people, to use great humanitie towards him while he liued, and afterwards to burie him with great pompe."[14]

With some variation, Latin citations in textbooks and the curricula of individual schools bear out Kempe's preference for epic as the favored genre for moral and political education. Lily's *Grammar* quotes numerous authors, but most frequently it cites phrases from Vergil, Ovid, Terence, and Cicero. The lesson on the impersonal verb is typical: "*Oportet me legere Vergilium*"—"It is good (or important, right, necessary) for me to read Vergil." The curricula do vary, but a fairly prominent consensus emerges about Latin literature: Aesop, Terence, Horace, Vergil, and Ovid were prominent authors for imitation across many schools. More important, almost every school aimed toward reading epic as a culminating achievement. First- and second-form boys read Aesop's fables, then moved to Terence and Horace; fifth- and sixth-form boys concentrated on memorizing and imitating Vergil and Ovid. By 1612, in Brinsley's *Ludus literarius*, the "Schoole Authors" boys were to have "translated" or to "have in hand" in the classroom begin with the easiest or "lowest" (*Pueriles confabulatiunculae*) and end with "Ovid's Metamorphosis" and "Vergil."[15] Given the school's aim of producing rhetorically capable gentlemen for the good of the "commonweal," it is hardly surprising that epic soon took pride of place. Then again, this is true only if one thinks of epic in its Vergilian mode and especially, as Heather James points out, the anodyne *reading* of Vergil as apologist for empire—a reading that emerged from the European tradition of appropriating *The Aeneid*'s translation of empire to legitimize state authority.[16] Ovid's well-known satire of the *pax romana* at the end of the *Metamorphoses*, never mind his fascination with what Vergil represents as the

politically damaging *furor* of desire, fits less happily into the school's announced ideological program.

Vergil's reputation as the poet of civic wisdom was further strengthened
by the overwhelming popularity of *Georgics* Book 4 for its extended comparison between a well-run state and a beehive. As Baldwin aptly observes, "probably no Elizabethan schoolboy escaped those bees—at least Shakespeare did
not."[17] Schoolmasters betray some nervousness about "unwholesome" content
in many heathen poets—the debate about the moral content of Roman poetry
never went away—but the epic that requires its hero to abandon Dido for the
sake of his nation usually escaped censure. In *The Governour*, Elyot recommends imitating Vergil especially because, like Homer, he is "like to a good
nurse." Ovid is a necessary evil: He helps "for understanding other authors"
but by contrast to Vergil has "little other learning . . . concerning other virtu-
ous manners of policy." Thomas Wolsey argues that a good curriculum requires students to imitate Vergil, "the first among all poets," right after Aesop
and Terence; responsive to the dictates of *actio*, he remarks that the "dignity of
his song, conducted with sonorous voice" will "give shape to the tender mouths"
and promote "the most elegant of pronunciation" among schoolboys.

We can, in fact, trace the preference for Vergilian precedent to particular
masters. In a series of classroom rhetorical exercises recorded in the notebook
of the Elizabethan schoolmaster John Conybeare, the response to the precept
"*labor omnia vincit improbus*" begins "*Vergilius Maro sui temporis illustrium
poetarum facile princeps*" ("Vergil was easily the first poet of his age"). No other
poet makes an appearance in these exercises.[18] As Baldwin discusses in some
detail, the class notes of a Winchester schoolboy indicate that his master,
Christopher Johnson, much prefers Vergil to Ovid; in this, he follows the
advice of the influential humanist headmaster John Sturm, according to
whom "*The Aeneid* of Vergil has all the virtues of heroic verse" necessary for
a boy's education, which should partake only of those poets who are "chaste,
pious, elegant, liberal."[19] Sturm recommended that boys read the *Metamorphoses*, but felt they could do it at home; Vergil, however, was suitable classroom material—advice to which Johnson evidently adheres. When Johnson
later publishes a Latin translation of Homer's *Batrachomyomachia* in 1580, he
announces in the preface that he has followed Horace's advice against word-
for-word translation.[20] Instead, he has taken the liberty of borrowing whole
and partial lines from Vergil to make his work more beautiful and pleasing.
(In doing so, Johnson exemplifies the kind of training he once inculcated in
others: He claims that such borrowing preserves Vergil's technique because

he, in turn, was imitating Ennius).[21] Finally, a collection of verses by the headmaster and several scholars of the St. Paul's School indicates how schoolmasters' preference for Vergilian epic might work in practice. Presented to Elizabeth in 1573, the volume opens with William Malim's poem setting out the theme of *translatio imperii* for his boys' imitation: First the master, then several scholars after him, praise Elizabeth for bringing a "second Rome" to England.[22]

Subject to Lily's maxim "It is good for me to read Vergil," schoolboys were drilled in the art of imitation and imbibed a system of training built around an ideal of devotion to the "good of the commonwealth" like that of *pius* Aeneas. Yet given the resonance between humanist admiration for Vergil's theme of civic duty and the school's announced goal of fashioning gentlemen for the good of the realm, there is something puzzling about the results of its training. Poems written by former schoolboys rarely followed anything like the model of *The Aeneid*. Rather, as literary history in the 1590s indicates, the school's training encouraged an outpouring not of epic poetry, but of epyllia—and epyllia of a distinctly Ovidian, erotic cast.

Before we turn to these, one ostensibly Vergilian imitation is instructive: Thomas Heywood's *Troia Britannica*.[23] Published in 1609, its prefatory verses refer to Britain as "Troy-novant" (41) and claim to praise "those Lordes which we from Troy deriue" (25). When Heywood cites precursors—"Homer . . . a Chronicler Diuine, / And Vergill, haue redeemd olde Troy from fire"—one expects that something of *The Aeneid*'s form, structure, hero, or plot will inform the poem.[24] Instead, *Troia Britannica* immediately swerves from Vergil to Ovid: Canto 1 begins not with arms and the man but with "The Worlds Creation" and descent from a Golden age. The connection to Britain remains as loose as the one in Ovid between the world's creation and Rome. Whereas Ovid arrives at Troy and Rome only in the last books, Heywood arrives at Britain only in the last two of seventeen cantos. His dilatory Muse sings a translation of empire in truly flippant Ovidian fashion—that is, only after "driving" "Through all past Ages, and precedent times, / To fill this new World with my worthless rymes" (59–66). Nor does Heywood ever offer a hero like Aeneas. Rather, he envisages an enormous cast of characters along the way. The poem's verse structure is the *ottava rima* of Ariosto, a poet similarly flaunting his divergence from Vergilian epic telos to follow the paths of Ovidian desire. And the preface, in which the poet suggests the allegiance to Vergil he fails to deliver, is the six-line stanza Heywood himself had already used for "Oenone and Paris" (the so-called "Venus and Adonis stanza"); Lodge and Marston use the same stanza form in their Ovidian epyllia. Even when invoked in its most recognizable and popular trope of *translatio imperii*, in other words, *The Aeneid* did not guide invention in nearly the way its position in the Elizabethan curriculum, training in imitation, or resonance with the school's ideological purposes suggest it might have done.

The best explanation for generic experiments by former grammar schoolboys is Richard Halpern's argument that training in rhetorical *copia* "atomized larger structures of meaning and ideological content," "resolved" the texts it taught "into generative strategies of style and dissociated bits of elocutionary material." A blissful disregard for ideological content does reign over hybrid generic forms in the period, as does a preference for "excerpts, ornaments, and fragments."[25] This argument explains why Ovid's skeptical critique of Roman rule, never mind his sexual content, could sit side by side with *The Aeneid* without provoking more than occasional and passing anxiety among teachers. John Brinsley is particularly enthusiastic about the capacity of both Roman poets to stir "invention": "Let them even strive, by imitation, to make Ovid and Vergil 'our own' for verse, as Tully for prose."[26] Charles Hoole agreed:

> I conceive it very necessary for scholars to be frequent in perusing and rehearsing Ovid and Vergil, and afterwards such kind of poets as they themselves are delighted withal either for more variety of verse *or the wittiness of conceit's sake*. And the master indeed should cause his scholars to recite a piece of Ovid or Vergil in his hearing now and then, that *the very tune of these pleasant verses may be imprinted in their minds*, so that whenever they are put to compose a verse, they make it glide as even as those in their authors.[27] (Emphasis mine)

Halpern's argument about the overwhelming desideratum of style, of course, is important for understanding the abundant quirks and oddities of humanist curricula. But it does not sufficiently explain why the poems and plays of former schoolboys show a specific preference for Ovidian eroticism over Vergilian *pietas*. In other words, if we accept the humanist cultivation of *copia* over content as sole explanation for the school's inconsistent ideological effects, we cannot fully explain why former schoolboys were so fond of turning epic convention away from the national, political, and moral themes for which it was praised into epyllia depicting the minute details of character, emotion, and desire. And while masters might well have presumed, or aimed for, the destruction of content in favor of rhetorical technique, that does not guarantee that their students encountered sexually charged texts like the *Metamorphoses* in so neutral or distanced a way.

The disciplinary setting for Latin learning that I examined in Chapter 2—the constant demand for the performance of eloquence and socially sanctioned affect under the threat of punishment; the master's role as exemplary mirror for a boy's imitation—suggests one further reason for Ovid's popularity among early modern schoolboys. Ovid's own training in the art of declamation left its mark all over the *Metamorphoses*: In dozens of programmatic scenes, Ovid assesses rhetoric's power and limitations in episodes of failed persuasion, unrequited demands rendered all the more compelling because they fail to achieve their intended goal.[28] The only recompense for rhetoric's limitations, in an Ovidian universe, is language's aesthetic aspect: As Apollo discovers, poetry is the sole consolation for oratory's failures. What I am suggesting is that the hallmark Ovidian moment of vocal failure—when characters like Philomela, Orpheus, Echo, Io, and Actaeon try, in vain, to *do* something with words, only to find that their own tongues betray them—offered his sixteenth-century English imitators myriad compelling ancient stories within which to recast the drama, fears, and desires of their own schoolroom performances. We have already examined a case in point: Gascgoigne's Philomela, a figure for a schoolboy's fear of his master precisely because the nightingale is trying to recover her voice by means of *pronuntiatio*, the school exercise designed to give agile movement to the tongue. Indeed, in the case of both of Shakespeare's epyllia, his protagonists have strongly Ovidian affiliations—not just in name or story, but in being forced throughout the narrative to confront the limitations of their own vocal power. Venus and Lucrece are trapped in situations in which their own attempt to persuade someone else ends only in words that escape, evade, distort, or otherwise frustrate the speaker's intentions. This predicament reveals something important about the place of Ovidian rhetoric in the history of the speaking subject. But its evident appeal to *so many* sixteenth-century poets and dramatists bears witness to the anxieties of the institutional setting in which Shakespeare practiced the art of imitation so well that his contemporaries praised him for the ability to reanimate Ovid's "witty soul."[29]

Preferences for Ovid over Vergil among former schoolboys, moreover, took a specific figural form—one in which literary and institutional history coincide. When poets in the 1590s avoid the national themes of Vergilian epic in order to imitate characters and affect from the *Metamorphoses*, they are practicing the art that Quintilian calls *prosopopoeia*. A trope that pervades the *Metamorphoses* as well as another Ovidian text frequently read and imitated at school, the *Heroides*, *prosopopoeia* consists in the art of personify-ing the voices of mythological as well as historical persons. It was one of the chief reasons Ovid became renowned for skill in the art of declamation. Humanist schoolmasters hoped to revive the Roman practice of declamation, and with it *prosopopoeia*, in year-end examinations as well as periodic public orations. Such impersonations called upon a student's skill as an imitator—and did so in ritualized social transactions in which the better the imperson-ation, the greater the reward.

Of advanced lessons in rhetoric drawn from "the post-classical work-books emerging out of Cicero and Quintilian" (i.e., Susenbrotus's *Epitome* and Aphthonius's *Progymnasmata*), Leonard Barkan observes that such texts "directed pupils essentially to place themselves in hypothetical or imagina-tive situations, sometimes historical, sometimes mythological, and to create their own Latin text. The resulting exercises were inevitably full of tropes, self-conscious about their status as discourse, and—most important of all—they amounted to dramatic impersonations."[30] One sees precisely such a dra-matic, self-conscious process of impersonation at work not just in advanced exercises in rhetoric, but also in the earliest forms of language instruction. The two mid-sixteenth-century *vulgaria* from the Magdalen School cited in Chapter 2 give a sense of how profoundly *prosopopoeia* inflected the school curriculum, even at the beginning stages of language acquisition. Both these *vulgaria* depart from precursors by making impersonations of familiar people the foundation for language learning. Earlier *vulgaria* offer fragments of Ter-ence or a series of moral *sententiae* for translation. Whittinton's 1520 text—the one that set off "the war of the grammarians"—insisted that learning is best done by rule or "precept" at the start; only later should a master offer particular classical examples. By contrast, both Magdalen *vulgaria* put imita-tion into immediate practice, setting sentences for translation that are *proso-popoeiae* in miniature. The vast majority of the selections for translation are either dialogues or monologues. And the characters offered for imitation are two: a schoolboy and his master.

Anticipating Colet's announced program of instruction, in which imi-tating others "more vaileth shortly to get the true eloquent speech than all the traditions, rules, and precepts of masters," the Magdalen *vulgaria* put into practice what English humanists were beginning to articulate as theory. These exercises have a deeply "dramatic quality," basing lessons in translation on a variety of voices that would seem familiar to young students.[31] For ex-ample, young boys were to render the following monologue into Latin:

All that was to me a pleasure when I was a childe, from iii yere olde to x, while I was undre my father and mothers kepyng, be tornyde now to tormentes and payn. For than I was wont to lye stylle abedde tyll it was forth dais. . . . What sport it was to take my lusty pleasur betwixte the shetes, to behold the rofe, the beamys. . . . But nowe the worlde rennyth upon another whele. For nowe at fyve of the clocke by the monelyght I most go to my booke and lete sleepe and slouthe alon. And yff oure maister hape to awake us, he bryngeth a rode stede of a candle. . . . here is nought els preferryde but monyshynge and strypys.[32]

Bringing mythological *prosopopoeia* home to England and turning it into the household drama of being forced to leave one's bed for the schoolroom, such introductory language lessons put *personae* before, or in place of, persons. Clearly, the *vulgaria* are indebted to the theory of language training Erasmus pursued in the *Colloquies* (1522)—a school text that became ubiquitous, teaching early modern students the art of conversation by way of short mono- logues and longer dialogues.[33] But the setting, characters, and situations in the early translation lessons of the Magdalen *vulgaria* are far more closely tied than the *Colloquies* to the specific environment of the English household, town, and grammar school. Which means that these exercises turned famil- iar situations into mise-en-scènes of dramatic personation, appealing to a child's familiar experience while at the same time estranging that experience, filling the social coordinates of everyday life with characters *qua* characters—voices to assume, or not, as need arises.

Most often, the *vulgaria*'s lessons required boys to practice translation skills while at the same time learning what it means to take up the place and voice of a *puer*, or Latin-speaking "boy." But at other moments, boys were asked to ventriloquize the master's voice:

I knowe that thou hast thy groundes of Elygansies right well. Therefor, go to it styll and thou shalt sone gete all that ever folows. There is nothynge, methynkyth, thou lackith nowe for to cum unto the best but only often and diligent exercise the which noryshith eloquence mervelously moche.[34]

In another example, a student took the "boy's" part again by translating a passage in which a student asks his teacher to forgive him for an unspecified lapse in behavior or diction: "Forgyve me this fawte, other for myn awne sake or for my mothers love. For I am of thes condicions, the more I am forgevyn, the lesse I fawte, and if ever I do another fawte, ye may well punyshe me for them both."[35]

In one of the more self-reflexive dramatizations of school social relations, a passage required boys to translate a schoolmaster's complaint. Adopting the master's voice once again, a student rendered the following lament into Latin: "I hade leuer teche in any place in the worlde then her at oxford." Narrating a rather lengthy grievance about another teacher's challenge to his authority over setting lessons in verse composition, the master then threatens to beat his student. Finally, he admonishes him to "play the man hereafter and not the boys."[36] In daily exercises such as these, a *puer* learned his Latin grammar through translation while at the same time coming to understand his scripted place in the world by imitating voices which purport to capture what counts as the "man's" or the "boy's" part. A dramatized relationship between master and student permeates translation lessons—be it in explicit references to beating or more generally by appeals to the strict sense of well-delineated hierarchy that pervades the text. Exercises that require students to impersonate the master's voice, that is, reveal how profoundly humanist language training installed a decentering imaginary practice in its schoolboy subjects. Learning what it means to *become* a "boy" means not only learning Latin, but also assuming a well-defined role within a social relation of hierarchy and address. In other words, assuming a Latin *ego* means putting such an ego in quotation marks from the beginning—and sometimes it means speaking in the voice of the other who monitors that ego's progress. Sometimes the examples solicit a boy's duty, obedience, and fear—at others, forms of commiseration and iden-tification with his master. As we saw in the Westminster "Consuetudinar-ium," a boy might well vacillate *between* affective and social scenes—identifying at some moments with his peers, at others with his master, or sometimes with both.[37]

These *vulgaria*, when understood within the larger humanist pedagogi-cal imperative for imitation, suggest a tropological specificity to what I earlier described as the school's theatrical *habitus*—inscribing what Bourdieu might describe as a "structuring disposition" toward personification, imitation, and (multiple) identifications in socially sanctioned form of address.[38] These re-peated acts of impersonation, moreover, reveal a structuring disposition to-ward performative self-reflection—toward monitoring one's success in the act of imitating while in the midst of speaking "as if" in the voice of someone else. At least two "pasts" are at work here: a transpersonal, classical past reactivated in Latin lessons, and the student's personal past as it intersects with the disciplinary and discursive practices of the school. The result, as Bourdieu observes, isn't a "mechanical determinism" but rather an identifiable set of historically specific constraints that, in "giving disproportionate weight to early experiences," limit the field of possible inventions and emotions. Such institutional constraints, in turn, ensured the "active presence of a past" that "tends to perpetuate itself into the future by reactivation in similarly structured practices."[39] But one of the structured practices that most tellingly illuminates the school's particular constraints, I suggest, are the personified pair, *puer* and *magister*, a boy and his master. A "boy" pleases, and eventually becomes, a "master" by imitating one—and by performing a succession of ancient literary and historical characters for his approval. The dynamic at work here is one that Slavoj Žižek might call "symbolic identification": a boy's desire for or identification with "the place from which he is seen," from which he is judged "worthy of love."[40] Boys who learned *amo magistrum* in their inaugural lesson in Latin grammar would, in other words, look to elicit the same emotion from their masters—to create an approved place for themselves in the school's social hierarchy by first performing for, and then identifying with, the one who sat in judgment of their daily performances.

With respect to *prosopopoeia*'s central role in the grammar school's *habitus*, surviving documents suggest tremendous continuity in habits of invention, written and oral, across the school forms. *Vulgaria* reigned in the lower forms but were then changed for Corderius's *Dialogues*, which were given to boys "for writing and for speaking Latine" by means of a series of personified pairs—speeches that were very often, as in the *vulgaria*, spoken by "the Maister" and "the Scholar" (or "the Boye").[41] Similarly, a variety of *personae* were necessary for exercises in letter writing (recommended by Erasmus and often begun on the model of Ovid's *Heroides*). And then, of course, *personae* were rendered more memorable still in the dramatic parts boys were required to play in school theatricals.[42] The most advanced rhetorical exercises, based on Aphthonius's *Progymnasmata*, built on long inculcated practice; as we will examine in detail in Chapter 5, boys were eventually set to imitate the *prosopopoeiae* of a series of emotional classical women—Hecuba, Niobe, Andromache, Medea, Cleopatra—as the basis for training in declamation. So recognizable was *prosopopoeia* as a school practice that Brinsley, in *Ludus literarius*, adapted it to his purpose of writing a treatise on pedagogical theory: he invented "Spoudeus" and "Philoponus" as the personifications through whom to dispense educational advice just as he made sure to translate Corderius's *Dialogues* for further school use. By the 1690s, the head boys of the Merchant Taylors' School competed for prizes on examination days by declaiming both Latin and English *prosopopoeiae* in the voices of townspeople, animals (especially horses and dogs), trees (the laurel, the birch or *betula*), and mythological characters (Apollo, Echo, Daphne, and Hermaphroditus).[43] Impersonation, in short, structured exercises across a range of school forms, a dominant presence that allows us to expand Joel Altman's insight into the shaping effect of *in utramque partem* arguments on the "Tudor play of mind." Constructing arguments on both sides of the question is clearly an important and influential habit developed from grammar school all the way through university. But I would argue that *prosopopoeia* is perhaps more determinative still, given its informing presence in earliest language lessons all the way to more advanced lessons in dialogues, letter writing, and (as we shall examine more closely in Chapter 5), declamation. Small wonder that Shakespeare conducts his *in utramque partem* argument about "love" and "lust" in *Venus and Adonis* by impersonating the voices for each side of the debate.

The distinction between acting and rhetorical performance, as Shadi Bartsch argues with respect to ancient Roman culture, may well have appeared "self-evident" to the elite groups who argued cases before the senate and the law court and from whom Roman schoolmasters inherited their curriculum. But it may not have been so evident to sixteenth-century humanist schoolmasters or, more important, to their students. In a Roman context, as Bartsch notes, the rhetorical practice that brings the orator into closest proximity to the actor is *prosopopoeia*, "the adoption of another person's voice and character." She suggests that one can glimpse the problem in Quintilian because he "both encourages and warns against the descent into histrionic talents."[44] As I detailed in Chapter 2, however, Tudor schoolmasters appear to have offered encouragement for such talent, and little or no warning about its dangers. Instead, they carefully inculcated a kind of shuttling back and forth between acting and oratory on the principle that both were crucial to cultivating "elegancy" of tongue and body in their students. The ordinances at Shrewsbury attest to the influence of theatrical practice on rhetorical training, setting down the rule that students must "declaim and play one act of a comedie" once a week on a certain day. In other words, the many *prosopopoeiae* at the heart of sixteenth-century epyllia in general and *Venus and Adonis* in particular attest to the classical rhetorical roots *and* institutional *habitus* from which dramatic impersonation grew.

School practices in *prosopopoeia*, moreover, meant that a *puer*'s "structuring disposition" toward impersonation for the sake of pleasing his *magister* was less dyadic than Žižek's model might suggest—and that it did not entirely conform to simple gender binaries. The address "to the place from which one is seen," it turns out, could set up a triangular relationship: In answer to a master's demand for him to perform eloquently, a boy might well impersonate the voices of ancient female, as well as male, characters.[45] Indeed, several school archives tell us that learning to play the part of a Latin-speaking *puer* took some unexpected turns—and anticipated the epyllion's swerve away from the obvious part of the "boy." In 1565, an eleven-year old student at the Winchester School, William Badger, wrote a poem entitled "Sylvia loquitur," in which he speaks as the "trembling" and "terrified" Sylvia and calls his schoolmates an "unhappy throng of boy-girls," the sound of their "laments" accompanying hers as a "chorus" whose sound rises to touch the stars ("plangitis," from *plango*, to strike or beat the breast in sorrow or mourning). The word he coins for his peers is neither the plural masculine *pueri* nor the plural feminine *puellae*; he coins, instead, the epicoene *puelli* ("*infelix turba puelli*").[46] He composed another Latin poem in two voices, a dialogue between Nero and Poppea; in it, the two discuss why Poppea no longer shares Nero's bed. As we've seen in the oration from Clarke, masters also did sometimes adopt female voices in public rhetorical performances. Nicholas Udall, for example, declaimed several times in the voices of the nine muses at Eton and in one of Elizabeth's processions. Beginning with "*Apollo loquitur*," Udall moved to "*Calliope loquitur*," and so on, until he'd delivered nine declamations, one in the voice of each muse.[47]

We have a more detailed record of a particular event at the Shrewsbury School in 1591. The boys staged an elaborate ceremony of farewell for their patron, Sir Henry Sidney. Gathered on a riverbank, the "scollars of the free scoole" were "apparelyd all in greene" with "greene wyllows uppon theire heades"—and bid farewell by impersonating the voices of nymphs. As Sidney sailed past, the boys made "lamentable orac'ons sorrowinge hys departure." One nymph appeared alone on the bank, and a witness recorded the final declamations and songs of their performance:

One boy alone:
O staye the barge, rowe not soe faste,
    Rowe not soe faste, oh stay awhile,
O staye and heare the playntts at last
    Of nymphs that harbour in thys isle.

Thear woe is greate, greate moane they make
        With doleful tunes *they doe lament*;
They howle, they crie, theire leave to tacke,
        Their garments greene for woe they rent.
O Seavern, turn thy streame quite backe,
        Alas why doyst thou us annoye,
Wilt thow cause us this Lorde to lacke
        Whose presince is our onelie joye?
But harke, methinks I heare a sounde,
        A wofull sounde I playnly heare;
Some sorrow greate thear hart dothe wound,
        Pass on my Lord, to them draw near.

Four boys appear in green singing:
O woefull wretched tyme, oh doleful day and houre
        Lament we may the loss we have, and floods of tears out poure.
Come nymphs of woods and hilles, come help us moane we pray,
        The water nymphes our sisters dear, doe take our Lord away.
Bewayle we may our wrongs, revenge we cannot take.
        O that the gods would bring him back, our sorrows for to shake.

One alone with musick:
O pinching payne, that gripes my hart, O thrice unhappy wight
        O sillie soule, what hap have I to see this woful sighte,
Shall I now leave my lovinge Lord, shall he now from me goe,
        Why will he Salop nowe foresake alas why will he so!
Alas my sorrowe doe increase, my hart doth rent in twayne,
        For that my Lord doth hence depart, and will not here remayne.[48]
(Emphasis mine.)

The witness to this performance writes that "so pytyfully and of sutche excel-
lency" was the nymphs' lament "that truly it made many bothe [those] in the
bardge uppon the water as also people upon land to weepe and my Lorde
hym selffe to change countenance."[49]

    Beyond the association between an adolescent boy and a nymph in Venus's
address to the "lovely" Adonis, such a moving rhetorical performance was clearly
worthy of other inventive, pleading nymphs in Elizabethan epyllia: for instance,
Beaumont's Salmacis or Heywood's Oenone. Like her sisters at Shrewsbury,

Oenone wears "willowes" on her "temples" as a sign of sorrow. Like them, she devotes considerable effort to persuading a man to stay and be "loving."[50] Given my earlier suggestion that the unintended effect of the school's rhetorical training was to shift poetic invention away from Vergilian epic duty toward Ovidian eroticism, it is perhaps important to notice several details about the way Heywood revises the story of Troy in his epyllion *Oenone and Paris*. First, he avoids any reference to the idea of *translatio imperii* but instead puts an erotic frame around the entire war. Second, Troy is the "matter" of Oenone's invention. Trying to persuade Paris to love her, Oenone represents Troy's fate as if it were one among several set topics for a rhetorical competition between the two of them—a device worthy of Quintilian. She begs Paris to return Helen lest "Whole worldes of warriours will beseige your citie" and predicts that if he remains with her instead, there will be "neither wracke, nor fatall ende to Troy" (15). Third, Paris veers between epideictic oratory ("Oenone fayrer than the dames of Troy") and forensic ("thou shalt see how well as I can cleare me," 33) when narrating the story of his choice between Juno, Pallas, and Venus. Heywood thereby produces an etiological, Ovidian version of Troy as a story that is not about nations or masculine civic duty but about desire's unpredictable historical effects. Paris claims, "Not I, but Cupid is to be condemned"—for Oenone's lament, but *also* for Troy's downfall and everything that resulted from it.

Like Heywood, many other poets in the 1590s avoided imitating the poem of civic duty most admired by their humanist masters—Vergil's *Aeneid*—and rarely took up the challenge of representing Aeneas's filial duty. Like their young counterparts at Shrewsbury, they preferred to imitate the voices of loving nymphs, goddesses, and women with a loss to mourn. On the few occasions when poets did invoke *The Aeneid*, the voice they were inclined to recall was that of Dido, the woman whose passion got in the way of Aeneas's civic duty.[51] In many of these cases, the "Dido" in question may derive less from *The Aeneid* than from her letter in Ovid's *Heroides*—another common school text. Despite the didactic models offered by masters and theorists of education, former students either passed over Vergil entirely in favor of Ovid or, on the rare occasions they took on a Vergilian voice, did so in one heavily inflected by Ovid's penchant for female monologues. Such a literary history suggests to me that school training in imitation may well have released identifications and emotions in its *pueri* that were at some distance from their masters' declared purpose.

I argued elsewhere that the tradition of transgendered *prosopopoeia* owes much to Ovid's own penchant for speaking in the voices of women, particularly as a way of commenting on problems of poetic authorship. But attributing this tradition to literary history alone ignores the institutional and material support the grammar school gave to it. The school's rhetorical training in eloquent Latinity required students to practice the theatrical art of cross-dressing alongside the art of Ovidian cross-voicing. It therefore seems to me that given the school's habit of cross-dressing in its theatricals, as well as its demand for impersonating female voices in poems and public performances—strongly allied to a "boy's" approval and social advancement—Ovidian epyllia like *Venus and Adonis* and *Oenone and Paris* demonstrate that the logical extension of school training in how to become a Latin-speaking gentleman was, in fact, not simply a theater, but a transvestite theater.

The Art of Loving Mastery

The vogue among former grammar schoolboys for speaking in the lamenting voices of women leads me back to Venus, Adonis, and the love lesson that asks him to imitate the example of an unruly Ovidian horse. Schoolmasters promulgated a myth of consolidation for their new curriculum, and contemporary critics often echo that myth. William Kerrigan, for instance, applauds the schools when declaring that the conversion of the English *I* into the Latin *ego* "was a wholly male achievement."[52] But the general proclivity in the 1590s for preferring Ovidian cross-voicing to Vergilian civic duty, and Shakespeare's (in)famous depiction of Adonis as "more lovely than a man," should warn us that the words *male* and *female* at school were rather less transparently referential than Kerrigan would have us believe. In a similar vein, Lisa Jardine and Anthony Grafton write that humanist pedagogy successfully "fostered in its initiates a properly docile attitude toward authority."[53] To counter such generalizing claims, I would like to look a little further into the institutionally sanctioned rhetorical forms and habits that inform Shakespeare's portrait of Venus, a failed *praeceptor amoris*, and of Adonis, an ambiguously gendered *puellus* who is less than persuaded by his Ovidian lesson in the passion of "love."

As is clear by now, Shakespeare leans heavily on grammar school training in *imitatio* in *Venus and Adonis* while also putting its formative lesson in *prosopopoeia* to work. But there are other more specific school exercises at work, too. First, one of Venus's opening gambits draws on a standard school theme set for composition: persuading a boy to marry and procreate. As

Baldwin points out, Venus's first argument, "Thou wast begot, to get it is thy duty. . . . By law of nature thou art bound to breed" (168, 171), was a deeply conventional school theme.[54] It is one that launches both the narrator of Shakespeare's sonnets and the debate over the nature of love between *Venus and Adonis*. The pro-and-con impasse of school training for *in utramque partem* argument structures the stalemate between Venus and Adonis, which Adonis calls to mind when he claims that he "hates her *device* in love" before launching into his own argument that she is talking about "lust" instead. Erasmus would have been happy: He was the one who recommended practice in writing speeches either for or against marriage as good training for boys learning to embellish a set schoolroom "theme" ("One should or should not marry. One should or should not travel—*all in suasory type*"; emphasis mine).[55] As the schoolmaster John Brinsley puts it, boys develop themes into declamations by developing a thesis "both Affirmatiue and Negatiue"; following Erasmus, he, too, gives as his example whether or not one should take a wife (*"uxor est ducenda, uxor non est ducenda"*).[56] Like most school themes, "affirmative or negative," the important lesson remains: A writer or speaker must demonstrate his ability to argue on either side rather than provide a final answer, and do so in a persuasive rather than merely speculative manner. Such a practice belies early twentieth-century critical attempts to argue that the poem endorses the "moral" solution to their lust/love debate.[57] As Altman suggests of sixteenth-century drama more generally, this institutional interest in persuasive force over resolution may help explain the famously unresolved nature of the love/lust argument between Venus and her reluctant pupil.

As rhetorical master, Venus tries every possible means to plead her side of the case. And her pupil is intensely aware that (among other things) his oratorical skills are not sufficiently developed to win the argument:

> More I could tell, but more I dare not say,
> The text is old, the orator too green,
> Therefore in sadness, now I will away . . .
> (805–7)

Adonis dismisses his would-be master's lesson twice as an "idle theme," an "idle, overhandled theme" (422, 770), theme being a term from early grammar school training. Set out by Erasmus in *Copia* and adapted to the themes of Aphthonius, such exercises were "preliminary to the full-fledged oration

on the authority of Quintilian."[58] In the end, Adonis feels unequal to the
task of countering his *praeceptor amoris* verbally; he says he prefers, like many
schoolboys surely did before him, to spend his time in sporting activity with
his friends rather than endure the tedium of his master's lessons.

But what of that lusty, rebellious horse that Venus tries to turn into an
example for her pupil's imitation? Here I would suggest that something of
the *puer* in Shakespeare's narrator emerges in the lengthy, self-promoting
ekphrastic turn that this classical allusion inspires:

> Look when a painter would surpass the life
> In limning out a well-proportioned steed,
> His art with nature's workmanship at strife,
> As if the dead the living should exceed;
> > So did this horse excel a common one,
> > In shape, in courage, color, pace and bone.
> (291-6)

While there are powerful literary reasons for the agonistic tenor of Renaissance *ekphrasis*,[59] the distinct preference for this mode in the epyllia of former
schoolboys is suggestive about the school's disciplinary practices and possible reactions to them. Once the narrator introduces the idea of instruction
and engages in the kinds of impersonations, tropes, and themes that were
engrained in the school's *habitus*, his rhetorical self-reflection turns into a
kind of showing off: This horse, we learn, "excels a common one" and even
improves upon nature. Read in light of the institution that taught boys to
imitate similar passages in their classical forebears, an agonistic ekphrastic
display like this one brings with it the external and internal rivalries implicit
in the school's social and personal scene with its decidedly punitive methods
for teaching Latin; a *magister* who sat in judgment; and divided, self-judging
schoolboy subjects who grew out of such daily training. The narrator, like any
schoolboy, has something to prove to his audience.

Given the structuring dispositions arising from the schoolroom, the narrator's implicit boast about his own rhetorical skill cannot surprise. Nor do
his bravura allusions to precursor Latin texts—the animals from *Ars amatoria*; the amorous bull from *Georgics* 3; and the hint that Adonis's horse resembles the winged horse that in *Metamorphoses* 4 carves out the Helliconian
fountain or "source" of poetry—that define Adonis's horse:

Sometime he scuds far off, and there he stares,
Anon he starts, at stirring of a feather;
To bid the wind a base he now prepares,
And where he run, or fly, they know not whether:
>   For through his mane and tail the high wind sings,
>   Fanning the hairs, who wave like feath'red wings.
(301–6)

The stallion's example and august genealogy may not do the persuasive work Venus hopes it will. But the stallion's demand for aesthetic appreciation beyond "mere" imitation betrays something of the agonistic scene, and jostling for position, that informed the institution in which the poem's author learned how to impersonate passionate figures from the Latin past.

The narrator's lengthy description, moreover, reminds us that the horse Venus tries to harness for her love lesson is *already an imitation*, not the animal itself: "Look when a painter . . . so did this horse." His ekphrastic comparison to painting, in other words, draws direct attention to the art of imitation. And it does so as a first step toward unfolding a character's relation to his/her own feelings. Venus expresses the urgency of her passion through this (imitation of a classical) horse; and Adonis defines his emotions by flatly refusing to assume the normative place in gender and desire that her proposed *exemplum* offers. When he declines to follow the "proceedings" of an "up prick'd" horse derived from a venerable group of precursor Latin texts, Adonis does something more than merely fail to measure up to a heteronormative understanding of nature represented by a "well-proportioned" stallion who "welcomes the warm approach of sweet desire." Worse than that, he won't bother to learn how to imitate the *representation* of "natural" masculinity that his master offers to him as a lesson in love. As a *prosopopoeia* or impersonation, in other words, Adonis animates the principle of refusal. As critics often note, Ovid's far older Adonis shows no such reluctance to Venus in the *Metamorphoses*. But Shakespeare's lovely *puellus* declines to take up the part already written for him in the text from which he comes—and declines further to learn a lesson derived from the texts his narrator is imitating. I would like to suggest that he is turning his back on more than sex. He also turns it on the language, lessons, and practices that sixteenth-century pedagogy indelibly associated, in the experience of its initiates, with eroticism and violence.

The poem takes a notoriously abrupt shift of tone and mood when Venus begins to mourn Adonis, so I will conclude by considering what Venus's expressions of grief can tell us about mastery and the passions at school. In a lesson from Aphthonius's *Progymnasmata* that we will examine in greater detail in the next two chapters, schoolboys learned how to invent emotional characters ("*passiva*") by memorizing and imitating a series of exemplary speeches from women mourning some terrible loss—most frequently of a child. Each of these speeches designed to illustrate "character making" (*ethopoeia*) bears a similar title: "the words Niobe would say over her dead children," "the words Medea would say over her dead children," "the words Andromache would say on the death of Hector," "the words Hecuba would say at the fall of Troy." Just as *Venus and Adonis* ends with reflections on both Venus's future and the future of "love," each of these mournful speeches is divided into comments on past, present, and future suffering—which Lorich highlights with prominent glosses: "*a presenti,*" "*ad praeteritio,*" "*a futuro.*" Almost all of these speeches, moreover, end with a rhetorical question that underlines the speaker's miserable prospects from this moment forward. Antiope demands, "What use is it to weep further?" Hecuba, "Why do I wail?" And Niobe, "Where shall I turn now? Where do I go?" Just before Venus begs Adonis to learn her "lesson" in love, Shakespeare represents her despair in rhetorical questions similarly directed to the future: "Now which way shall she turn? What shall she say? / Her words are done, her woes the more increasing . . ." (253–54).

Venus's despair, of course, only increases over the course of the poem until the narrator imagines a speech that Aphthonius might categorize as "the words Venus would say over the dead body of Adonis." At this point, the poem famously veers from satire to dwell on Venus's plight and feelings: "Dumbly she passions, frantically she doteh." She asks, "What face remains alive that's worth the viewing? / Whose tongue is music now?" (1059, 1076–77). As unresolved as any *in utramque partem* argument, the debate between the poem's two protagonists concludes only with a close-up account of the "variable passions" that "throng" Venus's "constant woe" (967). In the middle of inventing "the words Venus would say over Adonis's dead body," Shakespeare draws on a further technique in Aphthonius's chapter by inventing for her two different *prosopopoeia* to an abstraction: "O Death."[60] At the same time, the distinctly incestuous overtones that trouble the poem's modern readers shift to Venus's lament—a lament in which the narrator follows, as Apthonius recommended for effective depictions of character, "the motions" of the speaker's "mind in every respect" ("*prorsus animi . . . motum*"). Momentarily struck dumb in her passion, Venus looks on Adonis's body while the narrator attends to traumatic confusions of perspective that bewilder the goddess:

> Upon his hurt she looks so steadfastly,
> That her sight dazzling makes the wound seem three,
> And then she reprehends her mangling eye,
> That makes more gashes where no breach should be.
>> His face seems twain, each several limb is doubled,
>> For oft the eye mistakes, the brain being troubled . . .
> (1063–68)

This stanza prompts the question, whose wounds are these? The question arises more forcefully if we remember the rhetorical training this poem invokes, and on which early modern classicism relied: the demand for a transfer of affect from one party to another enforced at the end of a birch. As in the case of Philomela and Gascoigne's schoolboy, such transfers of affect efface differences, whether between male and female or person and text.

If we remember the several weeping mothers who speak over the bodies of dead children in Aphthonius's manual, Venus's "maternal" aspect becomes differently legible as a deeply engrained, institutional association between the Latin past and maternal grief. Boys who used Aphthonius's *Progymnasmata* to learn how to stir up passions in others by adopting ancient passions as their own had not been long separated from the home, and language, of their own mothers. Shakespeare's cross-voiced portrait of Venus's woe for the death of a young boy not yet out of puberty therefore conveys, with some eloquence, the cultural and institutional violence out of which sixteenth-century character was forged. It also reveals something of the unresolved contradictions that accompanied the gender categories masters were working so vigorously to establish.

Prying both characters away from the gendered moorings of his classical source—or rather, importing the scandalously polymorphous erotics from the other stories of Book 10 into the oddly (for Ovid) normative story of Venus and Adonis—the narrator reminds us of where he learned to imitate this story by casting one protagonist as rhetorical master and the other as her reluctant pupil. The narrator's decidedly violent turn in a story that gives two voices to the vicissitudes of *amor*, I suggest, is Shakespeare's way of interrogating the disciplinary practices of the institution in which he first encountered

Ovid. By impersonating the emotions of a "lovely" reluctant *puellus* and those of an aggressive female *magister*, framing their encounter as an argument on either side of a question about "love," and deploying the tropes of *ekphrasis* and *ethopoeia* to capture first Venus's erotic hope and then her despair, Shakespeare's narrator shows how much he has profited from that institution's technical rhetorical training. But at the same time, in the midst of stepping up to the challenge of impersonating the characters from an ancient precursor, the poem begins to unravel the hetero-normative story about gender that critics assume must have been set in place by the institution in which Shakespeare learned the art of classical *imitatio*. The polymorphous outpouring of fantasies and passions in *Venus and Adonis* exceeds the gender distinctions—as well as the preference for civic duty over eros—that schoolmasters claimed their Latin curriculum would impart. And the multiple voices through whom the poet tells this story suggest to me that the ego of the former schoolboy is both everywhere and nowhere in this poem, moving between active, passive, and impersonal positions much as the fantasizing patient who later gave Freud his unforgettable title, "A Child is Being Beaten." Perhaps the painful, emasculating death of Venus's truculent pupil is some kind of payment for his resistance. Or perhaps it is a fantasy testifying to the violence of the institution in which Shakespeare learned what it meant to be a Latin-speaking gentleman. I will venture one last observation about Shakespeare's portrait of the passions in *Venus and Adonis*: If a gentleman is being punished in this poem, then there is also someone there to mourn the inevitability of that violence.

Chapter 4

The Cruelties of Character in
The Taming of the Shrew

Utque quondam iuvenes, ita nunc, mea turba, puellae
Inscribant spoliis, "Naso magister erat."
"Just as young men once did, now let my claque of girls write upon the
bodies of their lovers, 'Naso was our master.'"
　　—Conclusion to *Ars amatoria*

Translations of Mastery

"Schoolmasters will I keep within my house." So Baptista's plan for proving himself a "liberal father / To mine own children in good bringing-up" in *The Taming of the Shrew* ushers in one of Shakespeare's most sustained engagements with the social aims, rhetorical techniques, and affective contradictions of early modern pedagogy (1.1.94–98). Critics have analyzed the numerous classical texts at work in the play as well as its overt interest in grammar school lessons: "shrew taming," as Leah Marcus observes, "is explicitly associated with humanist pedagogy."[1] To this we might add that such pedagogy is also associated with "swine" taming: The "jest" on the beggar, Christopher Sly, relies on the aspirations for upward social mobility that informed the humanist educational program from its inception. The Lord sets an assignment for his servants, calling on them to "persuade" Sly that "he hath been a lunatic" and that he is now a "mighty Lord" by means of a cross-dressed wife and a series of deceptions that culminate in a final, bravura rhetorical performance—their collective exercise in *descriptio* (also called *ekphrasis*) that features three "wanton" Ovidian "pictures" (Induction 1.30, 41, 59–60). Extending even to the sustained imagery that depicts taming / training as a kind of falconry—which George Turberville (whose translation of the *Heroides* is recalled in the play) understood to be a "humanist" sport—the texts and practices of the Latin schoolroom as well as its cherished social categories cast a very long shadow indeed over the induction, the main plot, and the subplot of the play.[2]

Understood in light of the schoolmasters who laid the groundwork for the tropological as well as transactional dynamics in its various scenes of instruction, *The Taming of the Shrew* raises complex questions in all three plots about rhetoric's practical efficacy in "training up" subjects to occupy different social stations by learning acceptable verbal, corporal, and affective behavior. From Tranio's opening advice for his master's study, that he "practice rhetoric" in his "common talk" (1.1.135), to the famous "rope-tricks" by which another servant claims that his "master," Petruchio, will "throw a figure" in Katharine's face to "disfigure" her (1.2.108–110), Shakespeare's early comedy puts humanist claims for the social utility of their training in rhetorical facility to the test. Indeed, all the schoolroom texts and lessons echoed in this play ought to remind us that one question it poses at every turn is, in fact, precisely how "subject" are those subject to others' instruction? And how stable are the new social identities to which they are supposed to be henceforth assigned? As I have been arguing, the humanist shift to imitation as the bedrock of grammatical and rhetorical instruction, as well as the contradictions between theory and practice in the schools, left unresolved problems worth further interrogation: Did masters achieve student hegemony more by consent or by force? Alternatively, could they really be said to achieve such hegemony at all? Such questions about the institutional parameters behind rhetorical performance and social force in *The Taming of the Shrew* offer a different historical and theoretical angle on what Robert Weimann calls "the process of the performer performing"—a crucial turn of attention for the many contemporary critics who try to grapple with this very popular play's heavy-handed ideological effects.[3] I concur with those who point out how often the play "flags performance, deception, and trickery" to demonstrate its awareness that gender and station are "socially scripted" rather than natural roles.[4] But in this chapter I will show that just as important as the commercial theater's practices and effects to such critique are those of the Latin grammar school. And I will argue, as well, that the play's engagement with schoolroom practice tests the limits of a sociological idea of adaptation to gender roles, challenging the stated ends of educational reform by staging repeated misfires between bodies and the genders putatively assigned to them.

The Latin schoolroom influences this play's reflections on rhetorical technique, discipline, and desire precisely because it undertakes a thorough-going interrogation of both the techniques and success of "mastery." "Master" and "mastery" carry many shades of meaning and social hierarchy in the play, of course, but I'd like to bring further attention to the crucial erotic, gendered, and rhetorical inflections that the shadow of the schoolroom *magister* gives to this word throughout.[5] As I pointed out in Chapter 1, Shakespeare conducts this inquiry through character types that actual grammar schools excluded: Baptista's two daughters and Sly, "a beggar and a tinker." Moreover, he directly and repeatedly brings such characters into revealing contact with one of his favorite Roman authors, Ovid: As the writer of the texts brought on stage for Bianca's seduction (*Heroides* in Act 3) and alluded to when Lucentio claims that he is "master of the *Art to Love*" (Act 4), Ovid is allied from the outset with persuasion, "music and poesy," and "pleasure" (1.1.34–39). But Ovid also provides Shakespeare with the literary and rhetorical template through which to explore the social transformations of Bianca, Sly, and Kate—three characters who should have little or no contact with Latin training. Now, the two Ovidian texts most prominent in *The Taming of the Shrew* had distinctly different profiles among educators: According to Erasmus, no epistle is more "chaste" than the one from Penelope to Odysseus in *Heroides*; but that is precisely the text Lucentio selects for their first translation lesson—not to teach Bianca but to seduce her. And according to numerous commentators, Ovid's *Ars amatoria* should not be taught to schoolboys, "lest in their tender years" they "drink in such corruption as shall be noisome unto them all their life after."[6] But in Act 4, Lucentio draws on Ovid's *praeceptor amoris* from the *Ars* to further his flirtation with Bianca. And though she most certainly shouldn't, Bianca apparently knows the scandalous Ovidian text that even schoolboys could not read for fear of "corruption."

One might expect Shakespeare's representation of contemporary pedagogy to reinforce the sense of gender hierarchy necessary to the plot of taming. But when Shakespeare draws on the texts and practices of grammar school training, a few surprises emerge for those interested in the effects that institution might have had on its subjects. That a father looks for teachers "fit to instruct *her* youth" is but the first and most obvious index of the many unexpected turns gender takes in Shakespeare's play, turns that self-reflexively remind audiences of the theater's practice of cross-dressing. As Patricia Phillipy cannily points out when arguing that Ovid's *Heroides* trouble the apparently smooth surface of male heroic dominance with the stone's throw of female lament, Lucentio's first move, upon falling in love with Bianca and deciding to disguise himself as a schoolmaster, is to speak not as heroic wanderer but as Dido begging for counsel from her sister:

> And now in plainness do confess to thee,
> That art to me as secret and as dear
> As Anna to the Queen of Carthage was:
> Tranio, I burn, I pine, I perish, Tranio,
> If I achieve not this young modest girl.
> Counsel me, Tranio, for I know thou canst.
> (1.1.152–7)

A few brief lines later, Lucentio-as-Dido suddenly casts himself as Jove to Bianca's Europa. These shifting allusions may suggest, in part, that Ovid's theme of constant metamorphosis defines the play's various meditations on gender. Similarly, the cross-dressed Bartholomew, outfitted "in all suits like a lady" according to the Lord's orders, reminds us from the start of the play that these are transvestite scenes of persuasion-as-instruction, indebted to the theatricality of the educational institution that made cross-dressing commonplace in a boy's early years of Latin education (Induction 1.106).

The Taming of the Shrew is fascinated with the idea of "mastery"—be it marital, rhetorical, social, or pedagogical. In fact, it puts the word *master* to the test over and over again, beginning with Petruchio's first appearance on stage with his "man," Grumio. We may begin by pressing the specifically institutional senses that accrue to this crucial word. The slapstick scuffle between Grumio and his "mad" "master" springs from three misinterpreted words— "knock me here"—a series of verbal misunderstandings that anticipate how deeply Petruchio relies on a contemporary pedagogue's two chief tools for achieving compliance: rhetorical power and the threat of violence. Both of which, of course, are captured by Grumio's apt nonce phrase for rhetoric, "rope-tricks."[7] In *Shrew*, as I have suggested about Tudor schoolrooms more generally, *mastery* remains a decidedly ambivalent term—one that, as Grumio's quibble on "knock" makes clear, is under contest and continued negotiation. I begin with the subplot, however, because it is primarily in Lucentio's attempt to seduce Bianca while disguised as a Latin schoolmaster that the texts and dynamics of contemporary education overtly enter the world of the play. By staging a commonplace school practice—a lesson in translation—as an attempted seduction, Shakespeare mocks school habits while once again forcing us directly to confront the erotics of early modern pedagogical practice.

I should note here that Lucentio's pedagogical disguise is but one of the most prominent examples of Shakespeare's career-long habit of associating "mastery" with "love." When read in light of the standard first lesson in the accusative case, *amo magistrum*, Lucentio's plot—to disguise himself as a Latin teacher to woo his student—is perhaps less surprising than one might hope it would be. Obedience and affective attachment—"love"—signal two terms schoolmasters frequently used to represent the appropriate pedagogical bond. But in this play, as in *Venus and Adonis*, Shakespeare explicitly weds the idea of love and mastery to the "magister" of Ovid's *Ars amatoria*. In so doing, he tests the claims to social utility on which contemporary pedagogy was founded.

In order to see what difference it makes that Ovid's "master of love" appears in *Taming of the Shrew*, however, I must first point out that two feminist critics have already begun a fruitful reassessment of the texts and transactions in Lucentio's schoolroom. Departing from the way Bianca is often portrayed as a "tractable, chaste, silent and obedient woman of the conduct books" and from the way the men in the play describe her—a girl who merely follows her tutor's lead in Latin translation—Patricia Parker and Heather James have recently taken another look at what Bianca says in her several scenes with her Latin master. Parker observes, "Bianca becomes the master of both her potential masters" in the "pivotal" dispute between Lucentio/Cambio (master of letters) and Hortensio (master of music), a reversal that anticipates her eventual revelation as "anything but a tamed wife by the play's post-marital end."[8] She draws attention to the play's swift move away from the elite connotations of education and the arts in the opening scene—Lucentio has come to "Padua, nursery of the arts" (1.1.2)—to "follow the path of *ars amatoria* instead." And Parker also points out that Bianca may well be mocking (in a way only those in the audience who had once been Latin scholars could find at all funny) Lucentio's mistake in claiming "for sure Aecides / Was Ajax" in the ostensibly obedient reply, "I must believe my master." Because Bianca goes on: "I must believe my master, else I promise you, / I should be arguing still upon that doubt. But let it rest" (3.1.54–5).

Similarly, Heather James observes that Bianca covertly, but effectively, derails Lucentio's position of mastery in the translation "lesson" by showing herself the better scholar of Latin grammar. Lucentio pays no attention to grammatical phrasing, and, as James observes, the meter is "hopelessly broken up" in his opening translation gambit:

> "*Hic ibat*," as I told you before—"*Simois*," I am Lucentio—"*hic est*,"
> son unto Vincentio of Pisa—"*Sigeia tellus*," disguised thus to get your
> love—"*hic steterat*," and that Lucentio comes a-wooing—"*Priami*," is
> my man Tranio—"*regia*," bearing my port—"*celsa senis*," that we might
> beguile the old pantaloon (3.1.31–6)

Bianca, by contrast, preserves "the syntactical integrity of Ovid's Latin" while "identifying the flaws" in Lucentio's "plan":

> Now let me see if I can conster it: "*Hic ibat Simois*," I know you
> not—"*hic est Sigeia tellus*," I trust you not—"*hic steterat Priami*," take
> heed he hear us not—"*regia*," presume not—"*celsa senis*," despair not
> (3.1.40–43).[9]

Given the disciplinary habits of the schoolroom in which Shakespeare and contemporaries first translated and imitated Ovid's *Heroides*, we would do well to take close stock of the resistant student, and unexpectedly accurate Latin scholar, in Bianca. The very first glimpse of this less than tractable Bianca emerges when she declares herself in charge of her own timetable:

> I am no breeching scholar in the schools,
> I'll not be tied to hours nor 'pointed times,
> But learn my lessons as I please myself.
> (3.1.18)

As I pointed out in Chapter 2, a strict schedule of days and hours was the lot of English schoolboys. But Bianca will have none of it. Accurate grammatical phrasing, a sense of her own schedule, and an ironic declaration of belief in her "master": Bianca's assertive, learned, and flirtatious utterances signal her proximity to the educational institution on which her seducer models his behavior, as well as her knowing refusal to conform entirely to his announced program. Indeed, the play charts her refusal to adopt schoolroom habits metrically. A Latin schoolboy would be very familiar with the rules of poetic meter, but in the moment she puts the school's daily regime aside, Bianca breaks the pentameter rhythm of her lines—and gives the four-beat line's definitive accent to "my*self*."[10]

Ovid's final appearance in Lucentio's amatory lessons occurs in a playful allusion to the prohibited *Ars amatoria*. Once again, Shakespeare makes the gendered and erotic connotations of "mastery" a central issue:

> *Lucentio:* Now, mistress, profit you in what you read?
> *Bianca:* What, master, read you? First, resolve me that.
> *Lucentio:* I read that I profess, *The Art to Love.*
> *Bianca:* And may you prove, sir, master of your art.
> *Lucentio:* While you, sweet dear, prove mistress of my heart.
> (4.2.6–10)

Here Bianca turns the question-and-answer method that schoolmasters often used in the lower forms on its head: Rather than submit to the formal demand implicit in the practice, she counters question for question. Were Lucentio the Latin scholar that Bianca proves to be, moreover, he might think twice before modeling himself after the narrator of *The Art to Love*. To understand why, it is important to remember that when Petruchio says he will counter Katharine by strict verbal opposition—

> Say that she rail, why then I'll tell her plain
> She sings as sweetly as a nightingale.
> Say that she frown, I'll say she looks as clear
> As morning roses newly wash'd with dew.
> Say she be mute and will not speak a word,
> Then I'll commend her volubility,
> And say she uttereth piercing eloquence.
> (2.1.168–174)

—he is clearly reversing an important Ovidian maxim from *The Art of Love*. In it, Ovid's narrator advises male lovers to follow a more politic rhetorical course, submitting in every case to a woman's lead:

> *Arguet, arguito; quicquid probat illa, probato;*
> *Quod dicet, dicas; quod negat illa, neges.*
> *Riserit, adride; si flebit, flere memento;*
> *Imponat leges vultibus illa tuis.*

("Blame if she blames, approve whatever she approves.
Affirm what she affirms and deny what she denies.
If she laughs, laugh with her; if she weeps, remember to weep;
let her impose her laws on your facial expressions.") (2.199–202,
    emphasis mine)

Petruchio's taming regime exactly reverses Ovid's recommendations in love's
"warfare" ("*militiae species amor est*"—"love is a kind of warfare"—2.233). Not
only does he invert the power dynamic, but he does so by means of words,
looks, and expressions—the mainstays of *imitatio* and *actio*. Joel Fineman
aptly remarks that "in ways that are so traditional that they might be called
proverbial, Shakespeare's *Taming of the Shrew* assumes—it turns out to make
no difference whether it does so ironically—that the language of woman is at
odds with the order and authority of man."[11] Perhaps irony in the play makes
no difference, though I might still argue upon that doubt. But there is some
difference between the nearly universal "proverbial" gender coding and the
specific textual model from which Petruchio's program springs—particularly if
we remember the pedagogical demand for verbal power, as well as for carefully
imitating the master's expressions and modes of speech, that informed Shakespeare's early institutional encounters with Ovid. Traditional these ideas may
be, but the institutional history and transactions of power revisited in any moment representing them may, in fact, make a great deal of difference. Schoolboys drilled in the arts of verbal, bodily, and affective imitation could hardly
help but notice that Ovid's advice to lovers puts a female "beloved" in the
master's exemplary position and turns a male lover into her imitating pupil.
But Lucentio doesn't seem to recall enough about the poem on which he models himself to know that it might be better to direct Bianca to texts other than
one that recommends a man let a woman's "laws" determine what he says, how
he looks, and what emotions he expresses. Bianca's arch response to his allusion—"and may you prove, sir, master of your art"—suggests it may already be
too late.

More important for the play's concern with the erotics of "mastery,"
Ovid does indeed declare himself *magister* in the art of love. But throughout
the *Ars amatoria*, his narrator is ludicrously unhelpful, dispensing advice
with little or no practical value in order to satirize a long tradition of previous
love poetry. The heavy irony of his self-portrait is perhaps most palpable when,
at the end of the poem, Ovid concludes, "*Naso magister erat*" ("Naso was master"). A deceptive boast, his final declaration brings the poem to a close after a

last bit of advice that decidedly undercuts the erotic wisdom it offers—as well as any man's claims to sexual mastery. He closes his advice to young women with recommendations for the most artful positions for achieving orgasm; the narrator hopes that female readers learn from his instructions how to feel "unstrung to the very depths of their frame" so that "the act delight" both partners alike ("*sentiat ex imis venerem resolute medullis / femina, et ex aequo res iuvet illa duos*" [3.793–94]). Yet the poem's "master" admits that a problem remains: "nature" has denied some women "the sensation of love." The solution?

> *Dulcia mendaci gaudia finge sono. . . .*
> *Tantum, cum finges, ne sis manifesta, caveto:*
>   *Effice per motum luminaque ipsa fidem.*
> *Quam iuvet, et voces et inhelitus arguat oris*
> ("Counterfeit that sweet bliss with a lying sound. . . .
> But when you feign, I caution you not to be too obvious:
> Win his faith by your movements and even by your eyes.
> Let your voice and panting breath make clear your pleasure.") (3.798–803)

With that last caveat, the narrator adds that it would probably be best if there were no light in the room so that the ruse remain well hidden. Only then does "Naso" declare himself "master." Though Lucentio wants to pattern himself on "the art to love," Bianca's reply, "may you prove, sir, the master of your art," reminds the audience—if not him—that the erotic *magister* in the *Ars amatoria* knows full well that he may be endlessly duped by women. Some may rival their would-be masters, in fact, in their ability to substitute rhetorical for sexual pleasure. Indeed, as Ovid points out, faking it requires the very vocal, corporal, and affective techniques required for effective oratory. The only thing left for the narrator to do after such an admission is to bring the poem to a close with the fervent wish that he and other men remain none the wiser. Perhaps Lucentio, in the end, may need to take this final magisterial lesson, choosing to turn a blind eye to the politic deceptions of a wife whose appearance of obedience so effectively conceals her actual feelings. Given this Ovidian subtext about the art of female deception, we might remember that while Erasmus praised the first Latin text in Lucentio's schoolroom—Penelope's letter to Odysseus as "chaste"—Penelope, too, was renowned for her skill in deceiving suitors.

Here it may be useful to note that *master*—the term under continued negotiation in the play and redolent of school hierarchy—is not quite as univocally gendered as is often assumed. Leah Marcus points out that "editors have traditionally adopted a number of emendations . . . that serve to simplify the play's gender relationships" in ways that uphold the very hierarchies that the play might, in fact, be eroding. Three times when the first folio "specifies 'Mistris,' editors have emended to 'masters' or 'master's'"—once when the folio's "mistris" shows Biondello choosing to show obedience to Bianca rather than to Lucentio; and again in the opening scuffle between Petruchio and Grumio in 1.2, the scene that introduces the struggle over the word *master* in the first place.[12] There is, in short, rather more gender confusion in this important word than contemporary editorial practice allows us to see.

That Bianca proves less tractable in her Latin lessons than she is often assumed to be, and is not entirely a foil for her "shrewish" sister in the schoolroom, should astonish no one. Other contemporary dramatic representations of Latin teachers and students portray scenes of instruction as fraught with conflict and hints of rebellion. Pedagogues, as Ursula Potter has shown, rarely fare well on stage; former schoolboys turned dramatists frequently made teachers the butt of their satire.[13] (We might also remember here the raucous satire of "Master Gill upon Gill" from Chapter 2). Thomas Ingelend's *The Disobedient Child*, a play staged at Cambridge in the 1570s, takes up the issue of contemporary pedagogy in ways that rely on classical rhetorical technique while at the same time dramatizing, with compelling force, a schoolboy's reasons for refusing to comply with a master's instruction. Ingelend's plot turns on a boy who refuses to go to school and the play's unresolved moral landscape, as Joel Altman's work should remind us, owes much to drilling in *in utramque partem* argument. On the one hand, the play concludes by suggesting that the Child's refusal was prompted by the Devil. Making a turn toward medieval morality plays, the final act brings the Devil onstage and cautions that because the Child escaped from a master's rod, he became stupid enough to marry a shrew—who beats him instead. Our final view of the protagonist as "The Husband" finds him in a condition as unhappy as Katharine's would-be music teacher:

> "Alas, alas, I am almost quyte dead,
> My wyfe so pytyfully hath broken my head."

> Here the Husbande must lye alonge on the grounde as thoughe hee were fore beaten and wounded.[14]

On the other hand, Ingelend spends considerable time airing the legitimate reasons for fear that made the Child so "disobedient." In the middle of the play, the Sonne explains his decision to flee to his father by painting a vivid picture of physical torment at the hands of a schoolmaster:

> *The Sonne*: At other boyes handes, I haue it learned,
> And that of those truelye most of all other
> Which for a certen tyme haue remayned
> In the house and pryson of a Scholemayster.
> . . . For as the Brute goeth by many a one,
> Their tendre bodyes both nyght and daye
> Are whypped and scourged, and beate lyke a stone
> That from toppe to toe, the skyn is awaye.
> . . . .
> of late dayyes I dyd beholde
> An honest mannes sonne hereby buryed
> Which throughe many strypes was dead and colde.
> *The Father*: Peraduenture the Childe of some disease did laboure
> Which was the cause of his Sepulture.
> *The Sonne*: With no disease surely, was he disquieted,
> As unto me it was reported. . . .
> Men saye, that of this man, his bloudy mayster
> Who lyke a Lyon most commonly frowned,
> Beynge banged up by the heeles togyther
> Was [ ] and buttocke greuouslye whipped.
> And last of all (whiche to speak I tremble)
> That his head to the wall he had often crusshed.

Ingelend's bald, no-exit picture of violence as social necessity—take your whipping early or you will certainly get one late—pulls against the play's final moral that the Devil is to blame for disobedience and ruin. So, too, does the protagonist's vivid description of a "crusshed" head, "strypes," flayed schoolboy "skyn," and a "dead and colde" boy "hereby buryed." Putting both sides of its central issue with some force, *The Disobedient Child* leaves the question of whether it is beneficial to go to school as unresolved as any Latin student trained to argue both sides of a case might have done. Contemporary audiences, in other words, would not only expect a certain amount of violence to attend representations of school training; they would be accustomed to seeing and hearing a good deal of resistance to the master's call.

Dost Thou Love Pictures?

The intimate connection between "love" and "mastery" that pervades Lucentio's translation lesson, as well as Lily's inaugural example of the accusative case, surfaces in a slightly different way in the Induction; once again, Ovid's precedent paves the way. When the Lord tries to translate Christopher Sly from "a beggar and a tinker" into "a Lord and nothing but a lord" (Induction 1.2.61) he puts another Ovidian representation of desire into service. The Lord's "jest" on Sly reminds us of humanist social aspirations—that schoolmasters intervened in social reproduction in order to train young boys up the ladder of social rank (with an eye, of course, to improving their own standing). The Lord's final and most effective technique for inducing Christopher Sly to believe he has risen above his former social position (beggar, cardplayer, pedlar, and tinker) is to describe a series of erotic pictures drawn from Ovid's *Metamorphoses*. That is, if Sly is to move up to the status of "mighty Lord," he must learn a lesson in classical desire.

In addition to flaunting the attractions of the cross-dressed Page, and therefore reminding us of sixteenth-century theatrical as well as school practice, the Lord's trick betrays something of its institutional genealogy because changing Sly's social status is negotiated not simply in relation to the classical past, but in relation to *imitations* of it that are elaborately framed as such. The several servants perform their parts under the watchful eye of their master, vying to fulfill the "instructions" he has set them by trying to "persuade" Sly into a new sense of himself (1.124). Before hearing the "wanton pictures" described so well, Sly speaks in prose and truculently clings to name, geography, education, and profession as fixed marks of identity:

> "What, would you make me mad? Am not I Christopher Sly, old Sly's son of Burton-heath, by birth a pedlar, by education a card-maker, by transmutation a bearheard, and now by present profession a tinker?" (Induction.2.16–22)

The deciding fiction that prompts his transformation upward follows from the query, "Dost thou love pictures?" Two servingmen and the Lord cooperate in performing an ekphrastic depiction of three scenes from the *Metamorphoses* which offer Sly the chance to see the "loves of the gods." After the *ekphrasis*, he begins to speak in verse with new questions about who "I" am:

> Am I a lord and have I such a lady?
> Or do I dream? Or have I dream'd till now?
> I do not sleep: I see, I hear, I speak;
> I smell sweet savors and I feel soft things.
> Upon my life, I am a lord indeed,
> And not a tinker, nor Christopher Sly.
> Well, bring our lady hither to our sight,
> And once again a pot o' th' smallest ale.
> (1.2.68–75)

At first glance, his transformation mocks the humanist effort to "train" young men "up" the social ladder by way of a classical education: Ovid substitutes for a former lesson in "card-making," and Sly still hankers after "small ale." Indeed, the Latin epic so prominent in school curricula comes on stage as "wanton pictures"—more in the guise of early modern pornography than worthy exemplar. Once again, Shakespeare irreverently turns the formal techniques of contemporary pedagogy quite explicitly into a matter of sex. But at the same time, he lends Sly a certain degree of eloquence. Rhetorical questions—"Or do I dream? Or have I dream'd till now?"—and a sense of wonder at "sweet savors and soft things" trace a transformation of Sly's mind and feelings. An encounter with an imitation of passionate alterity makes all the difference; Sly may experience new forms of desire and pleasure precisely by adopting the affective intensity of the classical past.

Sly's transforming burst of wonder, and of iambic verse, may also be indebted to grammar school training that was designed to teach students how to declaim. In the lesson on *ethopoeia*, or "character making," from Aphthonius's *Progymnasmata* examined in the last chapter, there are several telling observations about such a transformation up the social scale. The *Progymnasmata* was a popular post-classical manual in rhetoric, which the humanist scholar Reinhard Lorich significantly expanded with glosses, commentary, and, more important, numerous concrete examples of each technique offered to supplement Aphthonius's singular examples. Lorich's version of the *Progymnasmata* was only slightly less popular in the schools than Lily's *Grammar*; it went through over ninety editions between 1542 and 1689. As Donald

Lemen Clark argued in the 1950s, Aphthonius's manual probably thrived when so many others fell away precisely because of its evident practical value to teachers: At the end of each general lesson in this or that technique, Aphthonius provided at least one concrete example for student imitation. Lorich only amplified the text's pedagogical value by adding more such examples.[15] As Baldwin explains in some detail, Shakespeare was clearly familiar with Aphthonius's text: from the mock staging of Aphthonius's lesson in *narratio* in *Love's Labor's Lost*, Baldwin surveys numerous passages to conclude that Shakespeare "had from Aphthonius his fundamental doctrine of how to 'dilate' a story."[16]

In the lesson I think may be most at issue in Sly's transformation, Aphthonius opens with an outline of three kinds of *ethos,* or "character": First, one learns to capture emotional *ethos* (*passiua*) by imitating "the words Hecuba might utter at the destruction of Troy."[17] Second, one represents what is sometimes translated as "moral" character (*moralis*) by imitating "the words someone born inland might say on first seeing the sea." To preserve the Latin sense of *mores*—habit, custom, or tradition—I prefer to translate this type as "cultural" or "social" character. And third, "mixed" character (*mixta*) emerges in between; for instance, "the words Achilles might say at the death of Patroclus." "Taking counsel about what to do" reveals Achilles's "social" character; grieving for his dead friend reveals its "emotional" aspect.

The Aphthonian category that informs Sly's transition—"social character"—required students to invent speeches for a person confronted by something out of all previous experience: "what someone born inland might say on first encountering the sea." To put Sly's reaction to these pictures in Aphthonius's terms: "the words a beggar might say on first seeing the Ovidian gods." And though in this common school text the commentator, Lorich, largely abandons Quintilian's well-known distinction between moderate and extreme emotion to concentrate almost exclusively on intense feelings like those I will trace in the next chapter in relation to Hamlet and Lucrece, he does mention the distinction once, in passing. Moderate *ethos*, the gloss advises, may be conveyed by "the words a rustic might use when seeing a ship for the first time."[18] Something of this wide spread lesson in "character making," I suggest, emerges in the astonished queries Christopher Sly utters about the novel things he sees, smells, and feels.[19] Consonant with the *habitus* of school training in effective oratory, it is crucial that his speech convey not simply the speaker's thoughts, but his emotions as well. In all these examples of "social character," whether Aphthonius's rustic or Shakespeare's Sly, the affect seems to be astonishment or wonder.

The extended description of the painting representing three stories from Ovid's *Metamorphoses*, moreover, offers a fine example of what schoolboys practiced in the lesson immediately following the one on *ethopoeia*: the art called *descriptio* or ἔκφρασις. The chapter opens with the following: "A description is an expository speech, distinctly presenting to the eyes the thing being set forth" ("*Descriptio est oratio expositive, quae narratione id quod propositum est, diligenter velut oculis*"). The first category of things described so as to bring them to the reader's eyes is *personae*, by which Aphthonius primarily means literary characters: for instance, "how Homer describes Eurybates in the Odyssey."[20] Or, how the Lord and his servants describe three characters from the *Metamorphoses*, bringing Adonis, Io, and Daphne "distinctly" before Sly's, and our, eyes ("*diligenter velut oculis*") because they tell us they are describing a painting.

> *Second Servant*: Dost thou love pictures? We will fetch thee straight
> Adonis painted by a running brook,
> And Cytherea all in sedges hid,
> Which seem to move and wanton with her breath,
> Even as the waving sedges play with wind.
> *Lord*: We'll show thee Io as she was a maid,
> And how she was beguiled and surpris'd
> *As lively painted as the deed was done.*
> *Third Servant*: Or Daphne roaming through a thorny wood,
> Scratching her legs that one shall swear she bleeds,
> And at that sight shall sad Apollo weep,
> *So workmanly the blood and tears are drawn.*
> *Lord*: Thou art a lord, and nothing but a lord.
> Thou hast a lady far more beautiful
> Than any woman in this waning age.
> (Induction.2.47–61; emphasis mine)

The immediate effectiveness of this detour into ekphrastic description—Sly is persuaded, at least for now—stems from the rhetorical concept of "*enargeia*" (eventually attributed to painting in Renaissance pictorial theory). We learn that these "wanton pictures" are as "lively" as Aphthonius recommended for a good description; and from Lorich's added commentary in this chapter, boys read again that the art of effective *descriptio* depends on *enargeia*, or "liveliness." An effective orator, he remarks, is able to bring something "in colors before the eyes" "as if in a painting" (*tabula*). Lorich, the translator and commentator, warms to this topic: "Erasmus calls *enargeia* . . . not simply expounding a thing, but when, expressed by [rhetorical] colors we put it forward for the reader to see with his eyes." In other words, "The orator does not narrate so much as depict, *the reader does not read so much as see*" ("*ut nos depinxisse, non narasse, lector spectasse, non legisse videatur*"; emphasis mine).[21] For Ovid's ekphrastic "*verum taurum, freta vera putares*" ("a real bull and real waves you would have thought them," 6.104), for example, Golding also draws on this rhetorical ideal, translating the description of Arachne's tapestry with reference to its *enargeia*, or "liveliness":

> A swimming Bull, a swelling Sea, *so lively had she wrought*
> That Bull and Sea in very deede ye might them well have thought.
> (emphasis mine)

Apparently much taken by the affective efficacy of *enargeia*, Golding claims in his preface that "poets" know how the "simple white and blacke" of print will fail to "imprint" very much on the reader's "hart." Therefore, poets must use "comely colors" if they want to impress their images upon readers: "The Authors purpose is too paint and set before our eyes / *The lyvely Image* of the thoughts that in our stomacks ryse."[22]

Invoking such a visual ideal for his own description, the servant promises to "show" Io as she was "beguiled and surprised" and calls the work "as lively painted as the deed was done." (It is perhaps worth noting here that the Latin couplet Lucentio chooses for his translation lesson is drawn from an ekphrastic turn in Penelope's letter to Odysseus; she is describing Troy according to what she sees on a map he has sent to her). In the case of this ekphrastic description, I would note that the third servant is working to keep up with the Lord by imitating him, pointing out the picture's *enargeia* and therefore proving himself a worthy orator and obedient to his master. The Lord then concludes with a vivid description of what it would be like to "see" Daphne—compelling not in her beauty so much as in her pain:

> Or Daphne roaming through a thorny wood,
> Scratching her legs that one shall swear she bleeds,

And at that sight shall sad Apollo weep,
So workmanly the blood and tears are drawn.
Thou art a lord, and nothing but a lord.

"As lively painted as the deed was done" and "So workmanly the blood and tears are drawn": The Lord and then his two servants work to persuade Sly, and the audience, to *see* rather than hear the sedges that "seem to move and wanton with the wind," to "swear" along with an imagined spectator that he can see a painted Daphne "bleed"(1.2.56). The persuasive affective force here relies on the color of blood, the spectacle of tears—a "lively" evocation of eroticized pain that precisely corresponds to the dictates laid down for *ekphrasis* in sixteenth-century schoolrooms. Such is the final rhetorical flourish that persuades Sly to think about a new place for himself in the social world.

These lively descriptions, of course, are designed to induce Sly, like any early modern schoolboy, to turn to imitation—to mimic in the bedroom what the *ekphrasis* has just told him to "see." Because following on the heels of these Ovidian lovers, the Lord's servants tell Sly that he, too, has "a lady far more beautiful / Than any woman in this waning age." Negotiated across the *Metamorphoses*, Sly's translation to Lord derives humor from mocking the social status conferred by a Latin education. But it also alerts us to the complex libidinal effects and fantasies that might arise from such an education. The Lord and his servants offer three "lively" descriptions that tempt Sly into the position of voyeur/imitator. Yet these temptations to "see" hardly observe a heterosexual norm. The *ekphrasis* makes Adonis, as much as Io and Daphne, a visual object of desire. Taken together, the "wanton" pictures do not confer a single gender on the act of looking. In fact, the list *begins* with Venus watching the beautiful Adonis; the scene, as critics often remark, more likely recalls the predatory Salmacis of the *Metamorphoses* than it does Ovid's Venus.[23] And it is Venus's, or Salmacis's, panting desire that fills the landscape: The sedges "seem to move and wanton *with her* breath." Sly's new position as Lord may be evoked by a rhetorically accomplished piece of Ovidian erotica that remains true to Aphthonian instruction. But consonant with the attractions of a cross-dressed wife, the lesson invites him to take pleasure either as Apollo loved Daphne *or* as Venus loved Adonis. As one of the several desires offered for Sly's schoolboy imitation, Venus's love for Adonis (or for that matter, Salmacis's for Hermaphroditus) defies the reductive and fixed binary structure necessary to the plot of shrew taming.

In the Lord's elaborate jest, moreover, transvestite performance calls attention to itself as a gesture of obedience that wins the "love" of one's master, much as it would have done in school theatricals:

> Sirrah, go you to Barthol'mew my page
> And see him dressed in all suits like a lady;
> Tell him from me—*as he will win my love*—
> He bear himself with honorable action
> Such as he has observed in noble ladies
> Unto their lords . . .
> And if the boy have not a woman's gift
> To rain a shower of commanded tears,
> An onion will do well for such a shift,
> Which in a napkin close convey'd
> Shall in despite enforce a watery eye
> (Induction 1.104–127)

The method for winning the Lord's "love" divides the object of desire: Transvestism calls attention to itself and separates the object—Sly's cross-dressed wife—from any certain knowledge of gender (or from a sexuality determined by object-choice). It creates, as Tracey Sedinger writes in light of the anti-empiricist strain of psychoanalytic theory, an erotic scene "based not on a clear and distinct representation of the object, but on a moment that frustrates that representation."[24] The erotic scene thereby furthers the paradoxical ekphrastic demand to "see" what one is actually hearing. (To put the issue in Sly's words to his new "wife," "Come sit by us, and let the world slip" [2.136]). Like the ekphrastic detour claiming to paint a vivid canvas out of Ovid's written characters, Sly's cross-dressed wife participates in a collectively conjured fantasy of visual/erotic pleasure that "stages a moment of rupture *when knowledge and visibility are at odds.*"[25]

Indeed, the unfixed, labile erotic fantasy of these three disparate Ovidian stories and the cross-dressed Page hang over the play as a whole: We watch the story of "taming" as Sly watches it —a framed moment of theater going that keeps Sly from what he says he wants. "Madam, undress you, and come now to bed" (2.117). The "pleasant comedy" of wife taming helps the cross-dressed Bartholomew out of what he sees as a predicament; it means that Sly agrees to "tarry in despite of the flesh and the blood" (2.127). This unresolved detour (the frame never closes) further suggests that for Sly, as for Freud, "sexuality does not have, from the beginning, a real object" but consists, rather, in the fugitive substitutions of fantasy. At the same time, the Induction produces a desiring subject that is just as divided as erotic object: Much like Freud's inventive child in the beating fantasy, Sly may occupy his new, culturally marked place as a Lord by identifying himself with any and all positions—learning to imitate, whether successively or simultaneously, Ovid's weeping Apollo, bleeding Daphne, beguiled Io, and/or breathless Venus. In other words, and as I suggested in Chapter 3 concerning school practices and in the introduction concerning Bottom's dream, the grammar school's Latin curriculum may offer Sly a new social character—but it does so only by keeping that identity at a distance.

But why does the Lord conjure an image of Apollo weeping as Daphne bleeds? As I have been arguing, pedagogy's erotic aspect was neither exclusive to Shakespeare nor fixed with respect to gender roles; and it was, at the same time, shot through with intimations (if not always acts) of violence. The "ethos" in Aphthonius's lesson in *ethopoeia* is the Greek noun behind "ethickes"—a field of inquiry that, as one early seventeenth-century writer put it, "treat[s] of civil behavior and manners."[26] In the exemplary characters enumerated to define *ethopoeia*, however, behavior and manners are far from civil. Hecuba mourns the ruin of her city, Niobe and Medea mourn over the bodies of their children, and Achilles grieves for his dead friend. As I discuss further in the last chapter, Lorich's added examples for schoolboy imitation are rife with first-person speeches uttered at moments of death or brutality. In the description that prompts a speech suitable to what Aphthonius calls "social character," ekphrastic descriptions of sexual violence persuade Sly to move up the social ladder—"Am I such a lord?" Apollo's tears and Daphne's blood remind us that sixteenth-century pedagogy made pain inseparable from the rhetorical skill necessary to writing or performing such a scene. In both the content of the school text (Aphthonius's lessons in *ethopoeia* and *ekphrasis*) and the institutional setting in which a boy learned to imitate that text, we find representations of aggression and violence. Grammar school practice, in short, produced both writers and audiences for a commercial theater in which cruelty became central to representations of emotion and character. When the Induction draws on the school training that made this *ekphrasis*, and the "social character" of Sly, possible, we see that rhetorically capable subjects may take their place in the social world, and take their pleasure—whether aesthetic, sexual, or theatrical—precisely where someone suffers. Prompted by ekphrastic descriptions of classical scenes of eroticized violence, Sly's translation from beggar to lord does more than lay the groundwork for the play's interrogation of the humanist social agenda. It also anticipates the conjunction of "love" and "mastery" that dominates the play he is about to see—the tightly knotted connection between pleasure and pain in a comedy that juxtaposes its critique of humanism's socially scripted positions and emotions with spectacles and threats of violent punishment.

"Why Are Our Bodies Soft?"

Katharine, for her part, exacerbates Bianca's verbal sparring with her would-be master, turning to physical as well as verbal resistance. Anticipating the rhetorical wrangling with which she famously pays Petruchio back in kind, so deftly that he finds himself "Kated," Katharine shows herself the kind of student who turns her teacher's instruments and his words into weapons against him:

> *Baptista:* Why, then thou canst not break her to the lute?
> *Hortensio:* Why, no, for she hath broke the lute to me.
> I did but tell her she mistook her frets,
> And bow'd her hand to teach her fingering,
> When, with a most impatient devilish spirit,
> "Frets call you these?" quoth she, "I'll fume with them."
> And with that word she struck me on the head,
> And through the instrument my pate made way . . .
> (2.1.147–54)

Despite their father's declared alliance with these schoolmasters—"these are their tutors. Bid them use them well" (2.1.108)—neither daughter proves an entirely submissive pupil. The important point here is that both Katharine and Bianca answer their masters with the kind of verbal wit (and in Bianca's case, Latin facility) that might make a sixteenth-century schoolboy proud. In Katharine's rebellion against her tutor, moreover, one is prompted to ask, is she perhaps trying to move out of the student's role into that of the violent pedagogue? Certainly, Katharine will end the play by constructing a kind of school for wives. And to the extent that she resists her lesson by adopting the role of a punitive master, we should note that with respect to her music teacher, Katharine accomplishes this reversal by using specifically humanist techniques—*imitating* a schoolmaster's verbal skill ("Frets call you these? . . . I'll fume with them") and his penchant for physical coercion (he "bowed her hand" so she "struck me on the head").[27]

This master-pupil *agon* extends throughout the verbal sparring between Petruchio and Katharine, including their famous debate over what to name the moon and the sun.

> Petruchio: Good lord, how bright and goodly shines the moon!
> Katharine: The moon? The sun. It is not moonlight now.
> Petruchio: I say it is the moon that shines so bright.
> Katharine: I know it is the sun that shines so bright.
> Petruchio: Now, by mother's son, and that's myself,
> 　　　It shall be moon, or star, or what I list
> 　　　Or ere I journey to your father's house.
> 　　　Go on, and fetch our horses back again.
> 　　　Evermore crossed and crossed, nothing but crossed.
> Hortensio: *Say as he says*, or we shall never go.
> (4.5.2–11, emphasis mine)

Turning the Induction's scene of persuasion into verbal coersion, Shakespeare points here to yet another rupture, this one between what Petruchio "says" and Kate sees and "knows." As Laurie Macguire aptly points out about Katharine's submission to Petruchio's lesson in lingual obedience—

> But sun it is not when you say it is not. . . .
> What you will have it nam'd, even that it is,
> And so it shall be so for Katharine
> (20–23)

—not all may be settled. "Though Katharine is bombarded by her abbreviation 'Kate,' she later slyly reasserts the full form in the . . . scene in which she sanctions Petruchio's right to name everything."[28] In the moment of apparent capitulation, she claims the right to name herself "Katharine" (as I therefore have done throughout). This much studied battle over naming may owe something to the techniques contemporary pedagogues used to achieve mastery over student tongues: "Pronounce before them what they cannot" (John Brinsley). "Have them repeat over some ribble rabble" (Charles Hoole). "I say it is the moon" (Petruchio). "Say as he says" (Hortensio). The schoolmaster's disciplinary regime operated primarily by controlling what students might "say"—beginning with specific training in the art of *orthopoeia* ("right utterance"), vociferation, and reading "without boke" and ending in scripted speeches and theatricals. In a play invested in humanist pedagogy and its discontents, grammar school training casts a long shadow over their ongoing argument over whether to say "Kate" or "Katharine," "moon" or "sun." Underlying Katharine's imitative negotiations with Petruchio's "rope-tricks," too, is the knowledge shared by many members of the audience that Shakespeare is slyly inverting Ovid's advice to men in the *Ars amatoria*: Suit your words and expressions and affect to your lover's; imitate her well. Such a Latin subtext pulls against Petruchio's humanist program of verbal mastery.

The content of Katharine's final speech before Padua seems to put the obvious transvestite performance from the Induction to rest in its argument that the body is empirical ground for a woman's service to her "lord":

> I am ashamed that women are so simple
> To offer war where they should kneel for peace,
> Or seek for rule, supremacy, and sway,
> When they are bound to serve, love, and obey.
> Why are our bodies soft, and weak, and smooth,
> Unapt to toil and trouble in the world,
> But that our soft conditions and our hearts
> Should well agree with our external parts?
> (5.2.165–73)

Though this speech often convinces readers to reify a character once performed by a boy into the embodied referent "Kate" (even when reading "her" speech as mere politic submission), the history of school training in rhetoric suggests we think again. Sixteenth-century pedagogical practice, as well as the status of Katharine's speech *as* a speech delivered on a set topic designed to persuade the audience and so win a master's approval, means that the play once again underlines *the disjunction between seeing and knowing*—the condition of theatrical pleasure—that informs the *ekphrasis* to Ovid's *Metamorphoses*, Bartholomew's performance as Sly's "wife," and Katharine's capitulation in the naming contest over sun and moon. That is, by assuming the role of an orator whose task it is to persuade two audiences of her argument—in this case, "Such duty as the subject owes the prince, / Even such a woman oweth to her husband" (5.2.159–60)—Katharine shows herself well-schooled enough to engage in effective public declamation. And the fact that she is engaged in persuasive public argument before an audience of peers and a "master" would remind any contemporary audience member who had been to grammar school that "s/he" is a performer performing, an orator arguing a case from the body s/he does not have in order to succeed in convincing you that s/he does. Katharine engages in the kind of exercise in public argument, in other words, that masters commonly demanded a schoolboy perform effectively—without reference to a boy's actual convictions. In fact, the better s/he is at persuading her audience to believe her declared "obedience" to her master, the more "Katharine" reveals the benefits of rhetorical training commonly reserved to boys exclusively— boys who were, like the one who played "Katharine," well-schooled in the techniques necessary for playing female parts. Finally, the Shrewsbury School ordinances required a student to speak effectively on exactly the topic Katharine rehearses at the play's end. Upon a master's election, the ordinances state, he "shall make a Latin oration"; following that, "one of the best scholars shall welcome him with a congratulatory Latin oration, promising obedience on behalf of the school."[29]

Here important methodological and theoretical questions arise concerning the decisions that guide one's choice of historical context to bring to bear on the larger social texts and practices of which this play is a part. Questions about female speech and gendered violence have become central to feminist and new historicist criticism of *The Taming of the Shrew*. Historical accounts often read its verbal warfare in the context of early modern disciplinary rituals and discourses of normative gender ideology: With reference to the scold's bridle, conduct literature, household hierarchy and management, or the emerging commercial marketplace, critics are tempted to fix a determinate meaning for the play's "male" and "female" characters when deciding which historical frame best accounts for its depiction of gendered linguistic struggle.[30] Implicit in this decision is a tendency to elide the theatrical practice of cross-dressing, to proceed from text to context by sorting out the play's initial engagement with transvestite performance according to fixed identities that, even while acknowledged to be socially "scripted," can be mapped in direct, one-to-one relation to early modern men and women. But what if those "men" and "women" were themselves playing out the effects of certain privileged emotion scripts? Bringing school practices to bear on the verbal play and disciplinary action of *The Taming of the Shrew* has at least three advantages with literary, historical, and theoretical import. First, this comparison accounts for the play's evident interest in the efficacy of contemporary Latin pedagogy and "mastery"; its continued evocation of Ovidian texts concerned with *amor*, rhetoric, and imitation; and the way it deploys the specific rhetorical skills of *translatio* and *ekphrasis* in a critique of the reproduction of sanctioned social identities. Second, paying attention to the shadow the schoolroom casts over the play draws our attention to the fact that for contemporary audiences who had undergone training in Latin grammar and rhetoric, the actors' performances of gender, desire, and violence are just that—transvestite performances undertaken to produce convincing *effects* of character and the passions. Such convincing effects are created by revisiting the educational tropes and transactions that, as I have argued, bring into question the humanist claim that their Latin curriculum and methods of discipline would produce recognizable "gentlemen" for the good of the commonwealth. And finally, reading the play back into the institutional training that made its interrogation of "love" and "mastery" possible brings the anti-foundationalist implications of theories of performativity into everyday life, suggesting that rather than a sociological concept of gender identity, Kristeva's theory of the speaking "subject in process" or Lacan's that "the object *is* a misfire" offer more useful guides for historicizing the way *The Taming of the Shrew* participates in the larger social texts of gender and the passions that were under continued negotiation in sixteenth-century Britain.

If we remember the school's drilling in the art of arguing effectively on either side of a question, the ironic distance between speaker and speech that many hear in Kate's final speech attests to a larger institutional and cultural terrain: A potential distance between an orator's personal convictions and any given verbal performance was built into the educational practices at issue in Shakespeare's representation of gendered and erotic mastery. That so many modern readers have been inspired to question Katharine's sincerity is clearly an index of modern concerns. But at the same time, our persistent skepticism about what "Katharine" believes in relation to what she says reveals something telling about the institutional *habitus* that informs the play's depiction of verbal sparring for power. First, such reactions are picking up on a contradiction that humanist masters could not resolve in the tradition they inherited—the inevitable disjunction between a given rhetorical performance and what an orator thinks and feels. As we will examine in the next chapter in the case of the Player in *Hamlet* and Sinon in *Lucrece*, the institutional parameters informing the performance of "mastery" in this play means that "Katharine's" argument for "obedience" points out the rift between seeming and being. That is, this performance stages the question that school training in rhetorical facility could only exacerbate: How can one ever be certain whether or not a speaker's intentions lie elsewhere? Second, the modern tradition of wondering what "Katharine" really thinks (whether by critics or actresses playing the part) does more than revisit the problem inherited from classical rhetoric and made palpable in everyday life in sixteenth-century schools. It tells us that from this long-standing problem in the classical rhetorical tradition, vividly brought to life in the experience of schoolboys, Shakespeare derived a way to create convincing effects of character beyond even the specific lesson offered in Aphthonius. Declaring that one has "that within which passes show" (Hamlet); decrying the difference between a speaker and his words (Lucrece and Hamlet); turning the disjunction into a bravura performance that wins a master's approval—"Why, there's a wench!"—while prompting so many readers to interpret her unfathomable inwardness (Katharine): all these moments point to a distance between rhetorical performance and being. Each of these moments call attention to the former schoolboy who, by reengaging the school's tropological/transactional negotiations for power, creates the convincing *effects* of subjectivity and feeling for which he has so long been noted.

Chapter 5

"What's Hecuba to Him?"

Transferring Woe in *Hamlet, The Rape of Lucrece,* and *The Winter's Tale*

> *"Me miseram!" (Niobe)*
> *"O me miseram! . . . Sed quid lamentor?" (Hecuba)*
> *"O me miseram!" (Andromache)*
>   —Aphthonius, *Progymnasmata*

"More Woe Than Words"

The reality and spectacle of the master's birch—a figure that looms large in texts about the school as well as those written or used in it—has led me to focus often in the preceding chapters on the ways sixteenth-century teachers used violence, or the theatrical threat of it, to "train up" their Latin-speaking *pueri* as English gentlemen. But at this point in my analysis, it is useful to recall that humanist masters used imitation right alongside corporal punishment as a method for obtaining compliance with the school's linguistic and social regime. As we have seen, the author of "The Birch" joked that "whipping's used in mood & figure," and the unnamed schoolboy who wrote the Westminster "Consuetudinarium" similarly conceived of daily life according to the intertwined pair of flogging and imitation: "some" boys were "selected . . . to be examined and punished, others to be commended and proposed to imitation."[1] With respect to either of these paired techniques, I continue to stress daily material practice, "materiality" understood here to designate the school's discursive as well as corporal forms of discipline. The ever-present command to imitate or "follow" one's master as well as the precedent classical texts he taught may appear to be the gentler method for implanting the school's privileged social hierarchies, its codes for gentlemanly language, gesture, behavior, and affect. Gentler it may have been, but hardly less coercive.

Keeping in mind the depiction of schoolboys as "a companie of seven-yeare-olde apes" in *The Pilgrimage to Parnassus*, this final chapter aims to unfold what it means to think seriously about imitation as a disciplinary practice. It examines three of Shakespeare's texts from across his career to show how much each reveals about the unintended consequences, for the life of the passions and of gender, that could follow from the humanist demand that schoolboys learn eloquence by learning to mimic the voices and passions of others. One of the claims I have made is that it is time to reconsider whether the school's demand for imitation did, in fact, achieve a kind of "hegemony by consent" in schoolboy subjects rather than the mere politic appearance of it—or, for that matter, even more deep-rooted forms of opposition.[2] I therefore propose to look more closely, both historically and theoretically, at the affective textures one can detect in three representations of woe in Shakespeare's texts that either directly represent or draw upon early school practice. Understanding how early modern schoolboys experienced their teachers' favored social categories requires a detailed analysis of the assumptions about bodies and passions built into training in *imitatio*—which means, I suggest, that both school archives and the vernacular texts a Latin education made possible have much to reveal about the school's social as well as literary effects. To begin this analysis, I would like to take my cue from a young scholar who recorded a lesson in "Rhetorick" in the commonplace book he seems to have begun while still at school. He notes prominently on the page that in addition to verbal ability and bodily deportment, effective persuasion has one further requirement: good oratory involves an intimate emotional connection, or better yet, transfer of feeling, between speaker and audience. No less an authority than Cicero "saith yt is almost impossible for an Orator to stirre up a passion in his Auditors except he be first affected *with the same passion hymselfe*" (emphasis mine).[3]

School lessons in eloquence taught young orators that success was more than a matter of learning to imitate precedent Latin texts fluently and accurately. It also meant learning to feel for oneself, and convey to others, the many passions represented in them. At some odds with another influential, classically sanctioned view that we are subject to a lifelong struggle between the reins of reason and the horses of passion and appetite (the *locus classicus* being Plato's *Phaedrus*), school training in rhetoric encouraged young boys to experience and express precisely that aspect of the soul that strict moralists, from Plato to Thomas Wright, told them it was crucial to control. Wright, for instance, wrote *The Passions of the Minde in Generall* (London, 1601) "to direct the Reader to do something that may be either commodious to himself or profitable to the Commonwealth." On behalf of both personal and civic good, Wright warns that the "motions of the passions" are precisely what "blinde reason" and "seduce the will." Indeed, they are the "thorny briars sprung from the infected roote of original sinne."[4] Grammar school records reveal how assiduously school authorities worked to inculcate Christian precepts in their students. But the school's Latin curriculum and techniques for achieving eloquence nonetheless conveyed a few lessons that might impede reason's strict path to Christian virtue. Drilling in Latin oratory meant that young English gentlemen were frequently required to practice techniques for appealing to, and feeling, the "passions"—concentrating, in their daily exercises, on cultivating (and perhaps in some eyes, tempting) that aspect of themselves that Plato and many of their own contemporaries claimed could lead the soul to ruin. The classical tradition was hardly unified in its views on the place or value of the passions; nor, as we know well, did that tradition always sit easily alongside Christian doctrine. Humanist teachers who brought the art of imitating ancient texts into England for the good of the commonwealth inherited and then conveyed many of these contradictions.[5]

This chapter takes a close look at three portraits in grief: Lucrece, Hamlet, and Mamillius. In each case, Shakespeare represents "woe" in ways that raise a number of technical rhetorical concerns specific to school training—and in particular, to classical *imitatio* and its consequences. I examine all three characters in light of the role that imitation played in advanced lessons in Latin declamation (for Lucrece and Hamlet) as well as in elementary grammar lessons and bilingual vocabularies (for Mamillius). In each case, Shakespeare's meditation on the technique and possible effects of imitating *someone else's* passion—humanism's institutionalized method for achieving hegemony by consent rather than force—allows him to produce the effect of inwardness, of intense personal feeling, long recognized as characteristic of his texts. My primary purpose is to demonstrate how deeply the rhetorical, social, and libidinal opacities of early Latin training analyzed in Chapters 1 and 2 inform what we now recognize and describe as characteristically Shakespearean "subjectivity effects." I borrow Joel Fineman's phrase to acknowledge how far he shifted the contemporary critical terrain; but at the same time, I want to

bring institutional history and practice to bear on his argument that the sonnets' persuasive subjectivity effect is the consequence of literary history alone
(for the sonnets, Petrarchan *epideixis*). That is, we might profitably explore
how far Shakespeare's formal techniques for creating effects of personal character and feeling derive from the Latin grammar school's theatrical *habitus* and
its classically derived methods of rhetorical training (in which, for example,
practice in the art of *epideixis*, whether "praise" or "dispraise," was an important component).[6]

But I have a second, related aim. Hamlet's claim to possess "that within
which passes show" is a theatrical return to the rhetorical predicament Shakespeare explores in *The Rape of Lucrece*: "more woe than words." Both the trag-
edy and the narrative poem pause to define their titular character's passion in
light of the same question: How is it possible for anyone to imitate Hecuba,
Troy's exemplary grieving mother? Mamillius intensifies this fascination with
an ancient icon for maternal grief, dying from "mere conceit" of his own
mother's suffering—a mother whose return to her family is defined by several
other classical stories (Pygmalion's statue, Ceres, and Persephone). In an all too
brief encounter with Hermione's sorrow, Mamillius imitates his mother's passions so well that suffering carries him away altogether. I put these portraits of
woe, drawn from across Shakespeare's career, back into the institutional frame
that made them possible not simply to point out how important the school's
curriculum and forms of pedagogy are to the way Shakespeare represents character and the passions. More important still, I compare his narrative and dramatic portraits of grief to illuminate significant strains of resistance to the prized
social categories that schoolmasters claimed would necessarily follow from the
ability to transmit classical texts, and the affects portrayed in them, with convincing authority.

This resistance, I believe, is not unique to Shakespeare, although I would
argue that among contemporaries, he had a particularly canny ear for in-
congruities internal to the institution from which he benefited. I have already
suggested a number of contradictions between humanist theory and practice:
as just outlined, that between the transfer of emotion required of any good
rhetorician and the belief that the passions could "blind reason" and "seduce
the will" away from Christian virtue. Or, as discussed in Chapters 1 and 2,
humanist confidence in the beneficial effects of their classical curriculum and
modes of instruction did not always match school practice—a discrepancy
perhaps most glaring in that the shift to teaching by imitation did not entirely
supplant Latin lessons "well beaten in" to a student. Whether actual or virtual,

real or spectacular, flogging lingered in schoolrooms supposedly dedicated to the gentler pressure of imitation, despite calls like Richard Mulcaster's in *Positions* for less punitive forms of instruction. Additionally, Chapter 2 argued that the practical theatricality of everyday life in the schools pulled against the general theory of "mastery"—whether designating a unified gender or class identity—that humanists presumed when arguing that a Latin education would produce proper English gentlemen. In what follows, I propose that Shakespeare exploits, expands, and intensifies this last internal contradiction in ways that reveal a good deal about the school's effects on masculinity and the passions. In the case of the portraits of character and emotion under consideration here—Lucrece, Hamlet, and Mamillius—one finds a significant clash between the art of classical *imitatio* that sixteenth-century writers imbibed at school and the prima facie meaning of gender norms invoked by schoolmasters and theorists when promoting their new ideas about pedagogy. Shakespeare's portraits of the passions betray his debt to the inculcated practice of *imitatio* while remaining indifferent to the normative gender categories this institution claimed to establish in each student—categories crucial to its cherished distinction between "popular" and "elite" culture based on the seemingly natural, but actually historically specific, distinction between a "mother" and a "father" tongue.

Emotion, Character, Identification

To demonstrate what I mean by Shakespeare's fractious indebtedness to the Latin grammar school's disciplinary regime—or perhaps his fine-tuned ear for its internal contradictions—I would like to extend a discussion I began elsewhere. In *The Rhetoric of the Body*, I briefly observed that after her rape, Lucrece behaves much as any early modern schoolboy would, searching for classical exemplars to imitate and so find words to express her "woe." After failing to persuade Tarquin to desist with the prospect that he will turn himself into a "school where Lust shall learn" (617), and much to the disapproval of modern critics with an anachronistic distaste for Renaissance rhetorical display, Lucrece leans on a series of *prosopopoeiae* to ease her mind.[7] These formal exercises in personification and address allow her to imagine herself her own advocate in a courtroom trial. First she charges Tarquin with the crime— here one must remember that "epideixis" designates words spoken in *blame* as well as in praise—and soon animates three abstractions, accusing each of facilitating the rape: "O comfort-killing Night" (764ff), "O Opportunity, thy guilt is great" (876ff), and "Mishapen Time" (925ff).[8] Lucrece's experiment in forensic oratory fails to achieve a conviction or assuage her grief ("In vain I rail at Opportunity, / At Time, at Tarquin, and uncheerful Night" [1023–4]), so she chides her own verbal skill as well as the institution that taught the verbal art necessary for winning legal arguments:

> Out, idle words, servants to shallow fools,
> Unprofitable sounds, weak arbitrators!
> Busy yourselves in skill-contending schools,
> Debate where leisure serves with dull debaters;
> To trembling clients be you mediators.
>> For me, I force not argument a straw,
>> Since that my case is past the help of law.
> (1016–22)

Despite this outburst against forensic "argument" and the schools laying the groundwork for it, Lucrece's restless search for words that are not "in vain" (whether to ease her mind, express her feelings, or move her audience to revenge) continues along institutionally predictable lines. *Disputatio* and *comparatio* emerge in cognate translation—she "holds disputation with each thing she views" (1101) and "to herself all sorrow doth compare" (1102)—only to give way again to *prosopopoeia* and *imitatio*.[9] She turns aside from her own case to address two Latin precursors in order to imitate the passions of both: Philomela's "sharp woes" (1136) and Hecuba's "despair" (1447).[10] Indeed, William Weaver recently traced the thorough-going adaptation of "the rhetorical exercises and textbooks of Elizabethan grammar schools" in the poem to argue that Shakespeare develops, in Lucrece's voice, "a formal oration in the judicial genre."[11]

With regard to Lucrece's numerous choices of rhetorical form (whether generally forensic or specifically epideictic, perhaps in its "vituperative" mode from Aphthonius), her overall tone, and the poetic genre of complaint in which she and numerous other female characters participate in the 1590s, we might recall the Westminster "Consuetudinarium." In it, the student author's account of daily life at school makes "complaint" virtually synonymous with "accusation": the monitors "presented their complaints or accusations (as we called them) everie Friday morn" before "begging" and "prevailing" on behalf of those so accused.[12] Understood as phrases arising from schoolroom nomenclature, these terms suggest that the affect of "woe" we might interpret as intrinsic either to genre or gender—the sudden flowering of "female complaint" in the 1590s—had just as much to do with the content of the grammar school's Latin curriculum (its practical lessons in forensic argument) and its explicitly judicial methods for determining whether a boy would be punished or rewarded for performing those lessons.[13]

To modern readers, Lucrece's search for relief from the emotional dilemma of "more woe than words" follows a less than intuitively obvious path: "pausing for means to mourn some newer way" (1365), she looks twice to ancient precedent to help with her predicament. By means of apostrophe's "turn away" from the narrative at hand, as well as its implicit fantasy that a speaker may confer personhood on a dead, missing, or inanimate entity, Lucrece mirrors the poem's narrator when she looks to "imitate" precedent classical texts "well."[14] Her circuitous route through the characters of Troy—the city that would count as classical precedent in the poem's Roman setting—repeats the narrator's central act of impersonating legendary characters. And yet at the same time, this rhetorical detour allows Lucrece to experience her own shame and grief. As the narrator puts it, classical indirection allows Lucrece a "newer way" to find a path through the process of mourning.

Nor is Lucrece the only one in the poem to mimic a precedent model. The Trojan tapestry, a "well painted piece," offers Lucrece the precursors she needs. But the ekphrastic description tells us that the tapestry itself is already involved in acts of imitation. The waves of the river depicted in it mimic something else—in this case, the army fighting on its banks:

> And from the strond of Dardan, where they fought,
> To Simois' reedy banks the red blood ran,
> *Whose waves to imitate the battle sought*
> With swelling ridges, and their ranks began
> To break upon the galled shore, and then
> > Retire again, till meeting greater ranks
> > They join, and shoot their foam at Simois' banks
> > (1436–42; emphasis mine)

In *The Rape of Lucrece*, Shakespeare stresses imitation all the way down: Even the exemplary tapestry of Troy derives its "skillful" visual imagery from the "colors" of rhetoric, the Dardan's waves their movement from copying the action of armies.

Lucrece's decision to single out Hecuba from all the tapestry's "many Trojan mothers" for "some newer" way to grieve might well have pleased Erasmus, founding inspiration for Tudor pedagogy. In *De Copia*, Erasmus suggests that Hecuba would be a fine model from which to learn how to achieve the impression of great emotion. In this, he is very likely drawing on Lorich's Latin translation of Aphthonius's *Progymnasmata*. In the chapter on *ethopoeia*, Lorich seems to have been taken by Aphthonius's brief reference to Hecuba, since he invented an entire speech for her—"*exemplum, continens qualia verba dixerit post excidium Trojanum*" ("an example containing the words Hecuba would say after the fall of Troy")—where in the original Greek manual, Aphthonius had merely referred to her in his opening taxonomy of types of character. Read in light of both prominent school authorities, Erasmus in general and Aphthonius in practice, it is hardly surprising that Lucrece's desire to lend a tongue to the tapestry's "mute" imitation of Hecuba's "woe" anticipates Hamlet's complex reaction to the Player's imitation of Hecuba. For present purposes, difference of genre recedes before the habits of early Latin training: Both the narrative and dramatic encounters with Hecuba's grief have much to tell us about Shakespeare's reaction to the power and limits of classical *imitatio*— and much, too, about his habits for generating effects of character and feeling, whether in narrative verse or for the stage.

The speech Lorich invents for Hecuba ends on precisely the Ovidian note of rhetorical impasse that plagues both Lucrece and Hamlet: What can I say? Lorich's Hecuba concludes, "But why do I complain? . . . even when I can no longer speak with a human voice, I will never cease mourning with incessant barking" ("*Sed quid lamentor? . . . tamen ego quod humana voce non potero, id latratibus assiduis deplorare non sum cessatura*").[15] As occurs so often in the epic of a poet once well known in Rome for the art of declamation, the moment of metamorphosis captures a moment of vocal failure in which a gulf emerges between a speaker's feelings and what she can say about them. As passed on to English schoolboys in the form of rhetorical exercise in the art of character making, Hecuba's grief allows both Lucrece and Hamlet to address emotions from which they too feel at a certain distance, emotions that evade the grasp of language. Hamlet, weighed down by "blunted" "passion," becomes impatient with his inability to find words adequate to the cause, scorning his own limitations because he can "say nothing" about his own reason for woe. Similarly plagued by "more woe than words," Lucrece at first chastises her complaint for being "idle." But eventually she distinguishes herself from the painted imitation of Troy by claiming to "lend a tongue" to Hecuba's suffering and consequently her own. The painting's lively "colors" remain somehow insufficient to capture such a passion. This failure, in turn, allows Lucrece to better its imitation, to "tell" her own "sad tale" of Hecuba's sorrow—and thus, from a distance, to gesture to something of her own. As in the texts and daily exercises at school, Lucrece's renewed burst of feeling involves precedent Latin texts but also the discipline of word and gesture best suited to convey the passions represented in them. Lucrece involves herself in the tapestry's story by means of "words" and "looks," *imitatio* and *actio*: "she lends them *words*, & she their *looks* doth borrow" (emphasis mine, 1496–98).

In other words, Hecuba's provenance in Shakespeare's representation of grief not only stems from her presence in a widely circulated school text, but also bears traces of the larger disciplinary regime in which this text was used—a regime dedicated to inculcating in Latin-speaking gentlemen the affective, vocal, and facial techniques of *actio* alongside the linguistic skills necessary for *imitatio*. Both Lucrece and Hamlet begin by objecting to the specific techniques involved in the imitation enacted before them. Lucrece blames the painter for injuring his subject:

> On this sad shadow Lucrece spends her eyes,
> And shapes her sorrows to the beldame's woes,
> Who nothing wants to answer her but cries,
> And bitter words to ban her cruel foes;
> The painter was no god to lend her those,
> > And therefore Lucrece swears he did her wrong,
> > To give her so much grief, and not a tongue.
> > (1457–63)

From such perceived failure, Lucrece takes her own turn at imitation (i.e., "'Poor instrument,' quoth she, 'without a sound / I'll tune thy woes with my lamenting tongue'" [1464–65]). For his part, Hamlet finds new words and a "newer way" back to feeling from an encounter with the words, gestures, and looks of someone else trying to capture Hecuba's emotion. But by contrast to the painter's failure, in Hamlet's case the encountered imitation is flawed because it is too good. Complaining about the Player's "dream" of Hecuba's "passion," Hamlet objects to the practiced gestures and facial expressions the actor uses to create the impression that he is, as Cicero might put it, "affected with the same passion hymselfe" as Hecuba. And the apostrophe that in *Lucrece* renews the narrator's ekphrastic display of rhetorical ability and enables his character to imagine herself able to speak on behalf of Hecuba's "sad shadow" becomes, in *Hamlet*, a far-reaching question about the ethical implications of classical training: "What's Hecuba to him, or he to Hecuba, / That he should weep for her?" (2.2.559).

We should note that the Player's speech, much as the tapestry in the early narrative poem, rests on an important tenet in the classical rhetorical tradition: Words have the power to "move" others. Thus the Player tells us that Hecuba's "clamor" was powerful enough to "move . . . passion" even "in the gods" (2.2.518). Which is, of course, exactly what Lorich's Hecuba predicts for herself—even though she will be "deprived of sense" when transformed to a dog, Hecuba's noise will nonetheless move "the gods to compassion when they hear my afflictions" ("*quamuis aerumnarum miserti Dii me exaudierint*"). Drawing on rhetoric's emotional aim, the Player hints that the same transfer of affect will obtain between the Player and *his* audience. As if reacting to the idea of Hecuba's moving "clamor"—that passions may be relayed from one party to another by affecting sound—Hamlet turns detailed critic of *imitatio, actio,* and the possible consequences of rhetoric's moving power. If we remember the theatricality of school training in Latin grammar and rhetoric, we notice that Hamlet's objections have a certain technical precision with respect to *actio,* the relationship between word and gesture. As one schoolmaster admonished his class, students must learn from stage players "what must be pronounced with what expression . . . there should be in the voice a certain amount of elevation, depression, and modulation . . . the supplosion of the feel accommodated to the subject."[16] Others, as we have seen, designed specific exercises for training a would-be orator's voice—whether called "loud speaking" for modulations of tone or *orthopoeia* for drilling in pronunciation.[17] Hamlet rails against the "monstrous" implications of such technical training, objecting that the Player's well-honed accommodation between facial expression, voice, and gesture is "nothing" precisely because it is all summoned for a fiction, a "dream":

> Is it not monstrous that this player here,
> But in a fiction, in a dream of passion,
> Could force his soul so to his own conceit
> That from her working *all his visage wann'd,*
> *Tears in his eyes, distraction in his aspect,*
> *A broken voice, an' his whole function suiting*
> *With forms to his conceit?* And all for nothing,
> For Hecuba!
> (2.2.551–58; emphasis mine)

Hamlet's initial repugnance for the Player's well-honed rhetorical technique—for the moving expressions in "eyes," "visage," and "voice"—soon turns into a critique of his own inadequate language and movement. Indeed, as Heinrich Plett carefully describes, both this scene and Hamlet's instructions to the players bring on stage a long history of rhetorical theory about delivery (*actio/pronuntiatio*): for instance, Hamlet is questioning the power of "dreams" or visualizations that Quintilian outlined as an important aspect of an orator's training (in Quintilian, φαντασίαι).[18] First, Hamlet reviles himself for saying "nothing" despite his own "cue for passion" (561, 569). And when he does find his tongue, he judges his own words and gestures even more harshly than he did the Player's:

That I . . .
Must like a whore unpack my heart with words,
And fall a-cursing like a very drab,
A stallion.
(2.2.583–87)

Once he sees the Player imitate Hecuba's woe, however "monstrous" for conveying merely imagined experience with an all too convincing delivery, Hamlet thinks about and condemns his own errors in word and gesture, only to end by comparing himself with a spectrum of gendered figures for bodily and vocal excess (a "whore," a "drab," a "stallion").

However inadequate his words and gestures might be, Hamlet's quarrel with the Player's ability to imitate Hecuba's moving precedent so well nevertheless allows him, for a brief moment, to imagine he can "cleave the general ear with horrid speech"—a speech that will "amaze indeed/The very faculties of eyes and ears" (565–6).[19] In it, he aspires to what J. L. Austin might call a felicitous performative, dreaming that his "horrid speech" will "make mad the guilty"; it thus anticipates as rhetorical effect precisely what he designs his play to do to Claudius. For just such a moment, Lucrece achieves "words and looks" from Hecuba's story to convey her own "sad tales" to Troy's imagined receptive audience (1496). Observing previous imitations of Hecuba's passion, in other words, allows both Lucrece and Hamlet momentary escape from an impasse that is at once rhetorical and emotional. In both cases, it is the first or direct imitator—the painter, the Player—who is found wanting. Yet this initial attempt to mimic Hecuba's woe allows second-order imitators, Lucrece and Hamlet, to turn this perceived failure to personal advantage, to find new words and a "cue for passion" each claims as his or her own. (Pronouns are particularly confining here.) This may be a circuitous route to experiencing one's own feelings, but its obliquity tells us something important. These are not scenes about imitation or the passions *tout court* so much as they are a kind of meta-rhetorical commentary on the relationship *between* the two. By means of classical rhetoric's "lively" ability to "stirre up a passion," Hecuba's moving "despair" spreads to others—even to one who objects to the idea of miming her grief as merely "a dream" of passion. Both Shakespeare's narrative and dramatic meditations on the problems inherent in imitating someone else's passions draw on early school training in classical *imitatio*—indeed, on the same school text—only to end in an outburst of renewed "passion" in both speakers.

I am, in part, developing a historically and institutionally specific description of a textual, rhetorical, and transpersonal process reminiscent of what Linda Charnes calls "notorious identity"—the sense that a particular and affectively compelling identity emerges when one of Shakespeare's characters responds to the fact that his or her text has already been written.[20] The most succinct case in point Charnes offers is Cressid's horrified response to her own words: "Why have I blabb'd?" I recall Charnes's account of subjectivity effects alongside the school's pedagogical program to suggest that when read in light of school training, such hallmark self-reflection may be prompted by texts other than one's namesake. Another legendary story will do. Nor need this earlier story comport with assumed gender categories. In the case of both Lucrece and Hamlet, a precedent figure matters very much— and matters most when someone else is trying to *imitate* her. These encounters with Hecuba and her redactors, moreover, proceed according to the verbal and visual techniques of classical oratory's embodied training. "Voice," "visage," "aspect," "words," "eyes," and "looks" are exactly what schoolmasters tried to discipline, to teach their Latin-speaking *pueri* to "suit" precisely to the "conceit" of any given ancient story. In both *Lucrece* and *Hamlet*, failed "dreams of passion" allow a critical detour through Hecuba's woe. Studied and then undertaken through the allied disciplines of *imitatio* and *actio*, this detour revives previously "blunted" affect in each speaker, enacting a transfer of emotion between characters. "Weeping for Hecuba" becomes a way, however deviously, to turn a figure that weeps for others into a way of weeping for oneself and one's own cause for complaint. Here we encounter another instance of what I have called the habits of alterity implicit in school training. That is, this literary detour through Hecuba's passion may reveal something of the way ancient exemplars functioned in everyday life, providing an acceptable way for schoolboys to release emotions (like grief, despair, or rage) that the institution otherwise called upon them to suppress.

In addition, both meditations on the art of *imitatio* ask us to contemplate what seems to me a characteristically Shakespearean version of ethics—if one understands *ethics*, that is, in its derivation from Aristotelian *ethos*. As Lawrence Green describes, humanist scholars of rhetoric—from George of Trebizond to Juan Luis Vives and John Rainolds (Greek reader at Corpus Christi, Oxford)—gave priority, when reading Aristotle's *Ethics*, to his discussions of "character" (*ethos*) and "emotion" (*motus*). Sometimes emphasis falls on the orator's character and affect, sometimes on the audience's; in either case, Aristotle's humanist readers were deeply interested in the role that the passions played in acts of persuasion.[21] Trebizond prefaces his translation of the *Ethics* by praising the work for letting us "peer into, not just the secrets of Nature . . . but even peer into the hidden minds of men, into the private emotions of men." Rainolds's puritan version of Aristotle's notion of *ethos* strives, like Wright's treatise, for middle ground: Despite the "dangers" of reading pagan views on persuasion, Rainolds nonetheless argues that "*the passions must be excited*, not for the harm they do but for the good, so that they ward off vice, iniquity, and disgrace" (emphasis mine).[22]

Little of Aristotle's work entered grammar school curricula directly. But sustained interest among humanist scholars in what the *Ethics* said about *ethos* and the passions is suggestive for the institution they founded, particularly its often articulated Ciceronian belief that oratory's power to "move" audiences requires an orator to feel the affect in question himself as a prerequisite for conveying it to others. As the young author of the commonplace book cited earlier in this chapter dutifully records after his comment on the way persuasion requires a transfer of emotion between speaker and audience, "Cicero" said that "an oratour must first put on these passions which he would stirre in another, for passion conceived in the minde, is quickly formed in the speech and hence beget like impressions in others *by a subtil & lively contagion*" (emphasis mine).[23] Such early training helped institutionalize the aspect of rhetoric that Aristotle clearly understood: that *ethos* is intimately bound up with textures of emotional life, particularly the quicksilver transmissions of feeling that connect members of a community.

In Aristotle's handling of *ethos*, moreover, character appears predominantly as something *produced by* rhetorical performance. Remember that for someone like Vives, rhetorical training shaped students' characters, turned "beasts" into "gentlemen." In the school's classically derived rhetorical tradition, *ethos* was institutionalized on a daily basis as the product, the after-effect, of speech rather than the other way around. Because both scenes recalling Hecuba's grief allow Lucrece and Hamlet renewed access to their own emotions by taking an alternative route through someone else's, however, they begin to raise a more modern sense of *ethical* by suggesting that for speaking subjects, relationships to others are constitutive. Indeed, Hamlet's reaction moves in this direction. "What's Hecuba to him?" poses an impertinent schoolboy question about one of the humanist school's most important axioms: that only by imitating texts from the Latin past does a student become master of his own discourse and modes of self-representation.[24] Hamlet's ensuing question, "or he to Hecuba?" takes an even more expansive turn—changing his first query about the personal aspects of imitation ("what does this old text matter to me?") into a second one about his own insignificance to history, or to others in the world: Why, in any case, do I matter at all to the other, to the past, or to a woman with her own cause for sorrow?

With respect to the primary sense of *ethos*, these two meditations on Hecuba's grief stress a transfer of woe between parties; the very condition of personal feeling is that it moves between "characters." As I discuss in the next section with regard to Mamillius, the psychoanalytic term most pertinent to the relays of imitation I have traced here would be *identification*.[25] But the important point for now is this: The meta-rhetorical production of character and affect in Shakespeare's fantasy of Hecuba's "sad shadow" indicates that the regime of Latin rhetorical training forged eloquence in schoolboys by way of disciplinary structures (both real and imaginary) that involved more than one party. The actual, literal presence of another is not crucial: As I suggested in Chapter 2, the internal intrapsychic stage has already been set, the fantasy of address, audience, and judgment inculcated through daily practice in the school's theatrical *habitus*. Such an historically specific version of the fantasy of the "Other" to and through whom one proves oneself worthy of love (what Žižek calls "symbolic identification") means, of course, that both the texts of the classical past and the institutional scene of discipline and instruction were closely woven together in moving Renaissance performances of *ethos*.

As Keir Elam is careful to point out, however, Aristotle was quite clear about the distance between speech and *ethos*, a distance that raises a pressing moral and political problem—particularly for an institution devoted to shaping childrens' characters. "The most conspicuous Renaissance heir" to Aristotle's "unsentimental political philosophy" of *ethos*, he observes, is Machiavelli.[26]

Though perhaps less conspicuous, yet another heir to Aristotle's "unsentimental" view of *ethos* is the early modern grammar school.[27] Humanist training in classical rhetoric helped institutionalize, and thus realize in the everyday life of grammar school students, Aristotle's view that character is a rhetorical effect rather than prediscursive fact. And though Aristotle's texts were not taught at school, the lesson in *ethopoeia* from Aphthonius, who drew on Aristotle, was. The *Progymnasmata* turned *ethos* into a matter of daily exercises, a series of speeches boys learned by careful study and imitation. I suggest that it is the potential disjunction between speech and character in the rhetorical tradition—transmitted in very different ways by Machiavelli, Aphthonius, Erasmus, and humanist schoolmasters—that Shakespeare transforms into his vexed world of "seeming." This transformation is not merely a matter of intellectual history, but the result of a complex intersection between discourse, institutional training, and embodied experience.

Schoolmasters, one should note, betray a certain anxiety about the potential distance between speech and character that Aristotle and Machiavelli understood to be implicit in rhetorical facility. Given their often-stated mission that their methods for teaching Latin eloquence would profit the commonwealth by leading students along a path to wisdom and virtue, it is hardly surprising that they try (not always successfully) to assume a Ciceronian kind of moral seriousness on the topic. As one school text declares with bewildering circularity, "eloquans withowt wisdom doth a man but lityll good, for wisdom is the foundation of eloquens."[28] In *Positions*, Richard Mulcaster begins by asserting continuity rather than disjunction between character and speech, which leads him quickly into a kind of performative amplification of the point: The school's training will "profit my countrie . . . to haue her youth well directed in the tounges, which are the waies to wisdome, the lodges of learning, the harbours of humanitie, the deliverers of divinitie, the treasuries of all store, to furnish out all knowledge in the cunning, and all judgement in the wise."[29] But even here, in one of the period's more optimistic formulations about the school's social and personal effects, rhetorical training precedes and "directs" a student's character rather than the other way around. The disjunction between speech and character could not be simply wished away, particularly in an institution where boys were required on a daily basis to imitate multiple voices, whether in grammar lessons, declamatory performances "without booke," or stage plays. "Seven-yeare-olde apes" know the business of convincing mimicry very well. That such training in effective oratory walked a fine line between persuasion and deception may in fact explain the constant need one feels in Cicero's humanist followers to stress that eloquence and "wisdom" are one.

Read in light of the schoolroom and the classical rhetorical tradition on which it depends, however, *The Rape of Lucrece* refuses any such anodyne consolation about the connection between character and speech. The primary lesson Lucrece learns from Tarquin's "school" for "lust" and from the imitation of Troy on the tapestry is the distance between speaking and being. Sinon, Troy's effective orator and apt figure for Aristotle's "unsentimental political" view of *ethos*, is a revealing precursor for Shakespearean meta-rhetorical depictions of character. As Lucrece interprets Sinon's relevance to her own case, his appearance is a warning about the possible social and political consequences of expressive training in *actio*:

> "It cannot be," quoth she, "that so much guile" —
> She would have said, "can lurk in such a look";
> But Tarquin's shape came in her mind the while,
> And from her tongue "can lurk" from "cannot" took:
> "It cannot be," she in that sense forsook,
>   And turn'd it thus, "It cannot be, I find,
>   But such a face should bear a wicked mind.
>
> "For even as subtile Sinon here is painted,
> So sober-sad, so weary, and so mild,
> (As if with grief or travail he had fainted),
> To me came Tarquin armed to beguild
> With outward honesty, but yet defil'd
>   With inward vice, as Priam him did cherish:
>   So did I Tarquin, so my Troy did perish."
> (1534–57)

Sinon's moving affect—his seemingly "mild" and "sober-sad" weariness, his convincing imitation of "grief" and "travail"—turns as dangerously "subtile" in Shakespeare's hands as in those of the unknown schoolboy who recorded in his commonplace book that oratory moves the passions by means of a "subtil and lively contagion." Sinon does more than epitomize Tarquin's treachery: He also signifies oratory's stubborn "ethical" problem (in both its personal and social senses). As persuasive as it is deadly, Sinon's winning performance of grief stands against Hecuba's passion (as well as Lucrece's and Hamlet's) while reminding us, at the same time, of the extent to which questions about persuasion, character, and the affect in the classical rhetorical tradition were ones that the school's training could only perpetuate, not resolve. Hamlet defines inner life according to the famous, if less sinister, version of this same meta-rhetorical problem: "Seems, madam? Nay, it is, I know not 'seems' . . . I have that within which passes show" (1.2.76–86). But understood in institutional terms, Sinon's perniciously "honest" show of "grief," the Player's "monstrous" facility, and Hamlet's "that within" derive from the same inherited predicament—the potential gap between *ethos* and rhetorical facility that school practice gave authoritative sanction and permanence in the lives of eloquent young gentlemen.

The reflections on *imitatio* in *Lucrece* and *Hamlet* are suggestive about how unpredictable the dynamics of feeling and character might become in school training. In each text, the Ciceronian commonplace about rhetoric's "lively and subtil contagion" becomes manifest as subjects bond through "strong passions."[30] We enter a world in which confusions between text and person, as well as suspicions about a potential gap between speech, affect, and "that within," are pervasive.[31] Most important for my purposes, such moving passions are liable to be transmitted between parties (whether contemporary, historical, or legendary) without respect for distinctions of age, class, nation, or gender. In this instance, Shakespeare's two meta-rhetorical versions of Hecuba, "woe" connects characters without regard to the reductive gender divide that the schools were carefully designed to institute. In a labile transfer of feelings indifferent to normative early modern representations of appropriate gender roles, Shakespeare's persistent fantasy of Troy's grieving mother begins to suggest that the emotions released by school training in Latin could remain at some distance from the normative definition of the bodies its *pueri* actually inhabited.

The way Lorich expanded Aphthonius's *Progymnasmata* reveals a similar indifference to the gender distinctions I have just traced in *Lucrece* and *Hamlet*. And at the same time, his emendations give telling evidence about a consistent maternal underpinning to the classically inflected scenes of "woe" I am examining here (by "maternal," it should be clear by now, I mean what *counted* as maternal in the eyes of schoolmasters). Taking young students through lessons in such skills as *fabula*, *narratio*, *sententia*, and *chreia* ("anecdote"), the *Progymnasmata* also offered detailed discussions and illustrations of many techniques on vivid display in *Lucrece* and *Hamlet*: *descriptio* (also "*ekphrasis*"), *comparatio*, *vituperatio* (i.e. "dispraise"), *disputatio*.[32] In the lesson on *ethopoeia,* or "character making," he defines this figure as "*imitatio & espressio morum personae subiectae.*" And he illustrates *ethopoeia* with a passage about Troy, beginning his description of its three main types with the example of Hecuba's reaction to the city's fall:

> *Ethopoeia* may be pathetic [*passiua*], social [*moralis*], or mixed [*mixta*]. The *pathetic* are those that indicate the mind's movement at every point [*quae prorsus animi significant motum*]; e.g.: What words Hecuba would use after the sack of Troy [*ut qualia verba Hecuba faceret Troia subversa*]. The social are those which portray custom / habit only [*quae mores solos depingiit*]; e.g.: What someone from the mainland would say when he first sees the sea. The *mixed* are those that have both custom and emotion [*quae mores habet pariter & affectum*]; e.g.: What Achilles would say over Patroclus' body when resolving to fight; the deliberation according to customary tradition [*mores*], the emotion for a friend's death [*adfectum*]" (translation mine).[33]

Notice in this passage that the "pathetic" passions—*motum, affectum*—are conceived as internal movements of the mind caused by the spectacle of death (Hecuba's to Troy's ruin, Achilles over Patroclus's dead body). While there were many and varied passions to imitate in school texts (from *vulgaria* to colloquies, letters, and exercises in declamation), grief is the one prominently on display in this lesson. And in it, Lorich largely abandons Quintilian's steadying distinction between moderate and extreme emotion, because all but two of his eleven exemplary speeches are uttered by women in highly emotional states. In addition to imitating Hecuba's words, boys were to memorize and imitate a speech written to approximate what "Andromache might say, her fatherland fallen and husband murdered"; "what Antiope might say, carried away on the horns of the bull"; or "what Medea might say over her slain children" ("*Quae dixerit Medea, suos mactatura filios*"). Finally, Lorich's lesson in emotional character making concludes by pointing in the direction of another favorite Shakespearean author: For homework, a student should "consult Plutarch's *Life*" to find "the words Cleopatra would have spoken over Antony's tomb" ("*Quae Cleopatra ad Antonii sepulchrum. Vide Plutarchum in vita Antonii*"). In light of such antique forebears for schoolboy practice, small wonder that Shakespeare's Lucrece frets that her "woe" will become "a theme for disputation" (820–21).

Lorich evidently saw the advantages to Aphthonius's decision to conclude each general discussion with concrete examples for imitation. Though he adds many things to the fourth-century manual, including lengthy glosses, his main contribution was to add further practical examples at the end of each lesson. More to the point of the transgendered effects in Shakespeare's two reflections on imitating Hecuba, the single Aphthonian example that inspired Lorich to add so many other laments was that of another grieving mother who comes up in *Hamlet*: Niobe (i.e. "Like Niobe, all tears" 1.2.149). Offered as a lesson in imitation and memory to young schoolboys just parted from their own mothers, "the words Niobe would say over the bodies of her children scattered before her" is, in Aphthonius's terms, *"poeia passiua,"* an "emotional speech." It opens with her sense of grief: *"Me miseram!"* Boys were asked to read and translate a bereaved mother's inconsolable pain:

> What ruin among all others shall I now mourn, having once been famous for children am now bereaved of them all? . . . Where shall I, so unhappy, turn? To whom shall I go? [*Quo me vertam infoelix? Ad quae deflectar?*] What tomb big enough to commemorate so many dead children? . . . Yes, but why do I lament these things, when I can entreat the gods to transform me? I see one cure from my misery: to be changed in form, joining the things that have no life or feeling. And yet miserable as I am, I fear that even in that form I shall never stop weeping (translation mine).[34]

When inventing a speech to capture "the words Hecuba might say at the fall of Troy," Lorich replicates at least three aspects of Niobe's memorable lament. First, another mother grieves over multiple dead children: *"O me miseram,"* she exclaims, only to ask, "Where is Hector, where Polydorus, where Paris, Troilus, Helen, and my most beautiful daughter Polyixena?"[35] Second, Hecuba alludes, like Niobe at the end, to her distinctly Ovidian genealogy, predicting not simply her metamorphosis, but her transformation into an image of rhetorical impasse—a barking dog. And third, like Niobe—and later Hamlet in reflecting on such training—successive rhetorical questions convey the intensity of her passion (*"Sed quid lamentor?" "Quid Polidorem?"*).[36] Indeed, the many liberties Richard Rainolde took in translating this lesson into English in *The Foundacion of Rhetorike* (1564) speaks tellingly to the affective intensity of this particular school lesson: Rainolde defines "Ethopoeia" not simply as an imitation of a person, but as "a certaine Oracion made by voice, *and lamentable imitacion*, upon the state of any one" (emphasis mine). While cutting back the exemplary speeches to just one, Rainolde preserves only Hecuba as the one whose words will teach a boy how to invent *ethos*. And his emphasis falls decidedly on woe: He translates "*ut qualia verba Hecuba faceret Troia subversa*" ("the words Hecuba would say at the fall of Troy") to Hecuba's "*patheticall and dolefull oracion*" and creates his own title for her speech, "a lamentable Oracion."[37]

The school that separated boys from their mothers physically and linguistically could also preserve the figure, and emotions, of precisely those its students were forced to leave behind. Aphthonius's final allusion to Niobe as eternally weeping rock suggests that some passions persist beyond the character said to contain them, further moving those who come across her story. And Lorich's imitative allusion to Hecuba's final metamorphosis suggests the extent to which the passions may exceed the subject said to feel them. In passages such as these offered as lessons in the art of "character making," mothers become more than a boy's abandoned object. They granted Hecuba and Niobe a kind of permanence in the schoolroom precisely as affecting *subjects* worth studying and copying—women whose passions it is a Latin-speaking gentleman's task to imitate, feel, and convincingly move in others. (Here we might remember Venus, whose lament over the body of the youthful Adonis so abruptly shifts the mood and tone of *Venus and Adonis*.) A common school text like the *Progymnasmata* offered technical lessons in character making while echoing the persistent "sad shadow" of the grieving mothers it required young sons to abandon for the Latin world, and tongue, of men.

Mamillius

From a theoretical point of view, the relays of "woe" I have traced in Shakespeare's narrative and dramatic meditations on classical *imitatio* are reminiscent of the process Freud calls *identification*, a term for an interpersonal, volatile force that gives rise to quite unexpected bonds. Shakespeare's ongoing fascination with the question of how to imitate Hecuba's passions, if read alongside Aphthonius's popular lesson in character making, suggests that the grammar school's daily demand for imitation could also give rise to unexpected memories and affinities. Freud himself described identification as a form of "imitation" and made the important suggestion in *Interpretation of Dreams* that it follows a metaphorical logic of substitution and displacement.

Given the detour through Hecuba's grief and rage that allows both Lucrece and Hamlet renewed access to an affective response each reclaims as his or her own, it is crucial to stress that for Freud, identification is supremely indifferent to culturally sanctioned categories of gender or desire. With respect to the school's training, therefore, I use the term *imitation* to designate the formal, rhetorical practice for which "identification" might be the possible ethical, or characterological and affective, outcome. I am arguing that we should remain suspicious about which gender is at issue in any moment of imitation (literary as well as social) because such transfers of affect elide the difference between identities too easily assumed to be the "natural" source for this or that kind of feeling. Indeed, the idea of Hecuba's woe may be one of many classical screens that allowed former schoolboys to turn the culturally disreputable, "vulgar" bond between mother and son into narratives that could, in fact, be heard.

Attention to the multiple, and not necessarily compatible, identifications that Latin training mobilized in schoolboy subjects will help make Richard Halpern's insight about the school more concrete. The institutionalized demand for imitation allows us to "grasp" what Lacan calls the "Imaginary" and "Symbolic"—the subject's "phantasmatic relationship with governing models" and subjection to language—"as they *become practice*."[38] The Latin curriculum required students to imitate school contemporaries (the master, the master's surrogates, other exemplary students) as well as ancient authors, texts, and literary characters. "Governing models," both living and written, proliferated along the road to Latin eloquence; school texts and Shakespeare's tell us that they did so in a way that installed a deep, foundational indifference to distinctions between person and text, real and fictional characters, male and female feelings and desires. That a grieving Trojan mother should be the exemplar through whom both Lucrece *and* Hamlet recover their own feelings, or that Hecuba and Niobe were central to a common text used to train boys to imitate emotions persuasively, indicates that the school's institutionalized habits did not fix the cultural distinctions defining gendered, familial, or national identities so much as subject them to the vagaries of identification—to the accidents of personal history that have the potential to unravel totalizing, normative cultural narratives.

I turn to Mamillius's sorrow over his mother's disgrace in *The Winter's Tale* because through him, Shakespeare again touches on imitation in ways that suggest unexpected identifications. At the same time, his portrait of a young boy's overwhelming passions reactivates still earlier texts and lessons than those proposed by Aphthonius and Erasmus. Like Lucrece and Hamlet on Hecuba, Mamillius's modes of imitation ask us to think again about the bonds school training might forge in a new way between a sorrowing, retrospectively "vulgar" mother and her Latin-speaking son. But first, an important methodological distinction will clarify what kind of critical purchase I take a psychoanalytic term like *identification* to provide on the school's material and discursive practices (and perhaps more important, its unintended consequences). William Kerrigan tried to elaborate Ong's suggestion about the "male puberty rite" of a Latin education in light of psychoanalysis, calling the school a place for the "articulation of" a "male ego."[39] Kerrigan gives the following quasi-historical narrative about the school's psychological effect: "most boys . . . coming to a male teacher of the male tongue at seven or eight . . . had already completed the identification with their fathers that normally resolves the Oedipus complex." He therefore concludes that "the absorption of the vernacular *I* into the Latin *ego* was a wholly male achievement."

By turning Lacan's theory of an Oedipally inflected Symbolic order into a linear, chronological account of the stages of "normal" masculinity, Kerrigan considerably domesticates and flattens out the nuances of the theory he relies upon to tell his story of the Elizabethan "male" psyche. Psychoanalytic theory exceeds the contours of such a plot. Freud, for one, refused to adjudicate between the primacy of event and fantasy in psychic life. As his readers often note, the relentless search for origins in Freud's various case histories serves, in the end, to put the very idea of an original event from which all else follows into question. Laplanche extended Freud's work on the startling effects of "retrospective action." As we have seen with regard to several eroticized scenes of flogging, Laplanche argues that for speaking beings, the temporal gap between experience and understanding makes sexuality inherently traumatic—a "temporal succession of missed occasions" that arrive either too early or too late for sexuality, or its gendered coordinates, to emerge as anything other than a continual process of phantasmatic misfiring.[40] Lacan maintains that stories of origin produced after "the mirror stage" are recursive projections; in his view, representations of one's past are subject to the dislocating force of the future anterior (the famous formulation, "what I shall have been for what I am in the process of becoming"). Psychoanalysis, in short, cautions us to be wary of chronological or developmental narratives of "normal" or "resolved" subjectivity like the one that Kerrigan offers to explain the grammar school's production of properly masculine speakers of Latin. Rather, it suggests that for speaking beings, such chronological stories of origin are "rooted in illusion."[41]

Let me be very clear. I have no desire to object to Ong's insight that a masculinist *drive* animated the cultural and linguistic puberty rite of the Elizabethan grammar school. The schoolmasters' texts indicate that we write with considerable historical accuracy about their attempt to establish a culturally valued distinction between a mother and a father tongue. But I do want to question whether a finished identity or *ego* we can call definitively "male" was ever finally consolidated by the school's methods of induction into Latin. The crucial role that Hecuba plays in the meta-rhetorical scenes about both male and female grief begins to suggest that the many identifications and fantasies released by the school's training in *imitatio* exceeded the reductive gender categories that the schoolmasters explicitly set out to impart. So, too, might Shakespeare's habit of turning female characters as well as male ones into either students or teachers (Katharine, Bianca, Lucrece, Venus) lead us to reject a simple equation of schoolroom practice with commonsense notions of "maleness," whether modern or early modern. The Oedipal subjectivity Kerrigan takes as given in the school is what Freud understands, and Shakespeare dramatizes, as a *problem* in need of elucidation.

By contrast to the school's myth of consolidation, or to Kerrigan's echo of that myth, I have drawn on a non-normative account of psychoanalytic theory in order to put schoolmasters' claims about the effects of rhetorical training to the test of material, archival, and literary scrutiny. Chapters 2, 3 and 4 charted the theatrical and temporal dislocations integral to the daily, disciplinary regime organizing Latin learning, bringing "identity," "mastery," and normative assumptions about the difference between pleasure and pain into question. And my discussion of *prosopopoeia* in Venus and Adonis and *imitatio* in *Lucrece* and *Hamlet* pointed to the overlapping, contradictory identifications that the school's rhetorical training might forge—identifications that exceed a sociological definition of stable gender roles. The school's larger program (and not just its habits of corporal punishment), psychoanalytic speculation about the subject's rhetorical staging, the unsettling work of "deferred action," and jumbled collection of identifications at the heart of the "ego," all suggest that early modern as well as modern claims about gender identity in the "gentlemen" who attended school are rather more wishful than real.[42] As I see it, learning Latin rhetorical facility through the school's intense regime of imitation and punishment could not but aggravate the gap between a boy's experiences of bodies and emotions and his grasp of what such bodies and emotions signified in the social world around him.

The school's project of establishing a hierarchy of classical over popular culture, "paternal" over "maternal" spheres of influence, finds unusually plaintive expression in Mamillius, one of Shakespeare's most memorable depictions of a school-aged boy. In the middle of *The Winter's Tale*, Mamillius reminds the audience of the play's title. At the same time, these lines hint at a founding aim of humanist pedagogy: that education in a classical curriculum would produce a difference between "popular" and "elite" culture. To Hermione's request that he "tell 's a tale," her son famously responds, "A sad tale's best for winter. I have one / Of sprites and goblins" (2.1.25). Such a tale from a boy on the brink of puberty—who begins this scene flirting with his mother's ladies, commenting on the shape of their eyebrows and demanding not to be treated "as if I were a baby still" (2.1.5–6)—reminds us that schoolmasters were united in their contempt for any such vernacular tale. Education in a classical curriculum "was designed to alienate youth from more spontaneous forms of popular learning," from what Erasmus called "the stupid and vulgar ballad, or old wives' fairy rubbish."[43]

Indeed, there seems to me a telling connection between the playwright who loved fairy tales enough to write a play like *A Midsummer Night's Dream* and his character Mamillius, the young boy much devoted to vernacular stories. The last thing Mamillius does before disappearing entirely from *The Winter's Tale* is to whisper that story "of sprites and goblins" in his mother's ear. Of an age to be inducted into a Latin curriculum founded on disdain for such "fairy rubbish," Mamillius clings to vernacular tales his teachers would stigmatize as "popular and feminine."[44] And though she is encouraging her son to recite this story, Hermione also anticipates a Latin schoolmaster's demand for good oratory by praising his rhetorical skill:

Let's have that, good sir.
Come on, sit down, come on, and do your best
To fright me with your sprites: you're pow'rful at it.
(2.1.27–29)

A "powerful" narrator of the stories the school associated with feminine popular culture, Mamillius bears a name that echoes the Latinate institution in which boys of his age learned to substitute one language and set of stories for another. His much noted name does more than reveal that he is Hermione's boy. The masculine form of the Latin noun for "breast" (*mamilla*), the name "Mamillius" points beyond Hermione to the linguistic and cultural imperative that would soon take her away. Read historically, the Latin name ominously predicts Leontes's imminent demand for separation:

> "Give me the boy. I am glad you did not nurse him.
> Though he does bear some signs of me, yet you
> Have too much blood in him."
> (2.1.57–5)

Perhaps it does not go without saying in relation to this complaint that in the Galenic tradition, a woman's blood and her milk were interchangeable: As Isidore of Seville puts it, "whatever blood has not yet been spent in the nourishing of the womb flows by natural passage to the breasts, and whitening (hence *lac*, from the Greek *leukos* ['white'])."[45] Mamillius's name, both in its Latin provenance and its grammatical change of gender, recalls the institutionally corroborated paternal demand to abandon mothers, along with their English stories and signs, and replace them with the Latin "signs" of men.

When I say "paternal demand" or "the Latin world of men," I am invoking the obvious similarity between Lacan's theory of a paternally inflected Symbolic order and the school's Latin curriculum. These, however, are not theory-driven metaphors. The paternal inflection given to the school and its new language comes from the masters themselves. A long-standing topic or theme set for debate in school texts is whether a student owes more allegiance to his parents or his teacher; masters consistently represent themselves in loco parentis. In Lily's *A Short Introduction of Grammar,* the first lesson is how to decline the noun *magister.* The noun with which it is paired is *parens.* The commonplace substitution of "master" for "parent" does mean that masters sometimes represent themselves as mothers or nurses; the title of an introductory text like *Lac puerorum* ("milk for boys") obviously casts language teachers in a maternal light. While in Chapter 3 we saw that there were occasional, telling inconsistencies in school records about the masters' own moments of gendered self-representation, schoolmasters overwhelmingly preferred to refer to themselves as a boy's or the school's "father." The founding dean of the Westminster school wrote that he bore "the same affection" to the new school "as a father to his only son." The inscription on the seal from the Louth Grammar School similarly declared that "he who spares the rod, hates his son." A master here is *pater*: He is a father "loves" or "hates" his sons, demands only love and obedience from *filii.*[46]

Many of the vignettes in the texts schoolmasters wrote for language instruction accordingly pit the authority of a severe master's discipline against the coddling of a boy's indulgent mother. Most often in such lessons, a mother either distrusts the master's severity or gets a boy in trouble with her lenience. In an early *vulgaria* from the Magdalen School (the one most involved in early pedagogical reform), young *pueri* were asked to translate into Latin an English passage that depicts a master lamenting the fact that his former "mekenes and softnes" made his boys "moch the worse." Therefore, his fictional students admit that unless "we use our latyn tongue better then we were wont," "we shal be sharpely punysshede." A sentence for translation that soon follows tells of a mother's reaction to school discipline; she quarrels with the master and then her husband. The story is told in the voice of an unidentified first-person narrator who moralizes about the bad consequences of her domestic misrule:

> I wylly make youe an example by a cosyn of myne that [was sent] to his absey [i.e., ABC] hereby at the next dore. And if he come wepynge after his maister hath charade away the flees from his skynne, anone his mother loketh onn his buttockys yf the stryppys be a-sen. And the stryppys appere, she wepeth and waileth and fareth as she were mad [*ut que foret mente capta*]. Then she complayneth of the cruelte of techers, saynge she had lever se hire childe wer fair buriede than so to be intretide. These wordes thei speke and suche other infinite, and other while for the childrenys sake *their begynneth afray betwixte the goode mann and his wyffe, for what he commaundeth, she forbyddeth*. And thus in processe of tyme, when thei cum to age, thei waxe bolde to do all myschevousnes, settynge litell to do the greatest shame that can be. And at the laste, after ther merites, sum be hangede, sum be hedyde; on goth to nought on way, another way; and whan thei cum to that ende, then thei curse the fathers and mothers and other that hade rule of them in ther youghe.[47] (Emphasis mine.)

Much as in Thomas Ingelend's Cambridge play, *The Disobedient Child* (1570), the lesson in this translation exercise is grim. A mother weeps and defies the disciplinary rule of a schoolmaster and her husband, but her objections only lead her sons to ruin (heading and hanging).

In the same *vulgaria*, two further passages offered for translation from Latin to English lead in further, and not entirely compatible, ideological

directions. The first is a typical, if condensed, account of the school's pre-
dominant attitude toward the moral dangers of a coddling mother:

> *Matres . . . animant et verbis et rebus quo licenter omnia factitent. Ita*
> lasciuiis et licencia effeminati *fede preciptes eunt.* (emphasis mine)

> The mothers . . . bolde them both in worde and dede to do what thei
> list, and with wantonnes and sufferance shamfully they renne on the
> hede [i.e. let them run headlong].[48]

A budding Latin scholar must understand that "wantonness" and "shame"
derive, quite literally, *ex femina.* Lessons from mothers threaten boys with
becoming "*effeminati.*"

But in another passage a few sentences further along in the lesson, students found a rather different account of mothers and their passions. In this
passage, boys were to translate a moment of maternal grief that they would
find again in Aphthonius's examples of Hecuba and Niobe:

> A great while after my brother diede, my mother was wonte to sytt
> wepynge every day. I trow that ther is nobody which wolde not be sory
> he hade sen hir wepynge.

This persistent image of a mother weeping for her child occurs in a number of
standard school texts, offering fleeting acknowledgment of the founding cultural contract on which grammar school education was based. The "puberty
rite" of Latin training could begin only when sons left the care of English-
speaking women for the rule of a schoolmaster's rod.

Aphthonius's example of Niobe's woe does, of course, preserve a rather
suspect version of what counts as a "good" mother: one whose entire being is
exhausted in grief for lost children. Yet the affect in this passage from the
vulgaria indicates shared sorrow rather than censure or contempt: "I trow
that ther is nobody which wolde not be sory he hade sen hir wepynge." What
could be dismissed as mere women's tears is, nonetheless, an emotional reaction upsetting to everyone ("I trow there is nobody . . ."). When understood as
lessons demanded under the constant threat of a flogging, such discrepancies
ought to encourage further reflection about how young *pueri* experienced
their master's moralizing lessons about the difference between fathers and
mothers, or the necessary connection between masculinity and discipline.

Obedience and reverence for a master's authority might not be the first, or indeed the only, feelings generated by translating such sentences into Latin and back into English. If the theatrical role of the pedagogue in late sixteenth- and early seventeenth-century drama offers any index of possible reactions, we should remember that Shakespeare's pedantic Holofernes is not the only "ass" satirized in the dramatic texts of former schoolboys.[49]

In such an institutional and linguistic context, a fairly explicit kind of warfare between masters and mothers subtended both rudimentary and advanced lessons. There is nothing "subtil" about their representations of what choice a boy must make between mother and master to succeed at school and in life. The rhetorical "milk" boys drank at school was supposed to replace English with Latin, mother with father, "boy" with "*puer*," "milk" with "*lac*." But it is not merely the Latin derivation of Mamillius's name that recalls the humanist grammar school: Its designation of just one significant body part also recalls contemporary language training. As I observed in Chapter 1, bilingual vocabularies usually begin with nouns for all parts of the body; and the statutes of the Bangor Friar School require a kind of nightly schoolboy anatomy: "the schoolmaster . . . shall every night teach their scholars their Latin words with the English signification. . . . they shall begin with words that concern the head reciting orderly as nigh as they can every part and number of the body and every particular of the same."[50]

The bilingual vocabulary that Shakespeare most likely used at school lists many words for the male body but only one for the female body: *mamilla*. When it comes to the parts of the female body, however, one finds a consistent tendency toward euphemism in school texts. In John Stanbridge's early sixteenth-century *Vulgaria*, we see what was and what was not acceptable to say about bodies and genders within the humanist curriculum.[51] In an early vocabulary lesson, the *Vulgaria* prints a list of all parts of the body translated from English into Latin. And in all cases but two, the text pairs one Latin word with an English equivalent. It is possible to print, and to ask boys to memorize, the English words (and several synonyms) for all parts of the male body, including two Latin phrases for the "codde" and "a mannes yerde," one for "a stone," "the bladder," and even the "pype in a mannes yerde." "*Mamma*," "*mamilla*," and "*uber*" are the only nouns for women's bodies that receive an English equivalent: "pappe" or "teet." "*Uterus*" becomes a euphemistic "belly." Finally, after descending the male body in considerable detail, Latin alone will suffice for either "*vulva*" or "*matrix*":

Hec mammale	For a pappe
hec mamilla	For a lytel pappe/ or for ye teet
hoc vber/is	Idem
. . . .	. . . .
hic penis	For a mannes yerde
hoc membrum genitale	idem
hec ramex	For the codde
hic aquaticus	For the bladder
hec fistula vrine	the pype in a mannes yerde
. . . .	. . . .
Hoc scortum	For the codde
hic testiculus	For a stone
hic vterus	For a bely
hoc crus	For the thyghe
hec vulva	*Locus ubi puer concipitur*
hec matrix	*Idem*

This bilingual vocabulary for boys works hard to erase not only the female body, but also any English signs for it. Suppressing the English equivalent for both *vulva* and *matrix*, it tells boys in the father tongue that these are, rather, "*locus ubi puer concipitur*" ("a place where a boy is conceived" and "ditto"). Such an erasure is worthy of the paranoid world of *The Winter's Tale*, one in which Leontes's fear of Hermione's sexual maternal body prompts both jealous paranoia and a desire to cleanse his kingdom and family of any female taint: "hence with it and together with the dam / Commit them to the fire" (2.3.95–6).

A psychoanalytic account of Hermione's body—or, more accurately, her "breast"—in *The Winter's Tale* suggests that she can be recollected only recursively, through the retrospective distortions of the institutionally sanctioned language that separates her from her child only to give her back in altered form. As Laplanche describes this fundamental duplicity at the heart of object relations, the lost object continuously returns as "something else," a retroactive transformation that defines the lifelong fugitive substitutions of fantasy.[52] In the Shakespearean version of this duplicity, a mother returns only as lost to the language of fathers, the tongue that puts *mamilla* in place of "breast" and then changes its grammatical gender (*mamillius*). Laplanche theorizes that this recursive, socially determined "re-finding" of the lost maternal object has been, in practice, "Oedipal." Shakespeare stages this return as a nightmare of paternal rage that damages both mother and child—a rage that exacts the price of a dead son and a beloved mother's body lost until it can be made palatable again by art and time. Indeed, the classically inflected re-finding signaled by Mamillius's name replicates the work of the play in miniature—bent, as it is, on returning Hermione to the one who lost her only after she passes through the hands of Pygmalion, the Ovidian figure whose story draws attention to misogyny's shaping effects on both representations and perceptions of women.

Whether we consider the story itself or the language in which its author first encountered it, Shakespeare's imitation of Ovid's text draws attention to an abiding literary and institutional history in which classical rhetorical practice and a tradition of deeply entrenched misogyny are entangled in each other. And when we juxtapose these two discourses, literary and psychoanalytic, we encounter an early modern predicament rewritten in modern, theoretical form. Leontes's notable fear of a dangerous, "pre-Oedipal" fusion between mother and son ("yet you / Have too much blood in him") solicits an "Oedipal" intervention that in this period, with its educational hegemony of a father tongue, means a Latin (and hence socially sanctioned) story of sexual difference.

Despite his name, however, Mamillius can hardly be said to obey the call of the father tongue. Leontes himself tells us that his son clings to Hermione, understanding his mother's shame as his own:

> He straight declin'd, droop'd, took it deeply
> *Fasten'd and fix'd the shame on't in himself,*
> Threw off his spirit, his appetite, his sleep
> And downright languish'd
> (2.3.14–16; emphasis mine)

Of such a self-destructive melancholic turn, Freud might suggest that Mamillius negotiates loss by turning his anger at the precious lost object toward himself. Freud's return to the idea of melancholic identification in *The Ego and the Id* illuminates an important mechanism by which the ego is simultaneously constituted and fractured. Speculating that "identification may be *the sole* condition under which the id can give up its objects (my emphasis)," Freud makes melancholia constitutive of the ego and its "character."[53] And he turns the "resolution" of Oedipal conflict—the ostensible bedrock of masculinity—into a contradiction: To accede to the loss demanded of him, a son-in-the-making identifies with the woman he is enjoined to renounce.

Both the tale "of sprites and goblins" and the unassuaged grief of a boy named "Mamillius" stage the precise linguistic form of, but also the contradictions attending, his culture's demand for renunciation—its induction of young boys into their place as "male" by way of the Latin curriculum of the grammar school. Mamillius, in other words, is not quite "Oedipal" enough. His determined identification with Hermione—taking her shame and sorrow as his own—tells us that the "paternal" demand for such separation, however imperious, does not always mean that it happens. Or perhaps it means that it does not always happen in a socially *useful* way.

Hermione's son perishes rather than accept the loss required of him. Forced to choose between a mother's grief and a father's rage, the emotion that Mamillius imitates all too well is his mother's. When she objects to Leontes, "Sir, you speak a language that I understand not," I remember the grammar school and wonder, Whose voice is this? Perhaps it is neither mother's nor son's but both—a chorus objecting to the paternal language they "understand not." Indeed, Mamillius refuses consolation in a play otherwise devoted to it: "with mere conceit and fear / Of the queen's speed," he dies. He thereby obeys *and* refuses his father's injunction: He gives his mother up, but only by giving up himself. Mamillius's reply to his father's demand is, to say the least, unexpected. He declines to buy his identity—or survival—at the price of her loss. His melancholic refusal suggests that we may not know what we mean, or mean what we say, when we talk about the "all-male" affair of a Latin education.

The endlessly inventive child in Freud's essay "A Child Is Being Beaten" reveals the fluid, destabilizing potential of fantasy—its capacity to stage a series of overlapping and quite contradictory regressions and identifications. Reading Mamillius's refusal alongside the errant progress of discipline and identification in the scenes I have examined thus far suggests how thoroughly the grammar school's training—its demand for imitation paired with the constant threat of violent punishment—could exacerbate the split in identity and incoherence in gender norms that humanists claimed their curriculum would put in place. Indeed, a glimpse of this incoherence emerges if we turn to the difference between the text of *The Winter's Tale* and the material history of stage practices in the theater for which it was written. Stanley Cavell offers a moving argument about paternal grief in the play, pointing out that Mamillius is the one loss Leontes can never recover.[54] But both early modern theater practices and the school training that enabled the last act's classical fictions (of animated statues and family members who return from the underworld) suggest that *The Winter's Tale* does, in fact, try to offer some kind of compensation for Mamillius. And when it does so, the play's drive toward compensation extends beyond Leontes's losses to include Hermione's as well.

I have argued elsewhere for the telling pressure that maternal sorrow exerts in the play, particularly in Hermione's final speech: She casts herself as Ovid's Ceres, longing for the return of the daughter she lost to Pluto—the same daughter who herself invokes Persephone while distributing flowers in Act 4.[55] Both Hermione's final lines to her daughter, as well as that daughter's name, should remind us that because of the constraints on small theater companies, it is highly likely that the same boy actor who played Mamillius returned in Acts 4 and 5 to play "Perdita" (literally, "the girl who has been lost"). Read in light of school training, the associations revolving around this actor's return in the guise of a daughter provoke a number of questions: What has been lost and what returned to Hermione and Leontes when Perdita comes back to Sicily? The girl in the boy? The boy in the girl? The very opacity of these nouns at this point in my discussion indicates that the questions can no longer be asked this way—even though English offers few alternatives to such formulations. The recursive return of what Laplanche calls "something else" in the cross-dressed Perdita's "altered form" is evoked by early modern stage practice, as well as her Latinate name. Act 5 gives a child back to both Leontes and Hermione only as seen through the lens of several Latin stories about partial triumphs over death, stories that the play's author, moreover, first encountered at school. But the cost of this young actor's translation from "Mamillius" into "Perdita," from mother to father tongue, may well be registered in the memory of the school-aged boy she once played: the boy bearing a Latin name for his mother's suspect body; who clung to vulgar tales of sprites and goblins; and who identified so strongly with his mother's cause, "took it" so "deeply," that he "drooped" and died from "mere conceit" of her predicament.

Given the important connection between names, imitation, and resistance to the school's various forms of discipline in Shakespeare's representation of a child undone by sharing his mother's intense passions, there is one school play with another young boy very much worth comparing to Mamillius. In *Wit and Science*, an interlude written by the humanist schoolmaster John Redford for performance at school, a scene of pedagogical instruction turns the beating of poetic meter into a literal beating. A schoolmaster, Idellness, threatens a student with blows to the body to persuade him to pronounce the syllables of his name: "Ing-no-ran-sy." Idellness, moreover, was played by a cross-dressed boy, since Redford's version of a (suspect) schoolmaster is female. Idellness pursues her disciplinary task through the chief instruments of humanist pedagogy: persuasion and beating. Ignorance, for his part, takes a small step toward linguistic competence when the idea of the rod's sting induces him into a rhythmic enunciation of one syllable from that name: no.

> Idellness: shal I bete thy narse now?
> Ingnoranse: Vmmm
> Idellness: shall I not bete thy narse now?
> Ingnorance: Vmmm
> Idlleness: say no foole say no.
> Ingnorance: noo/ noo/ noo/ noo/ noo.

Pentameter is not far behind. Whether Ingnorance's "no" is the syllabic "no" that pays the price of admission to the school's paternally ordered symbolic economy or the "no" that *refuses* such an economy remains, to my mind, deeply uncertain. Ing*n*orance's "no," like Mamillius's name and fondness for "old wives' fairy rubbish," sounds a note as truculent as it is submissive. Such resistant obedience toward one's teacher, the form of one's name, or the form of one's favorite stories challenges any developmental account of the school's success in consolidating "masculine identity" around a fixed, hegemonic ordering of bodies and passions. Both Mamillius and Ingnorance respond to Latinate coercion with an imitation that defies as much as obeys the command that initiates it. When these school-aged boys respond to threatened violence, their forms of imitation evoke an unexpected intensity of feeling in their subjects that, if read carefully, troubles any claim—whether early modern or modern—about the school's seamless production of rhetorically capable "gentlemen" with a univocally "male" *ego*.

Notes

INTRODUCTION

1. For a reading of Freud's evolving thought on the topic, see Jean Laplanche, "Fantasy and the Origins of Sexuality," *The International Journal of Psychoanalysis* 49 (1968): 4.

2. My reading of Bottom's translation is indebted to many long discussions with Jonathan Lamb as we developed our course on metamorphosis.

3. See Chapter 5 for a full discussion of this commonplace.

4. For a complete discussion of Cicero's distinction between "*divisio*" and "*partitio*" as well as Shakespeare's knowledge of it, see T.W. Baldwin, *Shakspere's Small Latine & Lesse Greeke* (Urbana: University of Illinois Press, 1944) 2:111–112.

5. See Chapters 3 and 5 especially, where I outline the habits of personification and impersonation that were engrained in school lessons in grammar and rhetoric.

6. I rely here on the apt formulation of Diana Fuss in *Identification Papers: Readings on Psychoanalysis, Sexuality, and Culture* (New York: Routledge, 1995).

CHAPTER I

1. Since the records of the King's Free Grammar School in Stratford do not survive, and several recent studies suggest the important influence that a number of London schools had on provincial ones, I draw widely from many school archives and attend to several kinds of evidence from the boys rather than the masters: the exercises, books, and poems written for or by boys at school; which texts and practices appear to have been most widespread; and the rhetorical techniques that find clear reflection in the writing of former grammar schoolboys. The two most important recent summaries of what Shakespeare most likely read at school are Leonard Barkan, "What Did Shakespeare Read?" in *The Cambridge Companion to Shakespeare*, ed. Margreta de Grazia and Stanley Wells (Cambridge: Cambridge University Press, 2001), 31–45; and Colin Burrow, "Shakespeare and Humanistic Culture" in *Shakespeare and the Classics*, ed. Charles Martindale and A. B. Taylor (Cambridge: Cambridge University Press, 2004), 9–27.

2. Kent Cartwright, *Theater and Humanism: English Drama and the Sixteenth Century* (Cambridge: Cambridge University Press, 1999).

3. See Anthony Grafton and Lisa Jardine, *From Humanism to the Humanities: Education and the Liberal Arts in Fifteenth- and Sixteenth-Century Europe* (Cambridge, Mass.: Harvard University Press, 1986), 141–42. Like Burrow, I believe that "to argue whether Shakespeare's education was liberatingly dialectical" or "crushingly grounded in the authority of the classics" reduces the complexities of practice, reaction, talent, and memory to an unhelpful choice of either/or. Instead, this book pursues the gap between what Burrow calls "the august ideals of humanist education" and its "unintended consequences" ("Shakespeare and Humanistic Culture," 15) and does so with regard to what Shakespeare's classical training and practice can tell us about masculinity and the passions. For recent studies that take issue with the view of the school's authoritarian success in a variety of important ways, see Rebecca Bushnell, *A Culture of Teaching: Early Modern Humanism in Theory and Practice* (Ithaca, N.Y.: Cornell University Press, 1996); Jeff Dolven, *Scenes of Instruction in Renaissance Romance* (Chicago: University of Chicago Press, 2007); Alan Stewart, *Close Readers: Humanism and Sodomy in Early Modern England* (Princeton, N.J.: Princeton University Press, 1997); and Paul Sullivan, "Playing the Lord: Tudor Vulgaria and the Rehearsal of Ambition," *ELH* 75.1 (2008): 179–96.

4. The most influential statement of this view is Walter Ong, "Latin Language Study as a Renaissance Puberty Rite," *Studies in Philology* 56 (1959), 103–24. William Kerrigan proposes a psychoanalytic argument about the school's success at consolidating masculinity in "The Articulation of the Ego in the English Renaissance," in Joseph H. Smith, *The Literary Freud: Mechanisms of Defense and Poetic Will* (New Haven, Conn.: Yale University Press, 1980), 261–308. Not everyone agrees with this view of the school's seamless efficacy with regard to masculinity, either; here Stewart's *Close Readers* is the most important revision. As will become clear in Chapters 3 and 5 especially, my understanding of psychoanalytic theory differs considerably from Kerrigan's.

5. I rely on John Guillory, *Cultural Capital: The Problem of Literary Canon Formation* (Chicago: University of Chicago Press, 1993) and Pierre Bourdieu, *Distinction: A Social Critique of the Judgement of Taste*, trans. Richard Nice (Cambridge, Mass.: Harvard University Press, 1984).

6. See Daniel Wakelin, *Humanism, Reading, and English Literature (1430–1530)* (Oxford: Oxford University Press, 2007) for a detailed account of the possibilities opened in the fifteenth century by humanist reading and writing practices, understood as *studia humanitatis*, or the "self-conscious return to the classics." I do not attempt to adjudicate the accuracy of the humanists' historical claim about the difference between their forms of teaching and earlier practices; as Wakelin shows throughout, claims to "novelty" frequently and loudly accompany humanist polemic.

7. As quoted in T. W. Baldwin, *Small Latine & Lesse Greeke* (Urbana: University of Illinois Press, 1944), 1:95.

8. William Nelson, *A Fifteenth Century Schoolbook* (Oxford: Clarendon Press, 1956), 32. Nelson describes the battle between Whittinton, who argued for the primacy of rules and precepts, and Horman, who (along with Erasmus and Wolsey) argued for the primacy of imitation (1–15). *The Vulgaria of John Stanbridge and the Vulgaria of Robert*

Whittinton, ed. Beatrice White (London: Kegan Paul, Trench, & Trubner, 1932), collects the major texts in the controversy.

9. As Richard Halpern aptly observes, "imitation is a principle that animates not only humanist stylistics but also humanist pedagogy" (*The Poetics of Primitive Accumulation: English Renaissance, Culture and the Genealogy of Capital* [Ithaca, N.Y.: Cornell University Press, 1991], 29.

10. John Bullokar, *An English Expositor: Teaching the Interpretation of the Hardest Words Used in Our Language* (London: John Legatt, 1616), n.p.

11. One could construe "imaginary" in the strong, Lacanian sense, as has Halpern in suggesting the master operated as a kind of mirror for the schoolboy; see *The Poetics of Primitive Accumulation*, 25.

12. "*Pater: hunc filiolum meum ad te adduco, ut ex belua hominem facias*" (Juan Luis Vives, *Linguae latinae exercitatio*, sig. A 6r). Dean Colet wrote of his new school at St. Paul's that he would teach boys two things: to be "learned in Laten tung, but also instructe & informed in vertuouse condicions" (as quoted in Michael F. J. McDonnell, *A History of St. Paul's School* [London: Chapman Hall, 1909], 14). A series of related observations appears in Chapter 3 concerning the humanist preference for epic and schoolboy enthusiasm for epyllia.

13. Baldwin, *Small Latine & Lesse Greeke*; Donald Lemen Clark, *John Milton at St. Paul's School: A Study of Ancient Rhetoric in English Renaissance Education* (New York: Columbia University Press, 1948); R. R. Bolgar, *The Classical Heritage and Its Beneficiaries* (Cambridge: Cambridge University Press, 1954). More recently, see J. W. Binns, *Intellectual Culture in Elizabethan and Jacobean England: The Latin Writings of the Age* (Leeds, England: Francis Cairns, 1990), esp. 291–306.

14. Joel Altman, *The Tudor Play of Mind: Rhetorical Inquiry and the Development of Elizabethan Drama* (Berkeley: University of California Press, 1978); Emrys Jones, *The Origins of Shakespeare* (Oxford: Oxford University Press, 1977). Neil Rhodes recently revisited the structuring nature of *in utramque partem* argument to argue that "many of the concerns of new historicist and cultural materialist critics, and many of the contradictions they uncovered in early modern texts, can most usefully be understood in terms of the controversiality programmed by Renaissance rhetoric." ("The Controversial Plot: Declamation and the Concept of the 'Problem Play,'" *The Modern Language Review*, vol. 95, No. 3 [July, 2000] 609–22).

15. Clearly, I draw on Louis Althusser's conception of the school as an "ideological state apparatus" (*Lenin and Philosophy* [London: New Left Books, 1971]).

16. I borrow Joel Fineman's term from *Shakespeare's Perjur'd Eye* (Berkeley: University of California Press, 1986) to stress the difference a specifically literary and psychoanalytic understanding of Shakespearean character makes to a historical, institutional analysis of early modern subjectivity. As will become clear in Chapters 3, 4, and 5, my preferred terms are *ethos* and *character*, understood in relation to a common rhetorical manual in the schools (Aphthonius's *Progymnasmata*), as well as the classical rhetorical tradition, in which *ethos*, usually translated as "character," is a rhetorical effect rather than a prediscursive given.

17. Cartwright, *Theater and Humanism*, 1–12.

18. In *Close Readers*, Stewart argues that humanist teaching became a means of upward mobility for its practitioners that disrupted older, homosocial arrangements in the household by eliminating mothers as a mediating term. Grafton and Jardine discuss Henry VIII's reasons for developing a different educational model in *From Humanism to the Humanities*, 141–42.

19. Grafton and Jardine, *From Humanism to the Humanities*, xiv.

20. John Lawson and Harold Silver, *A Social History of Education in England* (London: Methuen, 1973), 103–10. The ordinances at the Shrewsbury School, for instance, call for fellowships to be given annually "with preference to 1. natives of Shrewsbury or 2. of its suburbs and the Abbey Foregate, being legitimate sons of burgesses if they shall be found meet" but that "the godliest, poorest, and best learned" were "to be preferred" (*A History of the Shrewsbury School from the Blakeway Mss., and Many Other Sources* [Shrewsbury and London: Adnitt & Naunton, The Square and Simpkin, Marshall & Co., Stationers Hall Court, 1899]), 46–52.

21. Halpern, *The Poetics of Primitive Accumulation*, 25. Arguing against any straightforward "economic functionalism" with respect to the school's ideological work, Halpern also points out that "humanism also sought to reform the behavior of ruling groups . . . in which the behavioral disposition of [what Richard Mulcaster called] 'the middle sort' was imposed on a relatively broad array of classes" (pp. 25–26).

22. Here Burrow's comments on the "shortcomings" implicit in the humanist desideratum of *copia* are particularly apt: "What was it for? If this question is asked at a merely instrumental level a number of problems immediately arise. It was to equip students with the *copia*, or fullness of language and knowledge, which would enable them to delight an audience, to persuade, to praise, or to obtain work as lawyers, secretaries to noblemen . . . But fullness of language has as its nightmarish double an ability to paraphrase, circumlocute, and ornament in a manner which serves no instrumental purpose at all." In this regard, Burrow adduces Hamlet's *in utramque partem* debate with himself —"to be or not to be"—as *copia*'s implicit nightmare: "sicklying o'er the name of action with the pale cast of words" ("Shakespeare and Humanistic Culture," 16–17). I would add that Dogberry is not far off, either.

23. On the difference between a "mother" and a "father" tongue, see Mary Ellen Lamb, "Engendering the Narrative Act: Old Wives' Tales in *The Winter's Tale, Macbeth*, and *The Tempest*," *Criticism*, 40.4 (1998): 529–53.

24. *As You Like It*, 2.7.146–7.

25. John Kendall, *Flowers of Epigrammes* (John Shepperd: London, 1577), n.p.

26. A skill like arithmetic—mocked in *The Lady of May* in Sidney's figure of the conceited pedagogue, Rombus—would have been necessary for trade, but it was deemed unsuitable for grammar schools and relegated to the petties. Vives and Mulcaster both complain about the attitude toward "reckoning," but their sentiments did little to change the curriculum. See Ursula Potter, "The Naming of Holofernes in *Love's Labour's Lost*," *English Language Notes* 38.2 (2000).

27. Ursula Potter, "Performing Arts in the Tudor Classroom," in *Tudor Drama before Shakespeare 1485–1590*, eds. Lloyd Kermode, Jason Scott-Warren, and Martine Van Elk (New York, N.Y.: Palgrave Macmillan, 2004, p. 145. She is drawing from John Lawson, *A Town Grammar School Through Six Centuries: A History of Hull Grammar School Against Its Local Background* (London: Oxford University Press, 1963), 121–22.

28. Halpern, *Poetics of Primitive Accumulation*, 24; Stewart, *Close Readers*, 104. For a contemporary example of a view much like Stewart's, see my discussion of Thomas Ingeland's 1570 Cambridge play, *The Disobedient Child*, in Chapter 4.

29. Ong, "Latin Language Study as a Renaissance Puberty Rite." As the passage from Ascham suggests, however, the triangular relays of homosociality could be abruptly short-circuited in the transmission of rhetorical facility—which means (as Stewart argues) that as an institution, the grammar school's relationship to normative gender categories requires closer, more particularized analysis than it has received.

30. Harold Newcomb Hillebrand, *The Child Actors* (Urbana: University of Illinois Studies in Language and Literature, 1926).

31. *The King's School Ely: A Collection of Documents Relating to the History of the School and Its Scholars*, ed. Dorothy M. Owen and Dorothea Thurley (Cambridge: Cambridge Antiquarian Records Society, 1982), 55–56. Apparently, official response to the complaint was minimal. For further information on the incident, see Potter, "Performing Arts in the Tudor Classroom," 162.

32. Richard Mulcaster, *Positions* (1581; rpt. London, 1887), 18.

33. I borrow this succinct formulation about rhetoric's two aspects from Harry Berger, "Narrative as Rhetoric in *The Faerie Queene*," *ELR Journal* 21 (1991): 3–48.

34. See Quintilian, *Institutio Oratoria*, 11.1.41. I will be exploring this declamatory technique in relation to the threefold distinction between *ethopoeia, prosopopoeia,* and *idolopoeia* that sixteenth-century schoolboys encountered in the widely distributed rhetorical manual, Reinhard Lorich's Latin translation of Aphthonius's *Progymnasmata.* "*Est quidem Ethopoeia, quae notam habent personam, mores solum effingit, ut qualia faceret verba Hercules, Eurystheo sibi imperante. Hic notus quidem est Hercules, dicentes vero effingimimus mores. Idolopoeia est, quae personam habet notam, sed defunctam, & loqui non potentem, quemadmodum en Demois Eupolis finxit . . . Prosopopoeia est, quando finguntur omnia, & mores, & personae, quemadmodum Menander fecit, argumentum. Argumentum enim nec rem, nec personam habet propositam, unde prosopopoeia est dicta: fingitur enim ipsa cum moribus persona*" (181).

35. Inscribed on the frontispiece of the 1592 edition in the British Library.

36. Baldwin is particularly detailed about variations on praise and dispraise, as well as Osrick's ostentatious display. From the perspective of structuring habits of thought, however, one should also note that in virtually every chapter Lorich divides his examples into positive examples and then others advanced "*a contrario,*" thus extending the rhetorician's ability to argue on either side of a given question into specific oratorical techniques.

37. See Kerrigan, "The Articulation of the Ego." My understanding of what psychoanalytic theory means for the social reproduction of sexual difference, however, differs considerably from his; see the analysis in Chapter 5.

38. See Barbara Freedman's account of the difference that psychoanalytic thinking introduces into the scene of pedagogy in "Pedagogy, Psychoanalysis, Theatre: Interrogating the Scene of Learning," *Shakespeare Quarterly* 41.2 (Summer 1990): 174–86. For a rhetorical understanding of the psychoanalytic scene, see Cynthia Chase, "Translating the Transference: Psychoanalysis and the Construction of History," in *Telling Facts: History and Narration in Psychoanalysis*, ed. Joseph H. Smith and Humphrey Morris (Baltimore: Johns Hopkins University Press, 1992), 103–26.

39. My understanding of the body's embedding in language draws on several theoretical discussions: Judith Butler's argument about citationality in which "matter has a history (indeed, more than one) and that the history of matter is in part determined by the negotiation of sexual difference. . . . Matter is fully sedimented with discourses on sex and sexuality that prefigure and constrain the uses to which the term can be put" (*Bodies That Matter: On the Discursive Limits of Sex* [New York: Routledge, 1993], 29); Julia Kristeva's theory of the semiotic and the abject maternal body as excluded margin of a paternal Symbolic order (*Revolution in Poetic Language* Trans. Margaret Waller [New York: Columbia University Press, 1984]); Jean Laplanche's theory of zoning and the way the "marks" of parental care organize a child's body around zones of exchange in which the vital order is "denatured" by a metonymic swerve from instinct to drive (*Life and Death in Psychoanalysis*).

40. See Dolven, *Scenes of Instruction*, p. 21.

41. *The Logic of Practice*, trans. Richard Nice (Stanford, Calif.: Stanford University Press, 1990), 54.

42. *Aphthonii Sophistae Progymnasmata* (London, 1572), 194. "*Erasmus secundo copiae vocat ἐνάργειαν cum. . . . Non simpliciter exponimus, sed seu coloribus expressam, in tabula spectandam proponimus, ut nos depinxisse, non narrasse, lector spectasse, non legisse videatur.*"

43. My list is certainly not exhaustive. For the role that both Terence's plays and the pseudo-Ovidian *Pamphilus* played in medieval and renaissance pedagogy, see Betsy Bowden, "Latin Pedagogical Plays and the Rape Scene in *The Two Gentlemen of Verona*," *English Language Notes* (December 2003): 18–32. She rightly points out that while Baldwin demonstrated how important Terence's five-act structure was to Shakespeare, he "evades the explicit sexuality" of these plays (30)—an evasion not exclusive to his treatment of Terence.

44. The Bangor Friar School statutes continue, "after that they shall teach the names of sickness, diseases, virtues, vices, fishes, fowls, birds, beasts, herbs, shrubs, trees, and so forth they shall proceed in good order to such things as may be most frequented and daily used" (quoted in George A. Plimpton, *The Education of Shakespeare: Illustrated from the Schoolbooks in Use in His Time* [London: Oxford University Press, 1933], 25). Such school practices influenced bilingual instruction in modern languages as well. The sections "The Members" and "Of Man's Body" in Claudius Holybrand's *The French Littleton: A Most Easy, Perfect, and Absolute Way to learne the French tongue* (London: Richard Field, 1602) suggest how explicitly Henry's seduction derives from the school's practice of

enumerating body parts ("the naile / un ungle," "the neck / le cou") as a basic language lesson.

45. On Shakespeare's "dark" and "deeply critical" reflection on the work of *translatio imperii* in *Titus Andronicus*, see Jonathan Bate, *Shakespeare and Ovid* (Oxford: Clarendon Press, 1993) and Heather James, *Shakespeare's Troy: Drama, Politics, and the Translation of Empire* (Cambridge: Cambridge University Press, 1997).

46. I cannot adequately address all these characters, though it will be clear that each casts a new light on the conventions of an education in Latin gentility. For a persuasive account of the historically contradictory figure that Othello strikes as an eloquent "barbarian," see Ian Smith, "Barbarian Errors: Performing Race in Early Modern England," *Shakespeare Quarterly* 49.2 (Summer 1998): 168–86.

47. See Heather James, "Shakespeare's Learned Heroines in Ovid's Schoolroom," in Martindale and Taylor, *Shakespeare and the Classics*, 66–88, as well as her incisive comments on Tamora's evident classical learning in James, *Shakespeare's Troy: Drama, Politics, and the Translation of Empire*.

48. Another widely circulated text, M. Whithal's 1554 was dedicated to helping young boys "avoid all Barbarisms and Anglicisms."

49. See Chapter 3 for further discussion of the place Vergil's *Aeneid* occupied in the humanist curriculum.

50. For an argument focused on the epistemological and narrative consequences of humanist pedagogy, the habits of reading it inculcated, and romance as the genre within which Lyly and Sidney explicitly "rejected the protocols of instruction bequeathed by their teachers," see Dolven, *Scenes of Instruction*. Though I concur with Dolven's insight about romance critique, I believe we can see similar veins of skepticism in a variety of Shakespearean genres and tropes. And my focus, by contrast, is on areas of early modern experience that exceed the domain of knowledge and skepticism—the affective, gendered, and sexual aspects of Shakespearean character.

51. For studies of the early modern "passions" from a variety of interdisciplinary perspectives, see Gail Kern Paster, Katherine Rowe, and Mary Floyd Wilson, *Reading the Early Modern Passions* (Philadelphia: University of Pennsylvania Press, 2004).

52. For different views of the strongly Ovidian aspect of Shakespeare's Roman archive, see Leonard Barkan, *The Gods Made Flesh: Metamorphosis and the Pursuit of Paganism* (New Haven: Yale University Press, 1990); Jonathan Bate, *Shakespeare and Ovid*; Heather James, *Shakespeare's Troy*; and Enterline, *The Rhetoric of the Body from Ovid to Shakespeare* (Cambridge: Cambridge University Press, 2000).

53. *The Oxford English Dictionary*.

54. The OED traces this sense of *affect* to the fourteenth century.

55. For a close discussion of Hooker in relation to *The Winter's Tale*, see David Ward, "Affection, Intention, and Dreams in *The Winter's Tale*," *Modern Language Review* 82 (1987): 545–54.

56. I should add that by "cause" I aim not to distinguish internal from external, subject from object, because Freud's work refuses such a distinction. See Jean Laplanche,

"Fantasy at the Origin of Psychic Life," *The International Journal of Psychoanalysis* 49 (1968): 110–135, and Jacqueline Rose, "Where Does the Misery Come From? Psychoanalysis, Feminism, and the Event" in *Feminism and Psychoanalysis*, ed. Judith Roof and Richard Feldstein (Ithaca, N.Y.: Cornell University Press, 1989), 25–39.

57. J. Laplanche and J.-B. Pontalis, *The Language of Psychoanalysis*, trans. Jeffrey Mehlman (Baltimore: the Johns Hopkins University Press, 1985), 14.

58. See Jean Laplanche, "Fantasy and the Origins of Sexuality," 4.

59. The formal mechanisms Freud posits for the way affect diverges from idea or event are three: "transformation" (translations into bodily symptom), "displacement" of energy (from one idea to another), and "exchange" (from one subject to another).

60. Bourdieu, *The Logic of Practice*, 56.

61. See Harold Fisch's helpful discussion of the way the term evolved, beginning with "character" as used in this latter sense in *King Lear* of *Measure for Measure*: "Character as Linguistic Sign," *New Literary History* 21.3 (Spring 1990): 593–606.

62. Aphthonius's ἔθος is not quite the same as Theophrastus's χαρακτήρ, though both derive from Aristotle, who used only the first term. Erasmus's interest in Theophrastan character would have been available to boys through *De duplici copia verborum ac rerum* (1512). But Aphthonius's lesson in ἔθος, while derived from Aristotle as well, diverges from Theophrastus's "character"; and I confine my study to the *Progymnasmata* because of its popularity for school use and its evident *practical* value to pedagogues teaching rhetorical technique by way of imitation. For a general explanation of the material in each chapter of Lorich's expanded edition of Aphthonius, see Clark, *John Milton at St. Paul's School*. For further discussion of *ethopoeia* in relation to Sly, Bottom, Lucrece, Hamlet, and Venus, see Chapters 3, 4, and 5.

63. Puttenham, too, defines *prosopopoeia* along Aphthonian lines as the personification of an abstraction. Sherry uses *prosopopoeia* as an umbrella term under which *ethopoeia* and *pathopoeia* fall; the first expresses habits (*mores*) and emotions (*affectum*) like "love for one's father," the latter more heated emotions (*vehementiorum affectuum*) (*A Treatise of Schemes and Tropes* [London: 1550], fol. xliii–xliiii). As I discuss further with respect to Venus, Lucrece, and Hamlet, Aphthonius himself did not make much use of Quintilian's distinction between mild and vehement emotion. In general, Sherry allies *prosopopoeia* with "Charactirismus / Effiction or pyctyure of the bodye or mind." He also preserves the close link in Aphthonius between *prosopopoeia* and description (*ekphrasis*): In both the school manual and Sherry's treatise, one follows close on the heels of the other. As a schoolmaster himself, Sherry reveals his pedagogic reasons on the title page: "Whereunto is added a declamacion, that children even strapt from their infancie should be well and gently broughte up in learnynge."

64. Here I would stress the pertinence of the Latin *motus*, or "motion," to the modern term *emotion*.

65. The OED cites Dryden as the first to use "character" in this sense: "He may be allow'd sometimes to Err, who undertakes to move so many Characters and Humours as are requisite in a Play" (1664) and ends with Dickens in 1882, "To no other author were his own characters ever more real."

66. Harold Bloom, *Shakespeare: The Invention of the Human* (New York: Riverhead Books, 1999).

CHAPTER 2

1. Halpern, *The Poetics of Primitive Accumulation*.

2. Edward Sharpham, *Cupid's Whirligig*, ed. Allardyce Nicoll (London: Golden Cockerel Press, 1926). Four schoolboys recite the following epitome of Lily's *A Short Introduction of Grammar*:

1. *Nomnatiuo hic, haec, hoc.*
2. A nowne is the name of a thing.
3. *Amo, amas, amaui, amare.*
4. In speech be these eight partes.

It is, of course, possible that the boys are imitating Lily's *Grammar* even as they appear to be reciting rules and precepts.

3. Lines 659–63. Erasmus's position on imitation became standard. In *The Education of Children* (London: by Thomas Orwin for John Porter and Thomas Gubbin, 1588), William Kempe writes that students "obseru[e] examples . . . in other mens workes" and make "somewhat of [their] owne . . . first by imitation, and at length without imitation" (F1v–F3v).

4. Thomas Elyot, *Boke Named the Governour* (New York: Garland Press, 1992), 19. Dean Colet wrote that "the master of the grammar school . . . shall be a good and honest man, and of much and well attested learning. Let him teach the boys, especially those belonging to the cathedral, grammar, *and at the same time show them an example* of good living. Let him take great heed that he cause no offence to their tender minds by any pollution of word or deed. Nay, more, along with the chaste literature let him imbue them with holy morals, and be to them a master, not of grammar only, but of virtue" (emphasis mine). As quoted in Michael F. J. McDonnell, *A History of St. Paul's School* (London: Chapman Hall, 1909), 20.

5. Anon., *A History of the Shrewsbury School*, 48.

6. As quoted in J. Howard Brown, *Elizabethan Schooldays* (Oxford: Blackwell, 1933), 41.

7. On exemplarity, see Timothy Hampton, *Writing from History: The Rhetoric of Exemplarity in Renaissance Literature* (Ithaca, N.Y.: Cornell University Press, 1990).

8. John Sergeaunt, *Annals of Westminster School*, (London: Methuen, 1898), 279–82. *Etoniana*, no. 10, July 15, 1907, records a "consuetudinarium" written by William Malim, headmaster at Eaton ca. 1560, for the information of Royal Commissioners who visited Eton in 1561. (Malim was Udall's student and equally renowned for beating; the pupils who escaped Malim's flogging prompted the dinner conversation about beating recorded in Ascham's *Scholemaster*.) Malim's text also elaborates the hierarchy of surrogate monitoring, though at Eton the boys appointed to oversee their juniors were called "*praepositores*," and

there seem to have been at least two in each form. At least two other schools (at Cuckfield in Sussex and at Saffron Waldon in Essex) explicitly modeled themselves on Eton's practices. The *Etoniana* also records a custom that was "peculiar to Eton and a few other schools in the 16th century" that is suggestive for several Shakespearean scenes: "in a medieval community a *custos* was a responsible officer (church warden, bridge warden), but the Etonian *custos* was practically the dunce. The opprobrious name could be acquired by talking in English, by making 3 mistakes in the repetition of a rule in grammar, or by making three misspellings in a written exercise" (139–40). John Brinsley elaborates this shaming ritual further: "it is a usual custom in schools to appoint *Custodes* or *Asini*, to observe and catch them who speak English in each form, or whom they see idle to give them the ferula, and to make them *custodes* if they cannot answer a question which they ask" (as quoted in Foster Watson, *The English Grammar Schools to 1660: Their Curriculum and Practice* [Cambridge: Cambridge University Press, 1908], 315). Such a custom of branding someone a "custos" or an "asinus" may explain why *ass* is the word Shakespeare frequently associates with those who have but tenuous command of their own discourse.

9. Anon., *A History of the Shrewsbury School*, 49.

10. McDonnell, *A History of St. Paul's School*, 126.

11. In *Copia*, Erasmus's lists suggest the habitual pairing of praise and blame when he discusses exercises based on Aphthonius—"Sometimes praise, vituperation, fable, similitude"—and those that teach invention: "sometimes the master will give as it were a declamatory theme in diverse kinds, as if he should order them to vituperate Julius Caesar, or praise Socrates . . ." (as quoted in Baldwin, *Small Latine & Lesse Greeke*, 1:88).

12. The ordinances at the Shrewsbury School similarly describe punishment as a timed, daily public spectacle: "The Second Schoolmaster shall comme to the schoole everie morning for the space of one weke before the bell cease, to th' intent to see the schollers singe and saie the nowe usuall praiers there reverentlie upon their knees, the which praier beinge ended, he shall orderlie call the Rolles for absents of the hole schoole, and punyshe them for negligence according to his discression and their deserts" (*A History of the Shrewsbury School*, 46–52).

13. The forms of coercion could vary; one suspects that often the spectacle and threat of punishment did their work as much as its actual execution. In 1635, a former pupil at Free School of St. Helens ca. 1635, Adam Martindale, wrote a retrospective, brief account of his course of study in which corporal punishment by the master is replaced by the more communal policing of "derision": "Mine exercises were usually a piece of Latin (of which he himselfe dictated the English) every day of the week . . . then an epistle wherein I was to follow Cicero, though (alas!) at a great distance. Then themes (as we called them) in the way of Aphthonius . . . and . . . good store of verses on the back side, most hexameters and pentameters, but some sapphics and adonics. All that were presumed by their standing able to discourse in Latin were under a penalty if they either spoke English or broke Priscian's head; but barbarous language, if not incongruous for grammar, had not punishing but derision" (as reported in Watson, *The English Grammar Schools*, 486).

14. Apparently, Friday was the day, at Eton and Winchester as well, when "all the offences committed during the week past were enumerated and culprits punished" (*Etoniana*, no. 10 [1907]: 139–40).

15. I draw here on Slavoj Žižek's notion of "symbolic identification" but leave open the question of whether the relationship is one of identification or desire, as it seems that either or both is possible.

16. I owe the suggestion about the scourge in contemporary satire to William Caroll.

17. See James A. W. Heffernan, *Museum of Words: The Poetics of Ekphrasis from Homer to Ashbery* (Chicago: University of Chicago Press, 1993).

18. W. J. T. Mitchell, *Picture Theory* (Chicago and London: University of Chicago Press, 1994), 164. As we will see in future chapters, Aphthonius's chapter on *descriptio* or *ekphrasis* brings the text/image dynamic that Mitchell's book examines directly into the school's social dynamics. Particularly compelling for these social relations, I might add, are what Mitchell calls "ekphrastic hope" and "ekphrastic fear."

19. Mitchell, *Picture Theory*, 172.

20. The *ekphrasis* of Busirane's tapestry written by one of Richard Mulcaster's former students is an obvious case in point. But so, too, are the ekphrases examined here from *Venus and Adonis*, *The Rape of Lucrece*, and *The Taming of the Shrew*.

21. Folger MS L.e.1189.

22. The best account of the texts concerning forms of voice control and gesticulation among ancient and Renaissance rhetorical theorists is Heinrich Plett's *Rhetoric and Renaissance Culture* (New York and Berlin: Walter de Gruyter, 2004). Interestingly, from the perspective of my argument about the transgendered habits of school training, he singles out Volumnia's instructions to Coriolanus on treating the plebs as a thoroughgoing lesson in *actio* (3.2.73–80)—one in which "the deictic 'thus' and 'here' indicate" that she "demonstrates for him, in some sort of theatrical rehearsal, details of his advanced rhetorical role" (p. 263).

23. In Lily's *Grammar* the section "De Orthoepia" on enunciation follows right after a lesson in writing letters: " . . . *hoc est emendate rectéque loquendi ratio, ab* ὀρθός *rectus, &* ἔπος *verbum. Hic imprimis curandum est,* ut praeceptores tenera ac balbutientia puerorum ora sic effingant & figurent *ne vel continuâ linguae volubilitate ita sermonem praecipitent, ut nusquam, nisi ubit spiritus deficit, orationem claudant . . . ad singulas quasque voces longa interspiratione, consilescant, ructu, risu, singultu, screatu, vel tussi, sermonis tenorem inepte dirimentes*" (emphasis mine). There follows a lesson in common mispronunciations of Latin words "*pro Multus . . . moultus /// pro falsus, faulsus,*" etc.

24. White, *The Vulgaria of John Stanbridge*, 114.

25. Richard Sherry, *A Treatise of Schemes and Tropes* (London, 1550), n.p.

26. Folger MS V.a.381, 97–99.

27. *Imaginary Audition: Shakespeare on Stage and Page* (Berkeley: University of California Press, 1989), 74–104. See a further unfolding of his conception of Shakespearean subjectivity —the way their acts of persuasion are simultaneously acts of self-persuasion

and judgment—in *Making Trifles of Terrors: Redistributing Complicities in Shakespeare* (Stanford, Calif.: Stanford University Press, 1997).

28. When Laplanche describes Freud's topographical and dynamic model, he writes in a way that is suggestive for the schoolroom: His "approach does not merely set up an interplay between the agencies. . . . Special importance comes to be assigned to the 'relations of dependence' obtaining between the various systems . . . the intrasubjective field tends to be conceived of after the fashion of intersubjective relations, and the systems are pictured as relatively autonomous persons-within-the person" (J. Laplanche and J.-B. Pontalis, *The Language of Psychoanalysis*, trans. Donald Nicholson-Smith [New York: Norton, 1973], 452).

29. Anon., *A History of the Shrewsbury School*, 46–52.

30. *Catechismus paruus pueris primum Latine . . . proponendus in scholis* (London: John Day, 1573). This copy is from the Folger Shakespeare Library.

31. I owe this suggestion to Peter Holland. For further description of classroom space and design, as well as the master's sometimes throne-like chair, see Ursula Potter, "Performing Arts in the Tudor Classroom," 147–48.

32. There are, however, a few important exceptions to this tendency. Recently, Ursula Potter pointed to training in *actio* and *pronuntiatio* as a "largely unexplored field of research" ("Performing Arts in the Tudor Classroom," 147). Potter documents the school's training in memorization, pronunciation, role-playing, and *actio* in order to argue that Tudor grammar schools were "fertile breeding grounds for the explosion of dramatic activity" in the sixteenth and seventeenth centuries. Leonard Barkan also points in this direction when he observes that the question-and-answer method of teaching at school made Latin something one "performed as a dramatic conversation" ("What Did Shakespeare Read?" in Margreta de Grazia and Stanley Wells, eds., *The Cambridge Companion to Shakespeare* [Cambridge: Cambridge University Press, 2001], 35). Neil Rhodes points out that our attention to Puritan attacks on the theater means that it "may come a surprise" in the current critical climate "to see how deeply rooted drama was in the educational system of Tudor England" (*Shakespeare and the Origins of English* [Oxford: Oxford University Press, 2004], 25). Though I concur with Rhodes's emphasis on the crucial importance of training in speech as well as writing in the schools, our conclusions about its effects differ. Finally, as Heinrich Plett describes, rhetoric took a long time to enter the world of Shakespearean criticism due to both paucity of materials and the general "disrepute" into which rhetoric "had fallen under the sway of idealistic philosophy" (*Rhetoric and Renaissance Culture*, 415). Now it is time to reexamine the institutional *habitus* by which Shakespeare and contemporaries were inducted into classical rhetorical training.

33. *A History of the Shrewsbury School* and Watson, *English Grammar Schools*, 315.

34. The student was Sir James Whitelocke, who entered Merchant Taylors' in 1585, and who was commenting on the frequency with which Mulcaster's boys acted at court (quoted in E. K. Chambers, *The Elizabethan Stage* [Oxford: Clarendon Press, 1923], 2:76). John Bale, *Scriptorum Illustrium Maioris Brytannie . . . Catalogus* (1577) , as cited in Hillebrand, *The Child Actors*, 700: "*ad formandum os tenerum & balbutiens, quo clarè, eleganter,*

& distinctè uerba eloqui & effari consuesceret. Plurimas in eius museo uidi ac legi tragoedias & comoedias, epistolas, orationes, congratulationes . . ."

35. As translated in T. W. Baldwin, *Small Latine & Lesse Greeke* 1:328.

36. Malim is quoted in *Etoniana*, no. 10, July 15, 1907, 159. Translation of Hoole's comment is Watson's, *English Grammar Schools*, 316.

37. As recorded in David Baldwin, *The Chapel Royal: Ancient and Modern* (London: Duckworth, 1990), 117–18. Though not exploring cross-dressing in any detail, Margaret Rogerson has usefully pieced together a great deal of evidence about the love for theatricals, and shared belief in their pedagogical efficacy, among provincial as well as London schoolmasters in "Provincial Schoolmasters and Early English Drama," *Leeds Studies in English* 29 (1998): 315–22.

38. T. W. Baldwin, *Small Latine & Lesse Greeke*, 1:90. Baldwin is summarizing Erasmus's advice in *Copia*; he then advises masters to draw comparisons between the boys in order to incite "a kind of emulation among them." David Bevington's insightful study of the semiotics of gesture in Shakespearean drama, for example, ignores school training and so derives the rhetoric of gesture from contemporary treatises in physiognomy and courtesy (*Action Is Eloquence: Shakespeare's Language of Gesture* [Cambridge, Mass.: Harvard University Press, 1984]).

39. Mary Thomas Crane, *Framing Authority: Sayings, Self, and Society in Sixteenth-Century England* (Princeton, N.J.: Princeton University Press, 1993), 3.

40. *Elizabethan Rhetoric: Theory and Practice* (Cambridge: Cambridge University Press, 2002), 11–47. Mack explains the precise techniques and forms of composition undertaken in the schools—amplification, moral sentences, letter writing, etc.

41. *Picture Theory*, 160.

42. Joseph Roach, *The Player's Passion: Studies in the Science of Acting* (Newark: University of Delaware Press, 1985), 33–38.

43. *Lac puerorum . . . anglice mylke for children* (Antwerp: 1507).

44. *Chirologia or The naturall language of the hand . . . Whereunto is added Chironomia: or, the art of manuall rhetoric* (London: Richard Whitaker at his shop in Pauls Churchyard, 1644), 115.

45. *Chirologia*, ibid.

46. I borrow freely from Barbara Freedman's discussion of the Socratic pedagogical "counter-tradition," in which, as she puts it, "rather than contrast ignorance and knowledge, Socrates emphasizes their constitutive and dynamic relationship" ("Pedagogy, Psychoanalysis, Theater," *Shakespeare Quarterly* 41, 2 [Summer, 1990], 175).

47. Roach, *The Player's Passion*, 44.

48. See Chapter 5 for a detailed discussion of the flogging scene. For the suggestion that the "shameful blots" on Ingnorance's face are part of Redford's attempt to "participate in social dialogue" over syphilis, see Todd H. Pettigrew, "Sex, Sin, and Scarring: Syphilis in Redford's Wit and Science" in *Tudor Drama Before Shakespeare, 1485–1590*, eds. Lloyd Kermode, Jason Scott-Warren, and Martine Van Elk (New York, N.Y.: Palgrave Macmillan, 2004), 213–27.

49. That the birch might be called the "master's daughter" suggests that the quarrel over Prospero's daughter in *The Tempest* would hardly have surprised contemporary audiences.

50. As quoted in Stewart, *Close Readers*, 98–99. The anecdote appears in McDonnell, *A History of St. Paul's School*, and Watson, *Richard Mulcaster and his "Elementarie"* (London: C.F. Hodgson & Son, 1893), 5. Mulcaster refers, in *Positions*, to his rod as "my lady birchely" (274).

51. My thanks to Leah Marcus for reminding me of the passage from the Psalms. While there is not room for a discussion here, the intimate connection between choir boys and schoolboys was long-standing—and in some early accounts the distinction is virtually nonexistent. See Baldwin, *The Chapel Royal,* and McDonnell's discussion of the way chorister and grammar schoolboy were one and the same at St. Paul's (15–20).

52. James Smith, *The Loves of Hero and Leander: A Mock Poem* (London, 1653). I thank Timothy Raylor for drawing my attention to this volume.

53. I am indebted to Alan Stewart for helping me reconstruct this line.

54. "The Birch" was written by Richard Halford (b. 1678/9; at Merchant Taylors' 1687–97; incorporated at Oxford, BA 1700; d. 1726). It appears in an unpublished collection of manuscript poems by various hands (presumably, by the boys themselves) that were composed and performed between 1694 and 1697 at the Merchant Taylors' School as a form of public examination ("A Collection of Verses, Orations, &c, Compos'd & Spoken by the eight upper Boys of Merchant Taylors' School, in London, upon certain public days of Examination or Election"). It is housed in the Merchant Taylors' School library.

55. In another ambiguous visual icon for school discipline, the seal of Louth Grammar School (1552) depicts a master with a boy on his knee, birch poised in midair. Six other boys watch the performance as the master pronounces a Latin lesson that informs all viewers, inside and outside the picture, that flogging and loving are the same thing: "*qui parcit virge* odit *filium*" ("He who spares the rod, *hates* his son"; emphasis mine); as depicted in Nicholas Carlisle, *A Concise Description of the Endowed Grammar Schools of England and Wales* (London: Baldwin, Cradock and Joy Subjects, 1818), 10. In almost all flogging scenes, signifiers for affective intensity like "love" and "hate" circulate with discussions of "wit" and "eloquence" and do so in ways that are erotically suggestive about the very hierarchy such punishment was designed to enforce.

56. I thank Donald Jellerson for bringing this poem to my attention at just the right moment.

57. Here we might see that Cynthia Marshall's account of an audience's pleasure in "shattering" in early modern theaters may well be expanded to include writing and reading poetry, particularly in moments of rhetorical or classicizing exuberance. See *The Shattering of the Self: Violence, Subjectivity and Early Modern Texts* (Baltimore: Johns Hopkins University Press, 2002).

58. In *Positions*, Mulcaster makes it clear that in his view, a boy's witnessing the punishment of "vice" or praise of "virtue" can be as effective as being subject to it (191, 3–6).

59. These questions arise from my understanding of retrospection and trauma as outlined by Jean Laplanche in *Life and Death in Psychoanalysis*, trans. Jeffrey Mehlman (Baltimore: The Johns Hopkins University Press, 1985).

60. Lacan's version of this problem appears most succinctly in "The Mirror Stage," *Ecrits*, (Paris: Editions du Seuil, 1966), 126–34.

61. Laplanche, "Fantasy and the Origins of Sexuality," 4.

62. For example: see Coppelia Kahn's revealing examination of one glaring conflict between classical and early modern culture—suicide—in *Antony and Cleopatra* (*Roman Shakespeare: Warriors, Wounds, Women* [New York: Routledge, 1997]).

63. See Eric Partridge, *Shakespeare's Bawdy* (London: Routledge, 2001), its most recent incarnation.

64. For specific readings of a few such moments, see Joel Fineman on Lucrece's discourse in *The Subjectivity Effect in Western Literary Tradition* (Boston: The MIT Press, 1991), 86–136; Harry Berger's reading of Isabella and Angelo in *Making Trifles of Terrors*, 212–22; and my "What 'Womanhood Denies the Power of Tongues to Tell,'" *Shakespeare Studies* (Fall 1999): 1–12.

65. A boy's buttocks, clearly a significant location for grammar school attention in these and a host of other stories, might be read in relation to Laplanche's discussion of "zones of exchange" that "attract the first erotogenic maneuvers from the adult. An even more significant factor, if we introduce the subjectivity of the first 'partner': these zones focalize parental fantasies. . . . So that we may say, in what is barely a metaphor, that they are the points through which is introduced into the child that alien internal entity which is, properly speaking, the sexual excitation" (24). An important difference, of course, is that Laplanche calls these the "marks of *maternal* care" because of modern parenting practices. But in the Tudor period, the grammar school intervened in the parenting function—indeed, masters portrayed themselves as paternal but occasionally as maternal, too—so that the gender of the parental figure attending to certain zones of the body and thereby lending those zones significance is difficult to specify. Because of this institutional intervention in child rearing, disciplinary or parental figuration could be as ambivalent as the fantasy of the "phallic mother" in psychoanalytic discourse.

66. Laplanche, "Fantasy and the Origins of Sexuality," 4.

67. This theory is not about sexuality in isolation from other aspects of psychic life. Laplanche is also talking about the emergence of subjectivity as such: "an intrusion from without into an interior which perhaps did not exist as such before this intrusion; we must reconcile the passivity which is implied by merely receiving meaning from outside with the minimum of activity necessary for the experience even to be acknowledged, and the indifference of innocence with the disgust which the seduction is assumed to provoke. . . . We have a subject who is pre-subjectal, who receives his existence, his sexual existence, from without, before a distinction between within and without is achieved" ("Fantasy and the Origins of Sexuality," 5). That sexuality is implicated in the very existence of the subject as such is why I find non-normative psychoanalytic theory crucial for the field of early modern studies, focused for so long on telling stories about the history of subjectivity.

68. The phrase is from Laplanche, *Life and Death*, 106.

69. "A Child is Being Beaten: A Contribution to the Study of the Origin of Sexual Perversions," in *The Standard Edition of the Complete Psychological Works of Sigmund Freud*, vol. 17, ed. James Strachey (London: Hogarth Press, 1974).

70. Both *mood* and *figure* were technical terms for kinds of syllogism in logic; "in mood and figure" designated "in due logical form," and *mood* was also used in grammar to indicate the various functions of a verb's conjugations. *Mood* seems to have been used fairly often in punning reference to its affective sense in the early seventeenth century (see *The Oxford English Dictionary*).

71. Thomas Nashe, *A Pleasant Comedie, called Summer's Last Will and Testament* (London: Simon Stafford for Walter Burre, 1600), 24.

CHAPTER 3

1. Jonathan Crewe adroitly summarizes the litany of critical unease about *Venus and Adonis* by pointing out that we are reading a sixteenth-century story about sexual harassment (*The Narrative Poems*, ed. A. R. Braunmuller, Stephen Orgel, and Jonathan Crewe [New York: Penguin Classics, 1999], 4).

2. This chapter expands a shorter essay originally published in *From Stage to Print: Rewriting Early Modern Stage History*, ed. Peter Holland and Stephen Orgel (New York: Palgrave Press, 2005), 173–90. It also takes inspiration from T. W. Baldwin's observation, years ago, that the debate between Venus and Adonis on procreation partakes of grammar school training in writing themes (*On the Literary Genetics of Shakespeare's Poems and Sonnets* [Urbana: University of Illinois Press, 1950]), 183–86. Though others pick up on Adonis's half of the relationship (see W. R. Streitberger, "Ideal Conduct in Venus and Adonis," *Shakespeare Quarterly* 26 (1975): 285–91), no one has extended the comparison to Venus.

3. See M. L. Stapleton, "Venus as *Praeceptor*: The *Ars Amatoria* in *Venus and Adonis*," in *Venus and Adonis: Critical Essays*, ed. Philip C. Kolin (New York: Routledge, 1997), 309–22.

4. *William Lily's A Short Introduction of Grammar, Compiled and set forth for the bringing up of all those that intend to attain the knowledge of the Latin Tongue.* Compiled in 1512 for St. Paul's School and printed shortly after, it remained in print and in school use for the next 150 years. As J. Howard Brown notes, while ordinary editions of books ran to 1,250 copies, Lily's *Grammar* had a print run of 10,000 (*Elizabethan Schooldays* [Oxford: Blackwell, 1933], 42). Tranio's first response to Lucentio's declaration that he is in love, for example, is a line from Terence, but it is probably recollected from Lily.

5. Sir Philip Sidney's *Astrophil and Stella*, poem 15. Echo runs throughout the *Rime sparse* as a figure for Petrarch's woe. See in particular poem 23 (the so-called "*canzone dei metamorfosi*").

6. On Adonis's hyper-masculine activities and the way hetero-normative expectations have shaped the critical tradition surrounding him, see Richard Rambuss, "What

It Feels Like for a Boy: Shakespeare's *Venus and Adonis*," in *A Companion to Shakespeare's Works*, vol. 4, *The Poems, Problem Comedies, Late Plays*, ed. Richard Dutton and Jean Howard (London: Blackwell, 2003), 240–58. Inversions of normative expectations for gender order, moreover, inflect the poem's word order—the example the editors of the Folger edition choose to illustrate such inversion is "*Hunting* he loved, but *Love* he laughed to scorn" (*Shakespeare's Sonnets and Poems*, ed. Barbara A. Mowat and Paul Werstine [New York: Washington Square Press, 2004], 347).

7. Jonathan Bate, *Shakespeare and Ovid* (Oxford: Clarendon Press, 1993, 54).

8. Early psychoanalytic and feminist studies tended to focus specifically on maternal power in the poem. See Coppelia Kahn, "Self and Eros in *Venus and Adonis*," *Centenntial Review* (East Lansing, Mich.) 20 (1976): 351–71; Wayne Rebhorn, "Temptation in Shakespeare's *Venus and Adonis*," *Shakespeare Studies* 11 (1978): 1–19; Alan Rothenberg, "The Oral Rape Fantasy and the Rejection of the Mother in the Imagery of Shakespeare's *Venus and Adonis*," *Psychoanalytic Quarterly* 40 (1971): 447–68.

9. *Suffocating Mothers: Fantasies of Maternal Origin in Shakespeare's Plays, "Hamlet" to "The Tempest"* (New York: Routledge, 1991).

10. Perhaps it does not go without saying that I understand such maternal figures not as unmediated expressions of the universal nature of the maternal body or mother-child relationship. Rather, I take them to be socially invested fantasies retrospectively imposed to *interpret* a relationship that both logically and chronologically precedes any child's understanding of the difference between mother and father, male and female. Such representations do not precede "the Law of the Father"—the imposition of what sexual difference means for societies organized around father power—but rather are shaped by it. They are projected back in time to explain an original state in which to say "My mother is a woman" has yet to make any sense. I borrow Constance Penley's formulation in *The Future of an Illusion: Film, Feminism, and Psychoanalysis* (Minneapolis: University of Minnesota Press, 1989), 27. For further discussion of the vacillation between Oedipal and pre-Oedipal registers in this poem, see my "Psychoanalytic Criticisms of Shakespeare," *Shakespeare: An Oxford Guide*, ed. Stanley Wells and Lena Cowen Orlin (Oxford: Oxford University Press, 2003), 450–71.

11. See A. F. Leach, *The Schools of Medieval England* (London: Chatto, 1915), 270.

12. *Orationes et Declamationes, Habitae in Schola Lincolniensi: Speech Day Proceedings in an English School 1624 and 1625*, ed. Charles Garton (London: Arethusa, 1972), 56.

13. *Ovids Metamorphosis translated grammatically . . . written chiefly for the good of the schooles, to be vsed according to the directions in the preface to the painefull schoole-master . . .* (London, 1618), 3–4.

14. *The Education of Children in Learning . . .* (London: Thomas Orwin, 1588), 4.

15. *Ludus literarius* (London: Humphrey Lownes, 1612), chapter 21.

16. James, *Shakespeare's Troy*, 1–18.

17. Baldwin, *Small Latine & Lesse Greeke*, 1:327.

18. *Letters and Exercises of the Elizabethan Schoolmaster John Conybeare, Schoolmaster of Molton, Devon, 1580 and Swimbridge, 1594* (London: Henry Frowde, 1905), 105.

19. John Sturm, trans. Baldwin, *Small Latine & Lesse Greeke*, 1:340–41.

20. Christopher Johnson, *Batrachomyomachia* (London: Thomas Purfoote, 1580), 3. See J. W. Binns, *Intellectual Culture in Elizabethan and Jacobean England: The Latin Writings of the Age* (Leeds, England: Francis Cairns, 1990), 229–30.

21. Ibid.

22. Royal ms. 12 A.LXVII, British Museum Library. One of Malim's verses reads, "*Tullius altisonis . . . dum scripta Maronis / Intonuit subito, o magnae spec altera Romae.*" A verse from one "Ioannes Pratt" then refers to "*Haec noua Trois super reliquas caput eriget omnes,*" while "Richardus Clercus" writes a brief poem in which Elizabeth's reign surpasses all others, particularly Troy and Rome: "*not ita . . . non ita . . . non ita. . . . Non ita Troia potens Priamo celebrata potenti / Non ita Caesareo numine Roma fuit. . . .*" "Edmundus Winchus" and "Thomas Sandersonus," who are clearly younger students less proficient at Latin, still try to continue the theme in short poems built around the idea of Britain as a second Rome or second Troy.

23. *Troia Britannica: or, Great Britaines Troy A Poem deuided into XVII. Seuerall cantons, intermixed with many pleasant poeticall tales. Concluding with an vniversall chronicle from the Creation, vntill these present times. Written by Tho: Heywood* (London: W. Iaggard, 1609).

24. Ibid. In "To the Right Honourable Edward Earle of Worcester," Heywood sets up the Troy story only to abandon it in the poem that follows:

> Homer (long since) a Chronicler Diuine,
> And Vergill, have redeemd olde Troy from Fire,
> Whose memory had with her buildings line
> In desolate ruyne, had not theyr desire
> > Snatcht her fayre Tytle from the burning flame,
> > Which with the Towne had else consumed her name.
>
> Had they survivude in these our flourishing daies,
> Your virtues from the auncient Heroes drawne,
> In spight of death or blacke obliuions rage,
> Should lieu for euer in Fames glorious fawne,
> > Rankt next to Troy, our Troy-novant should be,
> > And next the Troyan Peeres, your places free.

25. *Poetics of Primitive Accumulation*, 45–56. Daniel Wakelin points out that the solution of preferring style over matter emerges as early as the mid-fifteenth century, in an epilogue to a translation of Claudian (ca. 1445). In it, the translator styles Claudian a "maystyr" to his "chyld" poem: "loue not hys law/ love weel hys word" (*Humanism, Reading, and English Literature*, 71).

26. As quoted in Foster Watson, *English Grammar Schools to 1600*, p. 16. Wolsey's plans for the Ipswich School also recommend imitations of Ovid—both the *Fasti* and the *Metamorphoses*—but Wolsey pairs these texts with Horace's *Epistles* instead of *The Aeneid*.

27. Foster Watson, *English Grammar Schools to 1600*, p. 22.

28. This paragraph summarizes part of my earlier argument in *The Rhetoric of the Body*, especially Chapters 1 and 2.

29. Frances Meres, *Palladis Tamia. Wit's treasure being the second part of Wits commonwealth.* (London: P. Short, 1598), n.p.

30. "What Did Shakespeare Read?" in *The Cambridge Companion to Shakespeare*, ed. Magreta de Grazia and Stanley Wells (Cambridge: Cambridge University Press, 2001), 36. In a recent article, Paul Sullivan concurs that *vulgaria* also teach Latin vocabulary precisely by soliciting daily acts of impersonation. He is particularly struck by the wide spectrum of social roles the boys were asked to perform ("Playing the Lord").

31. William Nelson, *A Fifteenth Century School Book* (Oxford: Clarendon Press, 1956), xxv. The quotation from Colet and examples as recorded in Nelson.

32. As quoted in Nelson, 18.

33. During ten months in 1529, an Oxford bookseller sold 175 copies by Erasmus, 48 of which were the *Colloquies*. On the popularity of the *Colloquies*, see Craig R. Thompson, *Collected Works of Erasmus: Colloquies* (Toronto: University of Toronto Press, 1997), 39: xxxi–xxxvi.

34. As quoted in Nelson, 21.

35. Ibid.

36. "I hade leuer teche in any place in the worlde then her at oxford, wher I can teche nothyng that I thanke profitable for my scolares bot sum be agenst yt; I can consell nothyng but the consele the contrarie. I counsellyd you to make uersis thes holydays [and] when ye had mayde them to sett them vp apon this post. Ye began and there was no mane that was wise but he prasyd you for your begynnyng. I merwell grettly for what case ye seasyd from your purpose. Who conseled or feryd you from hit? I wene that hare brane feryd you that set vp versus here and presumptuosly commandyd to silens. In good feith if I knewe for a surty that you wer a-frayd for hym I wold sharpely punyse you everyone. Be-ware therefore lest any man fere you hereafter. If other that felow or anny trowbyll you, se that you make all to-gether insurrccion agenst hym, in the wich if my cownsell can do you any good you shall not lacke it. Therefor be wise, play the man hereafter and not the boys, as ye haue don in this mather" (as quoted in Nelson, *A Fifteenth Century Schoolbook*, 44).

37. See Chapter 2.

38. *The Logic of Practice*, esp. Chapter 3.

39. Ibid., 56.

40. *The Sublime Subject of Ideology* (London: Verso, 1989), 105. Here an ordinance of 1580, from the grammar school in Sandwich, read alongside the Winchester "Consuetudinarium" discussed in Chapter 2, gives a detailed sense of the reward structures that informed school training in how to become an effective public performer and helped generate the intense, career-long association I examine throughout between "mastery" and "love" in Shakespeare's texts: "everie yere once. . . . There be kept in the Schole disputacions, upon *questions provided by the Master*, from Seven or Eight of the Clock in the forenone till Nine or Ten of the Clock followinge; at which disputacions, I ordeine, that the Master desire the Parsons and Vicars of the Towne, with one or two other of

knowledge or more dwelling nighe, to be present in the Schole if it please them to hear the same. The disputacion ended, to determine which three of the hole number of several forms have done best by the judgements of the *Master* and learned hearers: and I ordeine, that the first allowed have a *Penn* of Silver *whole guilte* of the price of 2s. 6d.; the second, a *Penn* of Silver *parcel guilte*. . . . That the hole company goe in order decentlie by two and two unto *the Parish church*. . . . The three victors to come laste nexte to the Master and Ussher, and ither of them having a *Garland* on their heads provided for the purpose . . . and to saie or singe some convenient Psalme or Himpne . . . having some convenient rememberaunce and making mancion of *the Church, the Realme, the Prince, the Towne and the Fownder as shal be appointed and devised by the Master*" (emphasis in original). As recorded in Baldwin, *Small Latine & Lesse Greeke*, 2:378.

41. *Corderius dialogues translated grammatically; for the more speedy attaining to the knowledge of the Latine tongue, for writing and speaking Latine* . . . (London: Humfrey Lownes, 1614).

42. Baldwin lays out the texts for practice in letter writing based on the curriculum at Eton in 1530. *Modus Conscribendi Epistolas*, likely by Erasmus, sets out precisely the kinds of assumptions and habits that we have detected in the voices of the Magdalen *vulgaria*— and at the same time reinforces and extends the central place of "love" to the school scene of epistolary impersonation: A master should "exercise choice and care that he especially propose those" epistles "which allure that age with delightfulness as if baits . . . that will happen if they are either novel, or humorous, or in any other way connected with the interests of boys. These must be sought either from the fables of the poets or from the historians. . . . And of the first class are the *amatoriae* of Naso, in which perhaps it would not be safe to exercise callow youth. But the *Heroides* are more chaste, nor does anything forbid that this kind of thing be treated chastely and modestly. As if a wooer should go about the wooing of his girl with caressing letters; if Helena should deter Paris from an unlawful love. For the epistle of Penelope to Ulysses is wholly chaste, as also that of Acontius to Cydippe. If a wife should write to her husband lingering abroad that he should hasten home. . . ." (Baldwin, *Small Latine & Lesse Greeke*, 2:239–45). Baldwin notes that in 1528 "in the Ipswich-Paul's system," the fifth-form boys were introduced to the *Heroides* at the same time as they were set to imitate them for practice in the art of letter writing (242).

43. With sincere thanks to the curator of the Merchant Taylors' archives, Mr. Geoffrey Brown, for bringing the manuscript transcriptions of the school exercise day to my attention.

44. *The Mirror of the Self: Sexuality, Self-Knowledge, and the Gaze in the Early Roman Empire* (Chicago: University of Chicago Press, 2006), 158.

45. The appearance of female figures in schoolboy assignments came down from ancient and medieval practice. See Marjorie Curry Woods, "The Teaching of Writing in Medieval Europe," in *A Short History of Writing Instruction from Ancient Greece to Twentieth-Century America*, ed. James J. Murphy (Davis, Calif.: Hermagoras Press, 1990), 77–94, and "Weeping for Dido: Epilogue on a Premodern Rhetorical Exercise in the Post Modern Classroom," in *Latin Grammar and Rhetoric: From Classical Theory to Medieval Practice*, ed. Carol Dana Lanham (London: Continuum Press, 2002), 284–94. Lorich's expanded translation, and in particular his evident enthusiasm in this chapter

for speeches of female suffering, became standard fare after 1540 in schools across England. He thereby revivified and extended a practice that, as Woods notes, opened the possibility for "young male students" to "identify as much with the (usually female victims) as with the (male) perpetrators" ("Weeping for Dido," 290). Aphthonius's and Lorich's lessons, moreover, clearly are drawing on Ovid's own penchant for giving voice and sympathy to female suffering—and suggests one institutional reason that many Elizabethan authors so often read Ovid in precisely this way.

46. Additional ms. 4379, "Collection of themes and exercises, in Latin prose and verse, ca. 1565. Made by a scholar at Winchester School named William Badger, under the guidance of Christopher Johnson, Headmaster, 1560–79" (British Museum Library), p. 128.

> Quid initii vobiscii[ ] est infelix turba puelli
> Cur tam terrifico plangitis astra sono.
> En ego in toto en conpleto sylvia tremescens
> Terreor, ad sylvia[s] vociferante schola.
> Nam veluti caelo tonitrus mittuntur ab alto
> Mittitur a restro clamor in astra choro.
> Terque quaterque die nostras fremit aura per auras
> Wichamicique refert garrula verba gregis.

47. Royal ms. 18 A.LXIV, "A copie of diuers and sundry verses as well in Latin as in Englishe deuised and made partely by John Leland and partely by Nicholas Vuedale on the occasion of the coronation of Queen Anne Boleyn at the pageants exhibited by the Mayor and Citizens of London on Whitsun Eve, 31 May 1533." For the tradition at Eton, see Michael Meredith, *Five Hundred Years of Eton Theater* (Windsor, England: Eton College, 2001).

48. *A History of the Shrewsbury School from the Blakeway Mss., and Many Other Sources* (Shrewsbury and London: Adnitt & Naunton, The Square and Simpkin, Marshall & Co., Stationers Hall Court, 1899), 65–66. The records indicate that just six days earlier the boys dressed up in martial costume and marched around playing the part of generals, giving "warlike" speeches. My point is that their declamations covered a wide range of situations and emotions; they were asked to perform the emotions suited to a wide variety of situations, male and female.

49. That the gendered and sexual component to school training requires our critical attention becomes clear when one reads secondary accounts, which until recently have tended to pass over school transvestite practice in silence. In this case, for example, Joan Simon fails to note that the boys were dressed as nymphs (*Education and Society in Tudor England* [Cambridge: Cambridge University Press, 1967]). The Shrewsbury nymphs, moreover, are performing in a way that is consonant with contemporary Italian pedagogy. Based on Augustine's precedent—his famous confession that he wept for Dido at school— and the ancient practice he records in *The Confessions*, that he and his classmates had "to create and to recite" their own version of "women's laments from *The Aeneid*," Guarino

Guarini introduced a school practice that spread from Ferrara to northern Italy and France: Boys practiced similar rhetorical exercises, learning to recite the laments of goddesses and ancient queens. Such impersonations "of noblewomen *in extremis*" led to operatic libretti such as Monteverdi's *Arianna* (1608). See Ann MacNeil, "Weeping at the Water's Edge," *Early Music* 27.3 (August 1999): 406–17. In particular, MacNeil points out that the audience, who understood the conventions of the lament, *expected* to weep for Arianna and were recorded to have done so. Clearly, the Shrewsbury audience also understood the emotional terms of this performance, as well as the reaction appropriate to it. As the author of the school history is at pains to point out, the audience weeping on the riverbanks proves the "excellence" of the nymphs' performance. I am grateful to Marjorie Woods for bringing this article to my attention.

50. Here we may detect another interesting intersection with the emergence of opera, given that the Children of the Chapel Royal were frequently brought on stage in the last years of the sixteenth century to sing a lament.

51. Marlowe was not the only playwright to produce a play about Dido. William Gager's (1580–1619) *Dido* was performed at Cambridge; and John Ritwyse, headmaster of St. Paul's, wrote another *Dido*, which scholars performed for Wolsey between 1522 and 1532. This last is recorded in Watson, *The English Grammar Schools to 1660*, 323. See *William Gager: The Complete Works*, trans. Dana F. Sutton (New York: Garland, 1994).

52. For my full argument against such a view, see Chapter 5.

53. *From Humanism to the Humanities*, p. xiv.

54. Baldwin points out that Venus's premise here is a version of the school theme, "motiues to procreation as ye way to outliue time," with which the narrator of the sonnets opens his sequence (*Small Latine & Lesse Greeke*, 1:186).

55. Baldwin, *Small Latine & Lesse Greeke*, 1:88. See also Baldwin, *On the Literary Genetics of Shakespeare's Poems*, 44.

56. *Ludus literarius* (1612), 184–89; Baldwin, *Small Latine & Lesse Greeke*, 1: 339–40.

57. John Roe, editor of the Cambridge edition of the poems, implicitly recognizes the habit of mind born from such institutional training when he summarizes the poem's central dynamic—and the long-standing critical problem it generated for moral readings of its characters—as follows: "If we are to see an ideal principle in the poem it is this: not an approved human choice as represented by one of the protagonists more than the other, for the poem does not ultimately evaluate such things, but a balanced contemplation of feelings, motives, and actions from contrasting and opposing angles" (*The Poems* [Cambridge: Cambridge University Press, 1992], 5–6). See also Catherine Belsey's important critique of the critical tendency to resolve the argument between love and lust, "Love as Trompe-l'oeil: Taxonomies of Desire in *Venus and Adonis*," *Shakespeare Quarterly* 46.3 (Fall 1995): 257–76.

58. T. W. Baldwin, *Small Latine and Lesse Greeke*, 2:290. See also 1:84–88 for Erasmus's account of exercises in themes best suited to young minds—which he felt could be historical, fictional, figural, or drawn from *sententiae*. Baldwin also cites Hoole's thorough list, in *New Discovery* (1661), of all the ways that fifth- and sixth-form boys were to

be "employed weekly in making Theams and Verses, which they can never well do, except they be furnished with matter aforehand" (as quoted in *Small Latine and Lesse Greeke*, 2:290). One of Hoole's recommended sources for a boy's commonplace book, "Descriptions of things natural and artificial," suggests the extent to which Shakespeare's two ekphrases expand Ovid's couplet from the *Ars* into a lengthy ekphrastic description of the stallion and of Zeuxis's painted grapes.

59. See James A. W. Heffernan, *Museum of Words: The Poetics of Ekphrasis from Homer to Ashbery* (Chicago: University of Chicago Press, 1993).

60. See Chapter 5 for an outline of the distinctions Aphthonius draws between *ethopoeia*, *prosopopoeia*, and *idolopoeia*. Here I am using *prosopopoeia* in its narrow, Aphthonian sense as the personification of an abstraction, "something that is neither a thing nor a person."

CHAPTER 4

1. "The Shakespearean Editor as Shrew-Tamer," *English Literary Renaissance* 22 (1992): 180–92. For a reading less focused than mine on the gap between theory and practice in sixteenth-century pedagogy—in which the theater becomes successful pedagogue and the audience learns a lesson by taking Katharine as a disciplinary example of their own shortcomings—see Dennis S. Brooks, " 'To Show Scorn Her Own Image': The Varieties of Education in 'The Taming of the Shrew'," *Rocky Mountain Review of Language and Literature* 48.1 (1994): 7–32. Megan D. Little approaches Kate's education from the vantage of humanist pedagogy's promise for women ("The Persuasion of 'These Poor Informal Women': The Problem of Rhetorical Training in *The Taming of the Shrew* and *Measure for Measure*," *Explorations in Renaissance Culture* 33.1 [Summer 2007]: 83–108), which has the advantage of grappling with Katharine's considerable rhetorical power; but the reading also depends on reifying "Katharine" as female and turning attention away from the conundrum of "her" transvestite performance.

2. I draw on Patricia Phillipy's account of the way Ovid's *Heroides* function in the educational scene in " 'Loytering in Love': Ovid's *Heroides*, Hospitality, and Humanist Education in *The Taming of the Shrew*," *Criticism* 40.1 (Winter 1998): 27–53. On falconry as a humanist sport, see Richard Hosley, "Sources and Analogues of *The Taming of the Shrew*," *Huntington Library Quarterly* 20 (1963–64): 285–95.

3. *Author's Pen and Actor's Voice: Playing and Writing in Shakespeare's Theater*, ed. Helen Higbee and William West (Cambridge: Cambridge University Press, 2000), 3.

4. The first quotation is from Marea Mitchell, "Performing Sexual Politics in *The Taming of the Shrew*," in *The Taming of the Shrew*, ed. Dympna Callaghan (New York: W.W. Norton, 2009); the second, Jonath Gil Harris, "Materialist Criticisms," in *Shakespeare: An Oxford Guide* (Oxford: Oxford University Press, 2003), 475. Maureen Quilligan similarly argues for the play's performative awareness that "class" is a social identity that "can be learned (and unlearned)," particularly in the Induction, but does so by way of conduct

books rather than the grammar school ("Staging Gender: William Shakespeare and Elizabeth Carey," in *Sexuality and Gender in Early Modern Europe*, ed. James Grantham Turner (Cambridge: Cambridge University Press, 1993). See also Karen Newman, *Fashioning Femininity and English Renaissance Drama* (Chicago: University of Chicago Press, 1991), for whom "*The Shrew* both demonstrated and helped produce the patriarchal social formation that characterized Elizabethan England, but representation gives us a perspective on that system that subverts its status as natural" (50).

5. For example, Juliet Dusinberre reads the considerable ambiguity over power in the play in light of master-apprentice relations in Shakespeare's theatrical company ("*The Taming of the Shrew*: Women, Acting, Power" in *Studies in the Literary Imagination* 26.1 [Spring 1993]: 67–84.) My aim here is not to put one institution in place of another but rather to expand the philological and gendered resonance of the terms *master, mastery,* and *love.*

6. "*Modus conscribendi epistolas,*" as quoted in Baldwin, *Small Latine & Lesse Greeke*, 2.239; the second quotation is Thomas Becon in 1560, as quoted in Baldwin, 1.108-09. Baldwin points out that Ovid's *Ars amatoria* was singled out by name in an order by the magistrates of the Privy Council in 1582 (as *De arte amandi*); they judged it an exemplary "heathen" poem commonly "taught by schoolmasters unto their schollers" and therefore to be excised in favor of Christofer Ockland's *Anglorum prelia*. Baldwin's search of the curricula therefore uncovered no trace of the *Ars amatoria*.

7. On the way Petruchio asserts dominion by becoming an orator, see Wayne Rebhorn, "Petruchio's 'Rope Tricks': *The Taming of the Shrew* and the Renaissance Discourse of Rhetoric," *Modern Philology* 92 (1995): 294–327.

8. "Construing Gender: Mastering Bianca in *The Taming of the Shrew*," in *The Impact of Feminism in English Renaissance Studies*, ed. Dympna Callaghan (Basingstoke, England: Palgrave Macmillan, 2007), 193–209.

9. "Shakespeare's Learned Women in Ovid's Schoolroom," in *Shakespeare and the Classics*, ed. Charles Mardindale and A. B. Taylor (Cambridge: Cambridge University Press, 2004), 66–85.

10. With thanks to Leah Marcus, who generously commented on a draft of this chapter.

11. Fineman, "The Turn of the Shrew" in *Shakespeare and the Question of Theory*, ed. Patricia Parker and Geoffrey Hartman (New York and London: Methuen, 1985), 138–59.

12. Marcus, "The Shrew as Editor/Editing Shrews," in Graham Holderness and David Wootton, eds., *Shrew-Taming Narratives, 1500–1700* (New York: Palgrave-Macmillan/St. Martins, 2010) 84–100.

13. See Ursula Potter's account of Sidney's Rombus in Sidney's *The Lady of May* in relation to Shakespeare's Holofernes in "The Naming of Holofernes in *Love's Labour's Lost*," *English Language Notes* 38.2 (2000) 14–24.

14. Thomas Ingelend, *The Disobedient Child* (ca. 1570), ed. John S. Farmer (London: T.C. & E.C. Jack, 1908).

15. George Kennedy, *Classical Rhetoric and its Christian and Secular Tradition from Ancient to Modern Times* (London: Croom Helm, 1980) also points out the evident appeal of the appended examples to schoolmasters. And he singles out *ekphrasis* as the technique most likely to produce literary adaptations (164). In addition to the numerous Latin editions listed here, Richard Rainolde published a (very loose) English translation of the *Progymnasmata* under the title, *The Foundacion of Rhetorike*, in 1564.

16. Baldwin, *Small Latine & Lesse Greeke*, 2:320. The chapter on "Shakespeare's Themes" surveys each of Aphthonius's lessons and those passages in which Baldwin thinks Shakespeare is drawing on them. Leonard Barkan, "What Did Shakespeare Read?" in *The Cambridge Companion to Shakespeare*, ed. Margreta de Grazia and Stanley Wells (Cambridge: Cambridge University Press, 2001), discusses the proto-dramatic aspects of Aphthonius's text; he makes the important observation that this text would make students acutely tuned to the status of discourse *as* discourse.

17. From the 1566 London text in the British Library; translations mine.

18. Aphthonius, *Progymnasmata* (London, 1566), 181.

19. Here, of course, Bottom's astonished queries on waking from his encounter with the faeries—much like Sly's "do I dream?"—suggests that he, too, represents what Aphthonius and Lorich would recognize as "social character."

20. Ibid., p. 195.

21. Aphthonius, *Progymnasmata*, 281–82.

22. In "To The Reader," in *The fifteene bookes of P. Ovidius Naso; entituled, Metamorphosis* (London, 1612).

23. Shakespeare is likely recalling his own version of Venus as much as Ovid's, given the overt connections he makes between the goddess of Love and Salmacis in *Venus and Adonis*.

24. " 'If sight and shape be true': The Epistemology of Cross-dressing on the London Stage," *Shakespeare Quarterly* 48.1 (Spring 1997): 68. I am also indebted to Peter Stallybrass's work on the various prosthetic and visual/verbal indeterminacies characterizing the erotics of theatrical cross-dressing in the period. See "Transvestism and the 'Body Beneath': Speculating on the Boy Actor," in *Erotic Politics: Desire on the Renaissance Stage*, ed. Susan Zimmerman (New York and London: Routledge Press, 1992), 64–83.

25. Sedinger, "If sight and shape be true," 68.

26. John Bullokar, *An English Expositor: Teaching the Interpretation of the hardest words used in our Language* (London, 1616).

27. With thanks once again to my shrewd reader, Leah Marcus.

28. Callaghan, *The Taming of the Shrew*, 126.

29. *A History of the Shrewsbury School*, 46–52.

30. See Linda E. Boose, "Scolding Brides and Bridling Scolds: Taming the Woman's Unruly Member," *Shakespeare Quarterly* 42.2 (Summer 1991): 179–213; Frances E. Dolan, "Household Chastisements: Gender Authority, and Domestic Violence," in *Renaissance Culture and Everyday Life*, ed. Patricia Fumerton and Simon Hunt (Philadelphia: University of Pennsylvania Press, 1999); Karen Newman, "Renaissance Family Politics and

Shakespeare's *Taming of the Shrew*," in Marion Wynne-Davies, ed., *Much Ado About Nothing* and *The Taming of the Shrew* (Basingstoke, England: Palgrave, 2001); and Megan D. Little, "The Persuasion of 'These Poor Informal Women'."

CHAPTER 5

1. See Chapter 2.

2. I borrow Richard Halpern's apt distinction between the school's emergent and older forms of regulation as that between consent and force, though he acknowledges that the two forms coincided for some time (*The Poetics of Primitive Accumulation*).

3. Folger MS V.a.381, p. 94. This student takes as axiomatic the crucial connection between rhetoric and affect that Robert Cockroft traces through its various manifestations in the rhetorical tradition, including Peter Ramus (*Rhetorical Affect in Early Modern Writing*, esp. 38–82).

4. *The Passions of the Minde* (London, 1601), 1.

5. Sloane's introduction to his edition of *The Passions of the Minde* traces Wright's indebtedness to the classical rhetorical tradition, as well as his moderated departure from Ramism's narrow focus on style and action at the expense of the passions; see *The Passions of the Minde in Generall*, ed. Thomas Sloane (Urbana: University of Illinois Press, 1971), esp.12–15, 32–39). Sloane observes that while Wright "declines to discuss rhetoric at length," he does "provide in Book 5 a discussion of the rhetorical part historically known as 'action' (*actio, pronuntiatio*) under the head of moving the passions through the senses, and of the rhetorical parts of 'invention' and 'arrangement' (*inventio* and *dispositio*) under moving the passions through reason." *Elocutio* and *memoria*, the remaining two of classical rhetoric's five parts, "are dispersed throughout the book." Indeed, Wright's book makes "the very rationale of rhetoric . . . the instruction it provides in stirring the passions" (Sloane, 33).

6. Baldwin has an extended discussion of the way Shakespeare habitually translates Aphthonius's lesson in *epideixis* (*laus* and *vituperatio*), which he clearly knew, as "praise" and "dispraise" *(Small Latine & Lesse Greeke*, 2:332–336).

7. See Chapter 3 for my discussion of *prosopopoeia* across a variety of school exercises and sixteenth-century Ovidian epyllia.

8. Here our contemporary sense of *prosopopoeia* intersects with Aphthonius, who says that it is a trope that "invents both person and characteristics, as when Menander invented Argument. Argument is neither a thing not a person" (from the chapter on "Ethopoeia" in *Progymnasmata*).

9. Aphthonius's chapter on *comparatio* compares Demosthenes to Cicero and advises students to read Plutarch's *Lives*. As Donald Lemen Clark notes of Lorich's expanded chapter, comparison was already well engrained from writing themes; but in this text, "clearly the schoolboys were to compare historical, legendary, or fictitious characters whom they had met in their reading of school authors" (*John Milton at St. Paul's School*, 242).

10. On Shakespeare's ventriloquism and Lucrece as an author-surrogate in the poem, see Enterline, *The Rhetoric of the Body*.

11. "'O Teach Me How to Make Mine Own Excuse': Forensic Performance in *Lucrece*," *Shakespeare Quarterly* (59:4) 2008: 421–49.

12. See the full text in Chapter 2, "Imitate and Punish."

13. See, for example, *The Motives of Woe: Shakespeare and "female complaint"—A Critical Anthology*, ed. John Kerrigan (Oxford: Oxford University Press, 1991).

14. For a persuasive account of the way *prosopopoeia* in Shakespeare's sonnets produces unexpected answers from the ostensibly "silenced" Petrarchan woman, see Kathryn Schwarz, "Will in Overplus: Recasting Misogyny in Shakespeare's Sonnets" *English Literary History* 75.3 (2008): 737–66.

15. *Progymnasmata*, 197. Translations mine.

16. As translated in T. W. Baldwin, *Small Latine & Lesse Greeke* 1:328. See Chapter 2 for further discussion of *actio* and school discipline.

17. See previous discussion of exercises in "vociferation" in Chapter 2.

18. See Plett, *Rhetoric and Renaissance Culture*, esp. 437–45.

19. The pairing of "eyes and ears" is commonplace in descriptions of eloquence. In one sixteenth-century commonplace book, the writer discusses the orator's power in relation to speech and *actio*, the former related to reason and the ears, the second to passion and the eyes: "the reason is bycause as we have 2 sensces of disceplyne especially the eyes and the eares: reason entereth the eares: the passion wherewith the Orator is affected passeth by the eyes for in his face we discover it & in other gestures" (Folger MS V.a.381). For a thorough discussion of the difference between academic "presentational" acting style and popular "representational" style, see Peter Thompson's "Rogues and Rhetoricians: Acting Styles in Early English Drama" in *A New History of Early English Drama*, ed. John Cox and David Scott Kastan, (New York: Columbia University Press, 1997), 321–36. Clearly, Hamlet's speech has as much to do with acting styles; my point here is not to equate school declamation with acting in the commercial theater, but rather to trace Shakespeare's fascination with Hecuba's woe to its evident roots in school training—and to encourage further reflection on the nature of the connection between oratorical practice at school and acting in stage plays.

20. Linda Charnes, *Notorious Identity: Materializing the Subject in Shakespeare* (Cambridge, Mass.: Harvard University Press, 1993).

21. Lawrence D. Green, "Aristotle's *Rhetoric* and Renaissance Views of the Emotions," in *Renaissance Rhetoric*, ed. Peter Mack (London: St. Martin's Press, 1994), 1–26.

22. As translated in Green, "Aristotle's *Rhetoric*," 13.

23. Folger MS V.a.478, n.p. The reflections are part of the section entitled "De Rhetorica."

24. I am indebted to a conversation with Kenneth Gross.

25. Indeed, something very like what we would call "identification" surfaces in Wright's text. In a chapter about "policy" with respect to other men's passions and the way to "make friends or foes," Wright's answer is that one makes friends by imitating

their feelings: "because all likeness causeth love . . . if thou wilt please thy master or friend, thou must apparell thyself with his affections, and love where hee loveth: and universally, to smoothe other mens humours, plaineth the way to friendship" (*The Passions of the Minde*, 148–49).

26. Keir Elam, *Shakespeare's Universe of Discourse: Language-Games in the Comedies* (Cambridge: Cambridge University Press, 1984), 218.

27. See also Robert Cockroft, who discusses the history of the connection between *pathos*, *ethos*, and *logos* from the ancient period through the Renaissance, the importance of Aristotle's view of *ethos* in this tradition, and the central role that Aphthonius's chapter on *ethopoeia* played in transmitting this history to England (*Rhetorical Affect in Early Modern Writing*, [London: Palgrave Macmillan, 2003] 44–57).

28. See Nicholas Orme, *Education and Society in Medieval and Renaissance England* (London and Ronceverte: Hambledon Press, 1989), 20.

29. *Positions . . . which are necessarie for the training up of children* (London: Thomas Vautrollier, 1581), 5–6.

30. Folger MS V.a.478.

31. See Plett's discussion of the four types of orators, each of which turns on the possible difference between *ethos* and speech, as exemplified in *Richard III*, *Julius Caesar*, *King Lear*, and *Coriolanus* (*Rhetoric and Renaissance Culture*, 415–33).

32. Baldwin is particularly detailed about the technique of "division" from Aphthonius at issue in Hamlet's satiric reaction to Osric's "oration of praise" (*Small Latine & Lesse Greeke*, 2:330–33).

33. Aphthonius, *Progymnasmata*, 173.

34. Ibid., 178. "*Me miseram, quam aliam prae alia deflebo calamitatem, orbata nunc libris, quibus antea fueram insignis? . . . Quo me vertam infoelix? Ad quae deflectar? Quod mihi ad tot defunctos liberaos sufficiet sepulchrum? . . . Verumenimvero, quid ista queror ac deploro, cum a Diis, ut me in aliam naturam transmutem, impetrare liceat? Unum hoc miseriarum mearum video remedium, ut in alicuius, quod sensus viteque sit expers, formam commuter. Sed vereor misera, ne & sic quoque, quamvis mutata, inter lachrymas agere non cessem.*"

35. "*Filius fortisimus [occisus] ab Achille. O me miseram, quid Polidorum, quid Parin, quid Troilum, quid Helenum, quid dulcisimam filiam Polyxenam ad patris sepulchrum iugulat a commemorem?*" (188).

36. Ibid.

37. *The Foundacion of Rhetorike*, 54–55.

38. Halpern, *Poetics of Primitive Accumulation*, 29. His emphasis falls on the Imaginary; to it, as Chapters 1 and 2 makes clear, we must add the Symbolic.

39. William Kerrigan, "The Articulation of the Ego in the English Renaissance," in *The Literary Freud: Mechanisms of Defense and Poetic Will*, ed. Joseph H. Smith (New Haven, Conn.: Yale University Press, 1980), 261–308.

40. *Life and Death in Psychoanalysis*, trans. Jeffrey Mehlman (Baltimore and London: Johns Hopkins University Press, 1976), 43. For a full discussion, see pages 57–60.

41. The phrase is Jane Gallop's, *Reading Lacan* (Ithaca, N.Y.: Cornell University Press, 1987), 43.

42. When reading Freud's dream of Irma's injection, for instance, Lacan argues that the ruse of the consolidated "ego" given the lie by this dream means that our fiction of unity is little more than a "coat-rack" supporting the subject's multiple, often contradictory, identifications (*The Seminar of Jacques Lacan, Book II, The Ego in Freud's Theory and in the Technique of Psychoanalysis*, trans. Sylvana Tomaselli [New York: W.W. Norton, 1991], 157).

43. Halpern, *The Poetics of Primitive Accumulation*, 26.

44. Ibid., 27.

45. *Etymologiarum*, 11.1.77. On the fungibility of bodily fluids and corollary blurring of boundaries between the sexes that provides the medical context for the kind of anxiety Leontes shows here, see Thomas Laqueur, *Making Sex: Body and Gender from the Greeks to Freud* (Cambridge, Mass.: Harvard University Press, 1990), 35–43, and Gale Kern Paster, *The Body Embarrassed* (Ithaca, N.Y.: Cornell University Press, 1993).

46. See Watson, *English Grammar Schools to 1660*, 23.

47. William Nelson, *A Fifteenth Century School Book* (Oxford: Clarendon Press, 1956), xxiv, 52.

48. Ibid., 52.

49. Idleness, the master in John Redford's *Wit and Science*, is a case in point; I discuss this play further at the end of this chapter. So, too, is the later figure of Doctor Gill, master of St. Paul's, from *The Loves of Hero and Leander* (see Chapter 2). Ursula Potter provides a detailed and informative account of stage pedagogues in "Cockering Mothers and Humanist Pedagogy in Two Tudor School Plays," in *Domestic Arrangements in Early Modern England*, ed. Kari Boyd McBride (Pittsburgh, Pa.: Duquesne University Press, 2002), 244–78.

50. As quoted in Plimpton, *The Education of Shakespeare*, 25. From the body parts, boys were then to recite "the names of sickness, diseases, virtues, vices, fishes, fowls, birds, beasts, herbs, shrubs, trees, and so forth they shall proceed in good order to such things as may be most frequented and daily used."

51. *The Vulgaria of John Stanbridge and the Vulgaria of Robert Whittinton*. In another vocabulary, that of Lewis Evans's *A Short dictionary most profitable for young beginners* (London: Thomas Purfoote, 1581), a detailed translation of each body part from Latin into English gives female parts first, male second. The second is extremely detailed—"the coddes," "a stone," "the pricke," "the skinne that couereth the heade of a mans yarde," "the arse," "the hole" are all duly translated. By contrast, the female body parts are all versions of the same—pappe, dugge, teate, bosome—and represented by *mamma, papilla*, and *sinus*. Euphemism—"the lap" or *gremium*—takes care of the rest.

52. See Chapters 1 and 2 of Laplanche, *Life and Death in Psychoanalysis*.

53. *The Standard Edition of the Complete Psychological Works of Sigmund Freud* (London: Hogarth Press, 1974), 19:28–29.

54. *Disowning Knowledge in Six Plays of Shakespeare* (Cambridge and New York: Cambridge University Press, 2003).

55. *The Rhetoric of the Body*, 221–26.

Bibliography

MANUSCRIPTS

Additional ms. 4379. *Collection of themes and exercises, in Latin prose and verse, ca. 1565. Made by a scholar at Winchester School named William Badger, under the guidance of Christopher Johnson, Headmaster, 1560–79.* British Museum Library.

Folger MS V.a.381.

Folger MS V.a.478.

Royal ms. 12 A.LXVII. British Museum Library.

Royal ms. 18 A.LXIV. *A copie of diuers and sundry verses as well in Latin as in Englishe deuised and made partely by Jhon Leland and partely by Nicholas Vuedale on the occasion of the coronation of Queen Anne Boleyn at the pageants exhibited by the Mayor and Citizens of London on Whitsun Eve, 31 May 1533.* British Museum Library.

PRIMARY WORKS

Aphthonius. *Aphthonius sophistae progymnasmata. . . . Scholiis Reinhardi Lorichii Hamarii.* London: Thomas Orwin, 1596.

Ascham, Roger. *The Scholemaster.* Lawrence V. Ryan, ed. Ithaca, N.Y.: Cornell University Press, 1967.

Brinsley, John. *Ludus literarius: or, the grammar schoole shewing how to proceede from the first entrance into learning . . . intended for the helping of the younger sort of teachers.* London: Humphrey Lownes for Thomas Man, 1612.

———. *Ovids Metamorphosis translated grammatically . . . written chiefly for the good of the schooles, to be vsed according to the directions in the preface to the painefull schoolemaster.* London, 1618.

Bullokar, John. *An English Expositor: Teaching the Interpretation of the hardest words used in our Language.* London: John Legatt, 1616.

Bulwer, John. *Chirologia or The naturall language of the hand . . . Whereunto is added Chironomia: or, the art of manuall rhetoric.* London: Richard Whitaker at his shop in Pauls Churchyard, 1644.

Church of England. *Catechismus paruus pueris primum Latine . . . proponendus in scholis.* London: John Day, 1573.

Clarke, John. *Orationes et Declamationes, Habitae in Schola Lincolniensi: Speech Day Proceedings in an English school, 1624 and 1625.* Ed. Charles Garton. Buffalo, N.Y.: Department of Classics, State University of New York at Buffalo, 1972.

Conybeare, John. *Letters and Exercises of the Elizabethan Schoolmaster John Conybeare, Schoolmaster of Molton, Devon, 1580 and Swimbridge, 1594.* London: Henry Frowde, 1905.

Cordier, Mathurin. *Corderius dialogues translated grammatically; for the more speedy attaining to the knowledge of the Latine tongue, for writing and speaking Latine.* London: Humfrey Lownes, 1614.

Elyot, Thomas. *The Boke Named the Governour.* New York: Garland Press, 1992.

Evans, Lewis. *A Short dictionary most profitable for young beginners.* London: Thomas Purfoote, 1581.

Gascoigne, George. *The Steele Glasse . . . Togither with The Complainte of Phylomene.* London, 1576.

Golding, Arthur. *The fifteene bookes of P. Ovidius Naso; entituled Metamorphosis.* London: Thomas Purfoot, 1612.

Heywood, Thomas. *Troia Britannica: or, Great Britaines Troy; A Poem deuided into XVII. seuerall Cantons, intermixed with many Poeticall Tales. Concluding with an Universall Chronicle from the Creation, vntill these present times.* London: W. Iaggard, 1609.

Holt, John. *Lac puerorum . . . Anglice Mylke for chyldren.* Antwerp, 1508.

Holybrand, Claudius. *The French Littleton: A Most Easy, Perfect, and Absolute Way to learne the French tongue.* London: Richard Field, 1602.

Hoole, Charles. *A new discovery of the old art of teaching schoole in four small treatises.* London: J.T. Andrew Crook, 1661.

Ingeland, Thomas. "The Disobedient Child." In J. S. Farmer, ed., *Tudor Facsimile Texts.* London: Dryden Press, 1907.

Johnson, Christopher. *Batrachomyomachia.* London: Thomas Purfoote, 1580.

Kempe, William. *The Education of Children in Learning.* London: Thomas Orwin for John Porter and Thomas Gubbin, 1588.

Kendall, John. *Flowers of Epigrammes.* London: John Shepperd, 1577.

Lily, William. *Brevissima Institutio seu Ratio Grammatices cognoscendae, ad omnium puerorum utilitatem praescripta, quam solam Regia Maiestas in omnibus Scholis profitendam praecipit.* London, 1553.

———. *A Short Introduction of Grammar Generallie to be used, compiled and set forth, for the bringing up of all those that intend to attaine the knowledge of the Latin tongue.* London, 1557.

Mulcaster, Richard. *Positions wherein those primitive circumstances be examined, which are necessarie for the training up of children, either for skill in their booke, or health in their bodie.* London: Thomas Vautrollier for Thomas Chare, 1581.

Nashe, Thomas. *A Pleasant Comedie, called Summer's Last Will and Testament.* London: Simon Stafford for Walter Burre, 1600.

Petrarch, Francesco. *Petrarch's Lyric Poems: The Rime Sparse and Other Lyrics.* Robert Durling, trans. Cambridge, Mass.: Harvard University Press, 1979.

Quintilian. *Institutio oratoria.* Cambridge, Mass.: Harvard University Press, 1980.

Rainolde, Richard. The Foundacion of Rhetorike. London: John Kingston, 1564.

Redford, John. *Wit and Science*. London: Malone Society, 1951.

Sharpham, Edward. *Cupid's Whirligig*. Allardyce Nicolle, ed. London: Golden Cockerel Press, 1926.

Sherry, Richard. *A Treatise of Schemes and Tropes*. London, 1550.

Smith, James. *The loves of Hero and Leander: a mock poem: with marginall notes, and other choice pieces of drollery*. London, 1653.

Vives, Juan Luis. *Linguae latinae exercitatio*. London: Iohannis Harisoni, per Nicolaum Okes, 1612.

Wright, Thomas. *The Passions of the Minde in Generall*. Thomas Sloane, ed. Urbana: University of Illinois Press, 1971.

SECONDARY WORKS

Adelman, Janet. *Suffocating Mothers: Fantasies of Maternal Origin in Shakespeare's Plays, "Hamlet" to "The Tempest."* New York: Routledge, 1991.

Althusser, Louis. *Lenin and Philosophy*. London: New Left Books, 1971.

Altman, Joel. *The Tudor Play of Mind: Rhetorical Inquiry and the Development of Elizabethan Drama*. Berkeley: University of California Press, 1978.

Baldwin, David. *The Chapel Royal: Ancient and Modern*. London: Duckworth, 1990.

Baldwin, T. W. *Shakspere's Small Latine & Lesse Greeke*. 2 vols. Urbana: University of Illinois Press, 1944.

Barkan, Leonard. *The Gods Made Flesh: Metamorphosis and the Pursuit of Paganism*. New Haven, Conn.: Yale University Press, 1990.

———. "What Did Shakespeare Read?" In Margreta de Grazia and Stanley Wells, eds., *The Cambridge Companion to Shakespeare*. Cambridge, England: Cambridge University Press, 2001.

Bartsch, Shadi. *The Mirror of the Self: Sexuality, Self-Knowledge, and the Gaze in the Early Roman Empire*. Chicago: University of Chicago Press, 2006.

Bate, Jonathan. *Shakespeare and Ovid*. Oxford: Clarendon Press, 1993.

Belsey, Catherine. "Love as Trompe-l'oeil: Taxonomies of Desire in *Venus and Adonis*." *Shakespeare Quarterly* 46.3 (Fall 1995): 257–76.

Berger, Harry. *Imaginary Audition: Shakespeare on Stage and Page*. Berkeley: University of California Press, 1989.

———. *Making Trifles of Terrors: Redistributing Complicities in Shakespeare*. Stanford, Calif.: Stanford University Press, 1997.

———. "Narrative as Rhetoric in *The Faerie Queene*." *English Literary Renaissance* 21 (1991): 3–48.

Bevington, David. *Action Is Eloquence: Shakespeare's Language of Gesture*. Cambridge, Mass.: Harvard University Press, 1984.

Binns, J. W. *Intellectual Culture in Elizabethan and Jacobean England: The Latin Writings of the Age*. Leeds, England: Francis Cairns, 1990.

Bloom, Harold. *Shakespeare: The Invention of the Human*. New York: Riverhead Books, 1999.

Bolgar, R. R. *The Classical Heritage and Its Beneficiaries*. Cambridge, England: Cambridge University Press, 1954.

Boose, Linda E. "Scolding Brides and Bridling Scolds: Taming the Woman's Unruly Member." *Shakespeare Quarterly* 42.2 (Summer 1991): 179–213.

Bourdieu, Pierre. *Distinction: A Social Critique of the Judgement of Taste*. Richard Nice, trans. Cambridge, Mass.: Harvard University Press, 1984.

———. *The Logic of Practice*. Richard Nice, trans. Stanford, Calif.: Stanford University Press, 1980.

Bowden, Betsy. "Latin Pedagogical Plays and the Rape Scene in *The Two Gentlemen of Verona*." *English Language Notes* (December 2003): 18–32.

Brooks, Dennis S. "'To Show Scorn Her Own Image': The Varieties of Education in *The Taming of the Shrew*." *Rocky Mountain Review of Language and Literature* 48.1 (1994): 7–32.

Brown, J. Howard. *Elizabethan Schooldays*. Oxford: Blackwell, 1933.

Burrow, Colin. "Shakespeare and Humanistic Culture." In Charles Martindale and A. B. Taylor, eds., *Shakespeare and the Classics*. Cambridge, England: Cambridge University Press, 2004.

Bushnell, Rebecca. *A Culture of Teaching: Early Modern Humanism in Theory and Practice*. Ithaca, N.Y.: Cornell University Press, 1996.

Butler, Judith. *Bodies That Matter: On the Discursive Limits of Sex*. New York: Routledge, 1993.

Carlisle, Nicholas. *A Concise Description of the Endowed Grammar Schools of England and Wales*. London: Baldwin, Cradock and Joy, 1818.

Cartwright, Kent. *Theater and Humanism: English Drama and the Sixteenth Century*. Cambridge, England: Cambridge University Press, 1999.

Cavell, Stanley. *Disowning Knowledge in Six Plays of Shakespeare*. New York: Cambridge University Press, 2003.

Chambers, E. K. *The Elizabethan Stage*. Oxford: Clarendon Press, 1923.

Charnes, Linda. *Notorious Identity: Materializing the Subject in Shakespeare*. Cambridge, Mass.: Harvard University Press, 1993.

Chase, Cynthia. "Translating the Transference: Psychoanalysis and the Construction of History." In Joseph H. Smith and Humphrey Morris, eds., *Telling Facts: History and Narration in Psychoanalysis*. Baltimore: Johns Hopkins University Press, 1992.

Clark, Donald Leman. *John Milton at St. Paul's School: A Study of Ancient Rhetoric in English Renaissance Education*. New York: Columbia University Press, 1948.

Crane, Mary Thomas. *Framing Authority: Sayings, Self, and Society in Sixteenth-Century England*. Princeton, N.J.: Princeton University Press, 1993.

Cockcroft, Robert. *Rhetorical Affect in Early Modern Writing: Renaissance Passions Reconsidered*. London: Palgrave Macmillan, 2003.

Crewe, Jonathan, A. R. Braunmuller, and Stephen Orgel, eds. *The Narrative Poems (The Pelican Shakespeare)*. New York: Penguin Classics, 1999.

Dolan, Francis. "Household Chastisements: Gender Authority, and Domestic Violence." In Patricia Fumerton and Simon Hunt, eds., *Renaissance Culture and Everyday Life.* Philadelphia: University of Pennsylvania Press, 1999.

Dolven, Jeff. *Scenes of Instruction in Renaissance Romance.* Chicago: University of Chicago Press, 2007.

Dusinberre, Juliet.. "*The Taming of the Shrew*: Women, Acting, Power." *Studies in the Literary Imagination* 26.1 (Spring 1993): 67–84.

Elam, Keir. *Shakespeare's Universe of Discourse: Language-Games in the Comedies.* Cambridge, England: Cambridge University Press, 1984.

Enterline, Lynn. *The Rhetoric of the Body from Ovid to Shakespeare.* Cambridge, England: Cambridge University Press, 2000.

———. "Rhetoric, Discipline, and the Theatricality of Everyday Life in Elizabethan Grammar Schools." In Peter Holland and Stephen Orgel, eds., *From Stage to Print: Rewriting Early Modern Stage History*, 173–90. New York: Palgrave Press, 2005.

———. "Psychoanalytic Criticisms of Shakespeare." In Stanley Wells and Lena Cowen Orlin, eds., *Shakespeare: An Oxford Guide*, 450–71. Oxford: Oxford University Press, 2003.

Fineman, Joel. *Shakespeare's Perjur'd Eye: The Invention of Poetic Subjectivity in the Sonnets.* Berkeley: University of California Press, 1986.

———. *The Subjectivity Effect in Western Literary Tradition.* Boston: MIT Press, 1991.

———. "The Turn of the Shrew." In Patricia Parker and Geoffrey Hartman, eds., *Shakespeare and the Question of Theory*, 138–59. London: Methuen, 1985.

Fisch, Harold. "Character as Linguistic Sign." *New Literary History* 21.3 (Spring 1990): 593–606.

Freedman, Barbara. "Pedagogy, Psychoanalysis, Theatre: Interrogating the Scene of Learning." *Shakespeare Quarterly* 41.2 (Summer 1990): 174–86.

Freud, Sigmund. "A Child Is Being Beaten: A Contribution to the Study of the Origin of Sexual Perversions." In James Strachey, ed., *The Standard Edition of the Complete Psychological Works of Sigmund Freud*, vol. 17. London: Hogarth Press, 1974.

——— "The Ego and the Id." In James Strachey, ed., *The Standard Edition of the Complete Psychological Works of Sigmund Freud*, vol. 19. London: Hogarth Press, 1974.

Gallop, Jane. *Reading Lacan.* Ithaca, N.Y.: Cornell University Press, 1987.

Grafton, Anthony, and Lisa Jardine. *From Humanism to the Humanities: Education and the Liberal Arts in Fifteenth- and Sixteenth-Century Europe.* Cambridge, Mass.: Harvard University Press, 1986.

Green, Lawrence D. "Aristotle's *Rhetoric* and Renaissance Views of the Emotions." In Peter Mack, ed., *Renaissance Rhetoric*, 1–26. London: St. Martin's Press, 1994.

Guillory, John. *Cultural Capital: The Problem of Literary Canon Formation.* Chicago: University of Chicago Press, 1993.

Halpern, Richard. *The Poetics of Primitive Accumulation: English Renaissance Culture and the Genealogy of Capital.* Ithaca, N.Y.: Cornell University Press, 1991.

Hampton, Timothy. *Writing from History: The Rhetoric of Exemplarity in Renaissance Literature.* Ithaca, N.Y.: Cornell University Press, 1990.

Harris, Jonath Gil. "Materialist Criticisms." In Lena Cowen Orlin and Stanley Wells, eds., *Shakespeare: An Oxford Guide.* Oxford: Oxford University Press, 2003.

Heffernan, James A. W. *Museum of Words: The Poetics of Ekphrasis from Homer to Ashbery.* Chicago: University of Chicago Press, 1993.

Hillebrand, Harold Newcomb. *The Child Actors.* Urbana: University of Illinois, 1926.

A History of the Shrewsbury School from the Blakeway Mss., and Many Other Sources. Shrewsbury and London: Adnitt & Naunton, The Square and Simpkin, Marshall & Co., Stationers Hall Court, 1899.

James, Heather. "Shakespeare's Learned Heroines in Ovid's Schoolroom." In Charles Martindale and A. B. Taylor, eds., *Shakespeare and the Classics.* Cambridge, England: Cambridge University Press, 2004.

———. *Shakespeare's Troy: Drama, Politics, and the Translation of Empire.* Cambridge, England: Cambridge University Press, 1997.

Jones, Emrys. *The Origins of Shakespeare.* Oxford: Oxford University Press, 1977.

Kahn, Coppelia. *Roman Shakespeare: Warriors, Wounds, Women.* New York: Routledge, 1997.

———. "Self and Eros in *Venus and Adonis.*" *Centennial Review* (East Lansing, Mich.) 20 (1976): 351–71.

Kennedy, George. *Classical Rhetoric and its Christian and Secular Tradition from Ancient to Modern Times.* London: Croom Helm, 1980.

Kerrigan, John, ed., *The Motives of Woe: Shakespeare and "female complaint"—A Critical Anthology.* Oxford: Oxford University Press, 1991.

Kerrigan, William. "The Articulation of the Ego in the English Renaissance." In Joseph Smith, ed., *The Literary Freud: Mechanisms of Defense and Poetic Will.* New Haven, Conn.: Yale University Press, 1980.

Kristeva, Julia. *Revolution in Poetic Language.* Margaret Waller, trans. New York: Columbia University Press, 1984.

Lamb, Mary Ellen. "Taken by Fairies: Fairy Practices and the Production of Popular Culture in *A Midsummer Night's Dream.*" *Shakespeare Quarterly* 51.3 (Fall 2000): 277–312.

Lacan, Jacques. *Ecrits.* Paris: Editions du Seuil, 1966.

———. "The Ego in Freud's Theory and in the Technique of Psychoanalysis." In Jacques-Alain Miller, ed., *The Seminar of Jacques Lacan II.* New York: W.W. Norton, 1991.

Lacquer, Thomas. *Making Sex: Body and Gender from the Greeks to Freud.* Cambridge, Mass.: Harvard University Press, 1990.

Lamb, Mary Ellen. "Engendering the Narrative Act: Old Wives' Tales in *The Winter's Tale, Macbeth,* and *The Tempest.*" *Criticism* 40.4 (1998): 529–53.

Laplanche, Jean. "Fantasy at the Origins of Sexuality." *The International Journal of Psychoanalysis* 49 (1968): 110–35.

———. *Life and Death in Psychoanalysis.* Jeffrey Mehlman, trans. Baltimore: Johns Hopkins University Press, 1985.

Lawson, John. *A Town Grammar School Through Six Centuries: A History of Hull Grammar School Against Its Local Background.* London: Oxford University Press, 1963.

Lawson, John, and Harold Silver. *A Social History of Education in England*. London: Methuen, 1973.

Leach, A. F. *The Schools of Medieval England*. London: Chatto, 1915.

Little, Megan D. "The Persuasion of 'These Poor Informal Women': The Problem of Rhetorical Training in *Taming of the Shrew* and *Measure for Measure*." *Explorations in Renaissance Culture* 33.1 (Summer 2007): 83–108.

Mack, Peter. *Elizabethan Rhetoric: Theory and Practice*. Cambridge, England: Cambridge University Press, 2002.

Marcus, Leah. "The Shakespearean Editor as Shrew-Tamer." *English Literary Renaissance* 22 (1992): 180–92.

———. "The Shrew as Editor/Editing Shrews." In Graham Holderness and David Wootton, eds., *Shrew-Taming Narratives, 1500–1700*, 84–100. New York: Palgrave-Macmillan/St. Martins, 2010.

Marshall, Cynthia. *The Shattering of the Self: Violence, Subjectivity and Early Modern Texts*. Baltimore: Johns Hopkins University Press, 2002.

McDonnell, Michael F. J. *A History of St. Paul's School*. London: Chapman Hall, 1909.

Meredith, Michael. *Five Hundred Years of Eton Theater*. Windsor, England: Eton College, 2001.

Mitchell, Marea. "Performing Sexual Politics in *The Taming of the Shrew*." In Dympna Callaghan, ed., *The Taming of the Shrew*. New York: W.W. Norton, 2009.

Mitchell, W. J. T. *Picture Theory*. Chicago: University of Chicago Press, 1994.

Mowat, Barbara, and Paul Werstine, eds. *Shakespeare's Sonnets and Poems*. New York: Washington Square Press, 2004.

Nelson, William. *A Fifteenth Century Schoolbook*. Oxford: Clarendon Press, 1956.

Newman, Karen. *Fashioning Femininity and English Renaissance Drama*. Chicago: University of Chicago Press, 1991.

———. "Renaissance Family Politics and Shakespeare's *Taming of the Shrew*." In Marion Wynne-Davies, ed. *Much Ado About Nothing* and *The Taming of the Shrew*. Basingstoke, England: Palgrave, 2001.

Ong, Walter. "Latin Language Study as a Renaissance Puberty Rite." *Studies in Philology* 56 (1959): 103–24.

Orme, Nicholas. *Education and Society in Medieval and Renaissance England*. London: Hambledon Press, 1989.

Owen, Dorothy M., and Dorothea Thurley, eds. *The King's School Ely: A Collection of Documents Relating to the History of the School and Its Scholars*. Cambridge, England: Cambridge Antiquarian Records Society, 1982.

Parker, Patricia. "Construing Gender: Mastering Bianca in *The Taming of the Shrew*." In Dympna Callaghan, ed., *The Impact of Feminism in English Renaissance Studies*, 193–209. Basingstoke, England: Palgrave Macmillan, 2007.

Partridge, Eric. *Shakespeare's Bawdy*. London: Routledge, 2001.

Paster, Gail Kern. *The Body Embarrassed*. Ithaca, N.Y.: Cornell University Press, 1993.

Paster, Gail Kern, Katherine Rowe, and Mary Floyd Wilson, eds. *Reading the Early Modern Passions*. Philadelphia: University of Pennsylvania Press, 2004.

Penley, Constance. *The Future of an Illusion: Film, Feminism, and Psychoanalysis*. Minneapolis: University of Minnesota Press, 1989.

Pettigrew, Todd H. "Sex, Sin, and Scarring: Syphilis in Redford's Wit and Science." In Lloyd Kermode, Jason Scott-Warren, and Martine Van Elk, eds., *Tudor Drama before Shakespeare 1485–1590*. New York: Palgrave Macmillan, 2004.

Phillippy, Patricia. "'Loytering in Love': Ovid's *Heroides*, Hospitality, and Humanist Education in *Taming of the Shrew*." *Criticism* 40.1 (Winter 1998): 27–53.

Plett, Heinrich. *Rhetoric and Renaissance Culture*. Berlin: Walter de Gruyter, 2004.

Plimpton, George A. *The Education of Shakespeare: Illustrated from the Schoolbooks in Use in His Time*. London: Oxford University Press, 1933.

Potter, Ursula. "Cockering Mothers and Humanist Pedagogy in Two Tudor School Plays." In Kari Boyd McBride, ed., *Domestic Arrangements in Early Modern England*, 244–78. Pittsburgh, Pa.: Duquesne University Press, 2002.

———. "The Naming of Holofernes in *Love's Labour's Lost*." *English Language Notes* 38.2 (2000): 14–24.

———. "Performing Arts in the Tudor Classroom." In Lloyd Kermode, Jason Scott-Warren, and Martine Van Elk, eds., *Tudor Drama before Shakespeare 1485–1590*. New York: Palgrave Macmillan, 2004.

Quilligan, Maureen. "Staging Gender: William Shakespeare and Elizabeth Carey." In James Grantham Turner, ed., *Sexuality and Gender in Early Modern Europe*. Cambridge, England: Cambridge University Press, 1993.

Rambuss, Richard. "What It Feels Like for a Boy: Shakespeare's *Venus and Adonis*." In Richard Dutton and Jean Howard, eds., *A Companion to Shakespeare's Works*, vol. 4, *The Poems, Problem Comedies, Late Plays*, 240–58. London: Blackwell, 2003.

Rebhorn, Wayne. "Petruchio's 'Rope Tricks': *The Taming of the Shrew* and the Renaissance Discourse of Rhetoric." *Modern Philology* 92 (1995): 294–327.

———. "Temptation in Shakespeare's *Venus and Adonis*." *Shakespeare Studies* 11 (1978): 1–19.

Rhodes, Neil. *Shakespeare and the Origins of English*. Oxford: Oxford University Press, 2008.

———. "The Controversial Plot: Declamation and the Concept of the 'Problem Play.'" *The Modern Language Review*. Vol. 95, No. 3 (July, 2000) 609–22.

Roach, Joseph. *The Player's Passion: Studies in the Science of Acting*. Newark: University of Delaware Press, 1985.

Roe, John. *The Poems*: Venus and Adonis, The Rape of Lucrece, The Phoenix and the Turtle, The Passionate Pilgrim, A Lover's Complaint. Cambridge, England: Cambridge University Press, 1992.

Rose, Jacqueline. "Where Does the Misery Come From? Psychoanalysis, Feminism, and the Event." In Richard Feldstein and Judith Roof, eds., *Feminism and Psychoanalysis*. Ithaca, N.Y.: Cornell University Press, 1989.

Rothenberg, Alan. "The Oral Rape Fantasy and the Rejection of the Mother in the Imagery of Shakespeare's *Venus and Adonis*." *Psychoanalytic Quarterly* 40 (1971): 447–68.

Schwarz, Kathryn. "Will in Overplus: Recasting Misogyny in Shakespeare's Sonnets." *English Literary History* 75.3 (Fall 2008): 737–66.

Sedinger, Tracey. "'If sight and shape be true': The Epistemology of Crossdressing on the London Stage." *Shakespeare Quarterly* 48.1 (Spring 1997): 68.

Sergeaunt, John. *Annals of Westminster School.* London: Methuen, 1898.

Smith, Ian. "Barbarian Errors: Performing Race in Early Modern England." *Shakespeare Quarterly* 49.2 (Summer 1998): 168–86.

Smith, Joan. *Education and Society in Tudor England.* Cambridge, England: Cambridge University Press, 1967.

Stallybrass, Peter. "Transvestism and the 'Body Beneath': Speculating on the Boy Actor." In Susan Zimmerman, ed., *Erotic Politics: Desire on the Renaissance Stage,* 64–83. New York: Routledge Press, 1992.

Stapleton, M. L. "Venus as *Praeceptor*: The *Ars Amatoria* in *Venus and Adonis.*" In Philip C. Kolin, ed., *Venus and Adonis: Critical Essays,* 309–22. New York: Routledge, 1997.

Stewart, Alan. *Close Readers: Humanism and Sodomy in Early Modern England.* Princeton, N.J.: Princeton University Press, 1997.

Streitberger, W. R. "Ideal Conduct in Venus and Adonis." *Shakespeare Quarterly* 26 (1975): 285–91.

Sullivan, Paul. "Playing the Lord: Tudor Vulgaria and the Rehearsal of Ambition." *ELH* 75.1 (2008): 179–96.

Thompson, Craig R. *Collected Works of Erasmus: Colloquies.* Toronto: University of Toronto Press, 1997.

Thompson, Peter. "Rogues and Rhetoricians: Acting Styles in Early English Drama." In John Cox and David Scott Kastan, eds., *A New History of Early English Drama,* 321–36. New York: Columbia University Press, 1997.

Ward, David. "Affection, Intention, and Dreams in *The Winter's Tale.*" *Modern Language Review* 82 (1987): 545–54.

Watson, Foster. *The English Grammar Schools to 1660: Their Curriculum and Practice.* Cambridge, England: Cambridge University Press, 1908.

———. *Richard Mulcaster and His "Elementarie."* London: C.F. Hodgson & Son, 1893.

Weaver, William. "'O teach me how to make mine own excuse': Forensic Performance in Lucrece." *Shakespeare Quarterly* (2009): 421–49.

Weimann, Robert. *Author's Pen and Actor's Voice: Playing and Writing in Shakespeare's Theater.* Helen Higbee and William West, eds. Cambridge, England: Cambridge University Press, 2000.

White, Beatrice. *The Vulgaria of John Stanbridge and the Vulgaria of Robert Whittinton.* London: Kegan Paul, Trench, & Trubner, 1932.

Woods, Marjorie Curry. "The Teaching of Writing in Medieval Europe." In James J. Murphy, ed., *A Short History of Writing Instruction from Ancient Greece to Twentieth-Century America,* 77–94. Davis, Calif.: Hermagoras Press, 1990.

———. "Weeping for Dido: Epilogue on a Premodern Rhetorical Exercise in the Post Modern Classroom." In Carol Dana Lanham, ed., *Latin Grammar and Rhetoric: From Classical Theory to Medieval Practice,* 284–94. London: Continuum Press, 2002.

Žižek, Slavoj. *The Sublime Object of Ideology.* London: Verso, 1989.

Index

Acknowledgments

The inspiration for this book sparked as I was finishing the last one and thinking about the connection between ventriloquism, Ovid, and trauma. But the roots of the project run farther back than that, back to the many educational institutions, languages, and pedagogical scenes (both British and American) that made my inquiry possible. Fortunately for me, the resemblance between the matter and the author's schooling ends pretty much there, though I confess that a life time's experience as a student and teacher means that I remain fascinated by the potential gap between what schoolmasters thought they were doing and what students experienced and learned. Also fortunately for me, friends and colleagues were good enough over the years to be interested, or make a convincing show of being so, in the odd archival details and psychoanalytic speculation that kept arising from this research. My debts, in short, are legion—and keenly felt, as this book has been a long time in the making.

I owe three very long-standing debts: first and second to my Oxford tutors, Nan Dunbar and Miriam Griffin, who were very patient with the American scholar who fetched up on their door steps at Somerville College with very little Latin and, strangely, rather more Greek than necessary for entering the B.A. course in *Literae Humaniores*. The third is to Scott Mc-Millan, whose eternal curiosity about Hecuba's power over Shakespeare's imagination remained with me long after his graduate seminar on early modern drama finished. I am grateful to colleagues in the field who, when I first declared my interest in sixteenth-century pedagogy, had enough faith not to dissuade me from venturing into a massive archive when I was also trying to push my ways of reading in new directions. In particular, Harry Berger and Stephen Orgel gave me enormous latitude as I tried out new ideas. They both asked probing questions that shaped much that followed. Others—Peter Holland, Alan Stewart, Ann Rosalind Jones, Joe Loewenstein, Jim Carroll, Diana Henderson, Rick Rambuss, David Hillman, Peter Mack, Geraldine

Heng, Carla Mazzio, Heather James, Denis Flannery and Roland Greene—listened carefully, offered acute comments, and gave a fledgling project much needed support. Richard Halpern, whose own work on humanist pedagogy was an early inspiration, was similarly generous as I tried to figure out what a poststructuralist, psychoanalytic, feminist literary critic was going to "do," as he put it, "with facts." Lena Cowen Orlin read and listened to several parts of this book over the years, and was unfailingly generous in her moral and intellectual support. Elizabeth Harvey's comments on an early draft of chapters 1 and 2 were enormously helpful in guiding me forward. And when he heard the MLA paper that formed the basis for my reading of *Venus and Adonis*, Jonathan Gil Harris invented an apt mantra that I recited often to help keep matters in perspective.

The institutional and collegial support at Vanderbilt could not have been more generous. Paul Elledge, who once taught me Wordsworth and had just completed the evocative *Lord Byron at Harrow School* when I first arrived, graciously offered me all the names and addresses of the grammar school archivists in the U.K. who had once helped him. I would most especially like to thank Mr. Geoffrey Brown and Miss Elizabeth Wells, archivists at the Merchant Taylors' School and the Westminster School, respectively, for assistance in the initial stages of research and for bringing materials to my attention that profoundly shaped the questions I asked about pedagogical practice. Jerry Christensen read an early draft of what became chapters two and three; we started a conversation about acting and rhetoric that spurred me to important further thought and research. Over the years, my early modern cohort has been a source of tremendous intellectual support and comradeship: Kathryn Schwarz, Leah Marcus, and Katherine Crawford heard numerous presentations from this material without complaint and read drafts when their time was (inevitably) in short supply; their comments and suggestions improved this book enormously. Carolyn Dever read early drafts of chapters two and three; one of her questions in particular stayed with me and changed my direction at a crucial moment of writing. Cecelia Tichi was a steady professional beacon, cheerfully entering into numerous speculative discussions about an early article from the book that helped me plug on as we taught our seminar on empire. Over the course of researching and writing, Jonathan Lamb and Bridget Orr rallied round in difficult times abroad as well as at home. They know rather more about this project than anyone who isn't the author should. Discussions with Jonathan during our course on metamorphosis influenced the book in numerous ways, some of which I may no longer recognize. Colin Dayan offered steadying encouragement over the last five years, reading bits and pieces along the way and then the entire book in its last incarnation. It was endlessly clarifying to hear what parts spoke to her. And when I thought the manuscript was almost finished, Dana Nelson offered her fine editorial eye for the whole of it, helping me make the argument as good as it could be. I thank her now, though I was less grateful then, for judiciously prompting me to one final bit of writing—which became the introduction. Houston Baker graciously offered to read the final chapter; his response was just the kind of tonic a nervous author needed. While under serious deadlines of her own, Carla Kaplan came to my aid as I developed the final, public face for the project; she, Jonathan, Bridget, Colin, and Dana helped me, at last, to let it go.

The Folger Shakespeare Library asked me conduct a Faculty Seminar on the topic of early modern pedagogy, and I must thank the members of that seminar for making it such a vibrant scholarly and collegial weekend. I have been lucky enough to work with or alongside Elizabeth Hanson in various formal venues; her observations, offered from a slightly different angle, often helped me believe again, when faith flags as it will sometimes do, in the importance of the research I was undertaking. So, too, did the virtual assistance of Marjorie Currie Woods, whose own work on medieval schooling came to me later in the process and taught me much. To my indefatigable and meticulous research assistant, Donald Jellerson, I owe a great debt.

I must also thank a number of other organizations for supporting this research: a senior research grant from the American Council of Learned Societies and a visiting fellowship from Clare Hall, Cambridge, gave me necessary support for work in British archives; so, too, did a short term grant from the Folger Shakespeare Library allow me further time for archival research at home. An early fellowship at the Robert Penn Warren Center for the Humanities gave the project an important first push. And I must thank the literature faculties at several universities for invitations to present aspects of this research. The deeply engaged thoughts, comments, and queries from audiences at Smith College, Harvard, Johns Hopkins, Cambridge, Stanford, Emory, Texas at Austin, Chicago, Northwestern, Sydney, and Princeton Universities gave me enormous food for thought as I wrote, revised, and rethought my arguments. I thank the readers for the University of Pennsylvania Press for their generous commentary; their reports, and Jerry Singerman's advice, definitely improved this book. Finally, Michael MacDonald's keen and learned eye improved the manuscript enormously in the last stages. The remaining mistakes are my own.

For generous assistance with the pressing matters that come with serious physical set-backs I am indebted to my family and Mary Ellen, who rallied around. So, too, did to my cadre of fabulous girlfriends. Their generous concern for my physical and emotional well-being, as well as Ziggy's, means the world to me.